THE RISE OF WEST LAKE

A CULTURAL LANDMARK IN THE SONG DYNASTY

XIAOLIN DUAN

A CHINA PROGRAM BOOK

UNIVERSITY OF WASHINGTON PRESS
Seattle

The Rise of West Lake was made possible in part by a grant from the China Studies Program, a division of the Henry M. Jackson School of International Studies at the University of Washington.

Printed and bound in the United States of America

Composed in Minion Pro, typeface designed by Robert Slimbach

24 23 22 21 20 5 4 3 2 1

UNIVERSITY OF WASHINGTON PRESS
uwapress.uw.edu

LIBRARY OF CONGRESS CATALOGING-IN-PUBLICATION DATA
LC record available at https://lccn.loc.gov/2019034304
LC ebook record available at https://lccn.loc.gov/2019034305

COVER DESIGN: Stacy Wakefield Forte
COVER ILLUSTRATION: Formerly attributed to Li Song (傳)李嵩 (late 12th–early 13th c.), *Scenic Attractions of West Lake* (detail), ink and color on paper, 32.9 x 1581.1 cm. Freer Gallery of Art, gift of Charles Lang Freer (F1911.209).

The paper used in this publication is acid free and meets the minimum requirements of American National Standard for Information Sciences—Permanence of Paper for Printed Library Materials, ANSI Z39.48–1984.∞

To my parents

CONTENTS

ACKNOWLEDGMENTS

It has been a long ten-year journey since I started my first research on West Lake. I could never have even attempted, let alone completed, such a journey without the tremendous support, guidance, and good wishes of so many people in so many ways.

My deepest gratitude goes to my mentor, Patricia B. Ebrey. Her guidance sustained and nurtured me from the very beginning. Her unstinting support and mentorship helped me to put scattered thoughts and semicoherent drafts together and work through the various stages of this book. I am extremely grateful for her patience and thoroughness in providing constructive comments and direction.

I am also in debt to my mentors R. Kent Guy, Madeleine Yue Dong, Haicheng Wang, Shi-shan Susan Huang, Kyoko Tokuno, and David Spafford, who helped me conceptualize this project and advised me in the subsequent research and writing. They have broadened my vision by encouraging me to cross different intellectual boundaries into the fields of humanistic geography, art history, religious studies, and Japanese history.

My great appreciation also goes to my colleagues and friends from the University of Washington community: Chong Eun Ahn, Peyton Canary, Lin Chen, Xi Chen, Hsiao-wen Cheng, Chad D. Garcia, Qian He, Jeongwon Hyun, Gladys Ge Jian, Lily W. Schatz, Hsiang-lin Shi, Yingying Sun, Matthew van Duyn, Qian Yang, Sumei Yi, Xiaoshun Zeng, and Shuxuan Zhou, among others, for the discussions we shared and the many thought-provoking questions that came out of those conversations. Their unwavering emotional support and company have carried me through the most difficult times of research and writing.

Many scholars working in related fields and on similar subjects have read or heard parts of this work. I want to thank their meticulous readings of the early draft of this project and their honest and valuable comments. Each of them deserves much more than the brief mention I am giving here: Ian Chapman, Josh Yiu, Ronald Egan, Jenny Gavacs, Jeffrey Kinkley, Ellen Cong Zhang, Anne Gerritsen, Beverly Bossler, Liu Jingzhen, Christian de Pee, Iris

Ai Wang, Mahlon Meyer, Rebecca Scott, Pablo Celis-Castillo, Ariela Marcus-Sells, Hui-Hua Chang, Mary Jo Festle, David Fletcher, Pamela Winfield, Michelle T. King, and David Ambaras.

Earlier drafts of material for this book were presented at conferences and workshops in Ann Arbor, Beijing, Berkeley, Boston, Fort Worth, Leiden, Philadelphia, Richmond, Seattle, Tempe, and Washington, DC, between 2011 and 2018. I am grateful to all those who kindly and critically commented on my work presented on those occasions, including Maggie Bickford, Timothy Brook, Peter Carroll, Cao Jiaqi, John Chaffee, Kaijun Chen, Deng Xiaonan, Siyen Fei, Qiliang He, Li-Ling Hsiao, Amy Huang, Robert Hymes, Alister Ingles, Hui-shu Lee, Yiwen Li, Lin Hang, Zoe Shan Lin, Gang Liu, Victor Mair, Thomas Mazanec, Tracy Miller, Julia K. Murray, Susan Naquin, Elizabeth Parker, Benjamin Ridgway, Lu Sun, Xiaosu Sun, Chang Tan, Barend ter Haar, Brian Vivier, Xin Wen, Stephen West, Wu Ren-shu, Wu Ya-ting, Lei Xue, Zhaohua Yang, Ting Zhang, Zhao Dongmei, Yanfei Zhu, and Leah Zuo. A preliminary exploration of chapter 6 first appeared in the book chapter of the edited volume *Visual and Material Cultures in Middle Period China* (Brill, 2017). Many thanks to the editors and the anonymous reviewers for their valuable feedback.

The completion of the book is made possible by the Hsiao Endowment and Fritz and Boeing Fellowships from the University of Washington, a Blakemore Internship from the Seattle Art Museum, a Hultquist Fellowship from Elon University, sponsorship from the Lieberthal-Rogel Center for Chinese Studies at the University of Michigan, and the research fund from North Carolina State University. During my several trips to China, I could not have accomplished much without the timely and generous support from the West Lake Museum and the Zhejiang Provincial Library in Hangzhou.

I would also like to express my appreciation to those who have generously assisted me in preparing my manuscript. Immense thanks are due to the two peer reviewers of this manuscript for their careful reading and constructive comments, which helped tremendously in improving this work. I am also indebted to Ann Fenwick, who edited early drafts of the manuscript and offered valuable insights and guidance. I want to thank James Hargett for his helpful suggestions on publication. Thanks also to the Freer Gallery of Art, the Palace Museum, and the Bibliothèque Nationale de France for permitting me to use their images; also, thanks to Bill Nelson and Kailing Li for helping with the maps and illustrations. I have been fortunate to work with Lorri Hagman and her colleagues, Neecole Bostick, Michael O. Campbell, Beth Fuget, Kris Fulsaas, M'Bilia Meekers, Neal Swain, and Julie Van Pelt, at the University of Washington Press. Lorri has been a wonderfully attentive editor, and I am very grateful for her support in guiding me through this stressful but rewarding process.

Last, I reserve my fondest and deepest gratitude for my loving family: my parents and my husband, who have always been my unfailing source of love and confidence throughout the years. Their spiritual support has carried and accompanied me farther than I ever could expect to reach.

THE RISE OF WEST LAKE

INTRODUCTION

WEST LAKE, SITUATED NEXT TO THE CITY OF HANGZHOU, HAS been a cultural landmark in China since the Song dynasty (960–1279) and to this day remains one of the most visited scenic sites in the country. When the dynastic capital moved from Kaifeng to Hangzhou (known as Lin'an during the Southern Song, 1127–1279) during the mid-twelfth century, West Lake attracted visitors of all classes with its beautiful scenery and rich cultural traditions.[1] Touring around the lake inspired writings—from elegant poems to supernatural anecdotes—that reveal the range of people attached to this place. The lakeshore was crowded with peddlers, restaurants, and other establishments due to relaxed commercial regulation outside the city walls. Monasteries that dotted the hills around the lake drew pilgrims and tourists alike. The Ten Views of West Lake, ten four-character titles for specific scenic vistas, became a popular subject for poets and painters, whose works were charged with their emotional attachment to nature; these views continue to shape the gaze of sightseers right up to the present.

West Lake's development into a cultural landmark involved a complex historical process that was influenced by China's burgeoning Middle Period (800–1400) urbanization and increased exploration of the natural landscape, along with persistent and ongoing recording of this exploration within the Chinese cultural sphere.[2] Since the thirteenth century, the lake has served as a destination for tourist and cultural pilgrimage. Its fame also spread to Japan and Korea, consequently shaping landscape painting and garden design in those countries.[3] Ever since the dissemination of Marco Polo's writings about China, Europeans have also viewed West Lake as a symbol of Chinese urban culture.[4] When the history of West Lake is examined against the long-standing Chinese practice of creating cultural landmarks, several fundamental questions arise: What was distinct about the process of West Lake's transformation? How did visitors experience, alter, and perceive the natural landscape? How do we understand the complex meaning conveyed by the lake and the leisure sightseeing around it?

This book is both a history of West Lake and a case study of how famous Chinese sites were created through interactions between cultural norms and the natural landscape. It argues that West Lake emerged as a popular sightseeing destination in Song China and became a model for idealized nature that integrated spiritual pursuits and aesthetic desires. West Lake during the Song dynasty marked a significant moment in Chinese history: the natural landscape took an active role in shaping social activities and cultural identity instead of remaining a mere context for historical events or an aesthetic subject. Although this book concentrates on the Song dynasty, its discussion extends over a longer period, taking into consideration the cultural legacy of the Tang dynasty (618–907) and Five Dynasties (907–60) and also the Song dynasty's imprint in later times. Since the thirteenth century, Hangzhou and West Lake have served as icons of Chinese landscape appreciation, literary and artistic expression, and tourism. The cultural tropes that the lake embodied, such as the practice of naming scenic sites with titles like Leifeng Pagoda against the Sunset (Leifeng Xizhao), continued to inspire other places. The lake represented a powerful, unifying force in the formation of China's cultural geography and identity.

West Lake's emergence as a sightseeing destination took place in the very particular history of Hangzhou during its remarkable time as the de facto national capital. As leisure activities increased and the urban environment expanded, the lake was woven into the fabric of Hangzhou's city life both ecologically and economically. Studying West Lake involves a number of scholarly discussions and trends in the fields of urban history and cultural geography. By examining natural landscape in a suburban-urban context, this book contributes to the ongoing discussion of the traditional Chinese urban revolution by introducing the perspective of sightseers. Considering West Lake as a "sightseeing landscape" captures the moment and outcomes of a blurred division between nature and city. Furthermore, this approach enriches the growing literature of place studies with a historical viewpoint, emphasizing the importance of writing and layered cultural allusions in site making.

WEST LAKE AND HANGZHOU

West Lake is unique in that it was originally a natural part of the Zhe River (Zhejiang), also known as Qiantang River (Qiantangjiang), later became a freshwater lake that supported Hangzhou, and eventually developed into the city's "leisure zone."[5] This process involved complicated urban-rural interaction between Hangzhou and the adjacent West Lake, which shaped people's conception of nature and blurred the city boundary. These developments derived from and also contributed to the Southern Song's transitional status in the history of Middle Period China.

The natural geography of West Lake was formed over a long period. Archaeological evidence suggests that during prehistoric times, the region of West Lake was subsumed under the ocean. The lake started as a bay that connected the Zhe River and the East China Sea (Donghai). Gradually, the buildup of silt deposits separated the lake from the ocean, and by the fifth century CE, the lake had formed. Records from the Jin dynasty (265–420) do not mention a lake in that location, though they do offer detailed geographical information about nearby Wulin Mountain (Wulinshan).[6] When the lake was still connected to the river, the level and quality of the lake water changed with the tides. Deposits of silt eventually blocked the ocean waves and ultimately cut the connection between the lake and the river.

After its natural formation, the lake gradually became human-made nature. It was simultaneously a physically engineered natural feature and a conceptualized one as viewed through a cultural lens. The people of the city constructed nature through their presence and through the way they thought and wrote about it. On the one hand, the preservation of West Lake was achieved primarily through ongoing dredging projects. On the other hand, Chinese literati have long praised the lake for uniting heaven and humankind. West Lake therefore offers an excellent example of how an individual landscape has been brought under conceptual and aesthetic control while also being physically engineered.

Increasing interaction with the lake redefined the meaning of nature. In this context, nature is neither the pure natural landscape that literary works tried to concoct nor the constructed wildness that dominated this concept in the West.[7] In ancient China, the concept of nature was closely associated with the cultivation of land for agriculture and with practical observation of the physical environment. As intellectual historian Li Zehou argues, the traditional Chinese paradigm of "the unity of nature and man" combines the Confucian "humanization of nature" and the Daoist "naturalization of humans."[8] Aesthetic appreciation of the natural landscape in China began during the Six Dynasties (220–589), which witnessed the emergence of landscape poetry.[9] In Song times, this appreciation of landscape became popularized and commercialized.[10]

The appreciation of and increase in visits to West Lake were associated with the reconfiguration of urban space. In the field of urban history, one conventional approach is to treat the city as a unit and to investigate social structure and economic development within the city limits. Nevertheless, as environmental historian William Cronon argues, "The urban-rural, human-natural dichotomy blinds us to the deeper unity beneath our own divided perceptions."[11] While West Lake was one of Hangzhou's best-known features, it was a natural space linked to the city but not within its walls. Hangzhou's city walls—first built near the beginning of the seventh century and measuring about eleven miles in length, thirty feet in height, and about ten feet in width at the base—effectively blocked the view of West Lake from most parts of the city and thus demarcated a closed urban space.[12] But people's outings to the lake broke this separation intentionally and regularly.[13]

The development of Hangzhou and its outskirts benefitted from China's Tang-Song transition.[14] This time period witnessed a series of structural changes, including the institutionalization of the imperial autocracy, the use of the civil service exam to recruit talent, the growing circulation of culture via printing, and the monetization of the economy. These changes were particularly important for Hangzhou during the 150 years between the Jurchen conquest of north China in 1127 and the Mongol defeat of south China in 1276. During this period, southern China held for the first time more than 50 percent of the Chinese population, a majority of whom were immigrants from the north; numerous rivers facilitated transportation across regions; and an agricultural boom paved the way for accelerated urbanization.[15] This "medieval urban transformation" reached an extraordinary level in thirteenth-century Hangzhou. Located near the Zhe River and the southeast coast, and also on the south end of the Grand Canal, Southern Song Hangzhou attracted merchants from across the country (map I.1).

Hangzhou during the Southern Song also experienced both political and psychological turmoil; the lake was thus, for visitors, an escape from busy city life and worrisome political concerns. Hangzhou's hasty designation as the new temporary capital was controversial from the beginning. A short-lived peace treaty with the Jurchen did not protect the court for very long, and the Mongol invasion soon destabilized the dynasty. In their daily lives, residents of Hangzhou during the Southern Song were caught psychologically in a struggle between the uncertainty brought by the massive immigration from the north and the enjoyment of burgeoning luxury that went with it. The unfamiliar hustle and bustle of city life enhanced the sense of insecurity among literati and commoners alike. It was against this background that frequent excursions to West Lake first occurred.

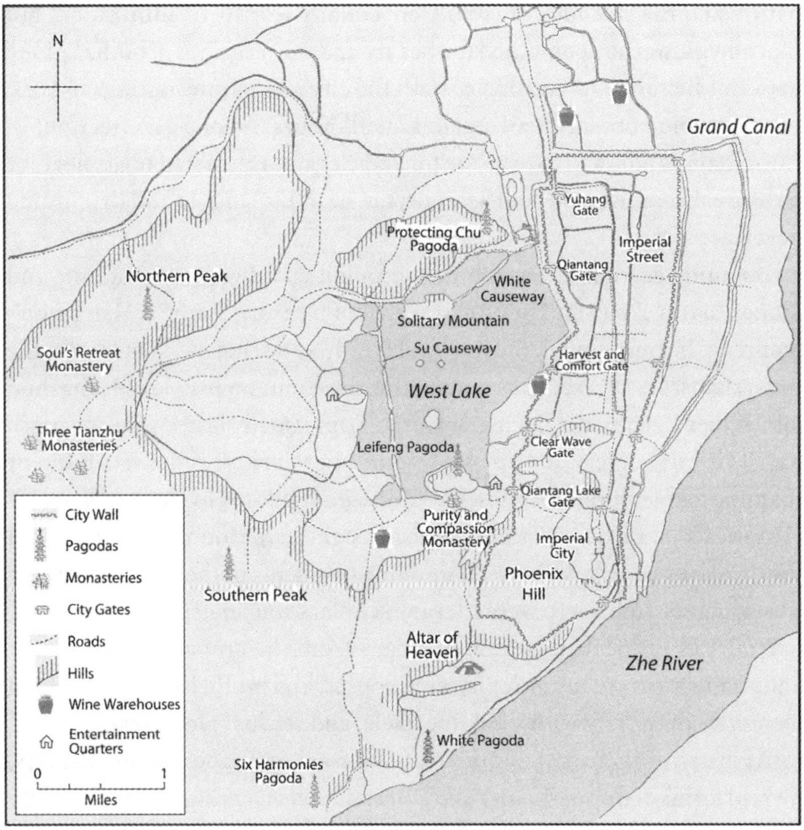

MAP I.1. West Lake and Hangzhou in the Southern Song (1127–1279). Cartography by Bill Nelson, 2019, after Hui-shu Lee, *Exquisite Moments*, 21.

SIGHTSEEING AND LEISURE

The lake became a destination for outings at the latest during the Tang dynasty, when a poem by Bai Juyi (772–846) first referred to it as West Lake.[16] The lake was originally referred to as Qiantang Lake (Qiantanghu), and the name "West Lake" came from its geographic position in relation to the city. Later, when the poet Su Shi's (1037–1101) comparison of the lake to the Lady of the West entered the vernacular as a famous saying, the lake was also called "Lady of the West Lake" (Xizihu).[17] During the Song dynasty, artistic and literary works dedicated to extolling urban life started to expand beyond the cityscape and incorporated the appreciation of natural beauty. The literatus Ouyang Xiu (1007–1072), for example, acknowledged that the beauty of nature and the splendor of cities were equally worthy of admiration, but that only Hangzhou combined the beauty and the pleasures of both.[18] Along with this literary appreciation of both the city and nature, outings to West Lake became popular in all seasons, at all hours. As one gazetteer put it, "Mountains and waters are beautiful and elegant. Decorated boats float for pleasure throughout the four seasons; the sound of singing and drumming never stops."[19]

Booming economic development brought city dwellers extra time and money to travel outside the city in search of pleasure. Early in Hangzhou's tenure as the new capital, the imperial family and scholar-officials were the main sightseers at West Lake. Gradually, the common people of Hangzhou joined them, especially during festivals. Trips usually lasted a day or half a day. This kind of leisure trip was referred to as *you* or *youye* (strolling or roaming for pleasure) in traditional Chinese as opposed to *xing* (traveling).[20] Historical documents usually refer to the sightseers around Hangzhou and West Lake as *youren* (sightseers) or *duren* (residents of the capital). Among this group of sightseers were literary scholars touring specific locales of note, urban residents in search of escape from the pressures of daily life, and connoisseurs of restaurants, wine houses, and brothels, who connected memories of the city with food, spectacle, and sensual pleasures.

Along with increasingly frequent sightseeing in and outside the city, myriad forms of infrastructure and entertainment catering to a wide variety of tastes and budgets became available. Scenic spots were constructed as a series of attractions; the series—and generally the order of viewing and the route of sightseeing—was standardized and reproduced in journal narratives, literary works, and visual images. The new career of tour guide developed to serve the tourists; seasonal markets and specialty stores also emerged. Furthermore, people started to pursue an authentic travel experience and therefore emphasized the value of localness and personal interaction with the physical sites. These quests fueled what sociologist John Urry and environmental scientist Jonas Larsen call the "romantic gaze," meaning a focus on idealized places through a cultural lens.[21] Touring the lake thus bridged the material enjoyment of sightseeing and the sensory experience of the landscape.

Pleasure and leisure activity have only recently received scholarly attention, and most scholarship concentrates on the late Ming (1368–1644) development of leisure life.[22] Echoing social and cultural historian Li Hsiao-ti's discussion of leisure (*yile*), this book takes sightseeing, along with its necessary infrastructure, as a focus for the examination of social complexity in a transitional period.[23] It examines excursions as class-specific and identity-constructing activities. Through leisure mobility, people seek connections with their own individual lives, so not everyone has the same experience at the same site.[24] Through excursions, emperors sought to demonstrate their political legitimacy, monks at their lakeside temples evoked religious teaching, merchants discovered opportunities for profit, and literati entered into dialogues with the lake's cultural past. Although usually motivated by the pursuit of pleasure, these recreational trips and excursions held complex meanings.

The history of sightseeing thus foreshadowed the complexity of tourism and preceded West Lake's intensity of meanings in late imperial China and today. Over the course of history, tourism has developed from occasional excursions into a global industry. Tourism, however, is by no means a modern development. As anthropologist Pál Nyíri argues, mass tourism has gone through "a series of staggered configurations," which included both historical and contemporary conditions.[25] In other words, modern tourism is rooted in and has been significantly shaped by premodern leisure sightseeing.

Scholars from diverse fields have examined tourism and excursions as cultural phenomena that both reflected and reshaped the very culture that attracted tourists. Social historians have revealed the influential role of travel in shaping identities;[26] sociologists have explored the social and psychological desires that fuel tourism.[27] The Song dynasty witnessed the nationwide development of traveling, which has attracted social and cultural historians in the past two decades. Wu Ya-ting examines the Song dynasty travel culture from the perspectives of movement and information networks; Ellen Cong Zhang discusses travel in the context of social and cultural integration.[28] Literary historian James M. Hargett explores the history of travel literature in imperial China and suggests that the Song dynasty scholar-officials' trips were usually regarded as a leisure activity, which was different from their predecessors.[29] Inspired by this scholarship, this book focuses on short-distance, pleasure-driven sightseeing activities and the formation of a cultural landmark with an assemblage of scenic sites. The development of sightseeing around West Lake during the Song dynasty is not entirely unfamiliar to scholars, but in general, previous discussions merely mentioned the lake's popularity or noted that literati added to its fame.[30] To bridge this gap, this book focuses on how West Lake was experienced and perceived in exploring the importance of sightseeing in physically and conceptually shaping the natural environment.

Historians of China have generally agreed that sightseeing became a culturally approved activity for the gentry during the sixteenth century.[31] By this period, a standardized list of *mingsheng* (famous scenic sites) had been established through literary traditions that constantly referred back to Tang-Song cultural figures.[32] Indeed, a similar phenomenon had already started around West Lake before the sixteenth century. Unlike its late imperial counterpart, Song dynasty sightseeing featured imperial spectacles and the formulation of literary conventions. It also created the model of an idealized human-constructed "sightseeing landscape" for Ming and Qing (1644–1911) cities. Similar sites such as the Long Causeway (Changdi) in Yangzhou, Tiger Hill (Huqiu) in Suzhou, and Black Tortoise Lake (Xuanwuhu) in Nanjing all functioned as "leisure zones" for their respective cities.

SITE MAKING AND PLACE STUDIES

Increased popular mobility of people spread the fame of West Lake. Enclosed by hills and gardens, the lake offered limitless possibilities for social and cultural engagement: "imperial outings and illicit trysts, puppet plays and official banquets, accomplished music and practiced crime, poetic competitions and vulgar commerce, weddings, and funerals."[33] The lake functioned as an arena where knowledge was reconfigured, aesthetic standards were contested, and commercial development was hosted. The history of sightseeing around West Lake can no longer be understood as an independent or solely leisured phenomenon. Instead, it was intimately woven into the formation of West Lake as a famous place and thus casts light on place studies.

The combination of lake, mountains, architecture, commercial activities, literature, and religious practices made West Lake a unique locale for visitors. What distinguishes West Lake from many other Chinese landscapes was its place in cultural tradition created by the renowned literati who wrote about it. In addition, royal patronage of Buddhism, which started during the Wuyue Kingdom (907–78) and was enhanced by the imperial family during the Southern Song, also established West Lake's identity as a religious center. Throughout history, most well-documented places benefited from only a few of these features, or, like Mount Tai (Taishan) and Mount Putuo (Putuoshan), did not emerge as multifaceted destinations until the late Ming or Qing.[34] West Lake, however, was one of the few sites that developed as sightseeing centers during the Song dynasty as a result of the convergence and interaction of political, commercial, cultural, religious, and environmental elements.

Place studies, derived from local history studies, constitutes a new research trend that no longer regards place as mere context for the discussion of other historical issues; instead, it sees place as an essential field for the production of materiality and the construction of discursive boundaries.[35] In the field of imperial Chinese history, scholars have researched specific prefectures and their local elites.[36] While these works focus on a city, a village, or a county, some scholars have recently narrowed the focus to a single place, such as a mountain or even a pavilion, initiating a trend toward place studies.[37] Compared to previous studies of local history, place studies directs more attention to the centrality of physical environments, both natural and human made. This approach explores how humans record, utilize, and conceptualize the physical place. Place is usually defined as a meaningful space that is central to people's immediate experiences of the world. While "space" has volume and allows movement, "place" indicates pause and provides security.[38]

Drawing from scholarship on place studies, this book examines the practice of site making. The making of sites is a cultural process very much associated with the practice of *seeing* these sites, which involves the active pursuit of scenic spots and the romantic gaze on these spots. Those who visually grasp a landscape also simultaneously experience a preordained vision acquired from the culturally bound previous depictions of this landscape. These sites become ephemeral through cultural engagement with physical places. Place making is the process through which the identity of a place is derived; the consequent formation of subjective and emotional attachment to place is usually called "sense of place." The sense of place varies depending on the individual and encompasses a diversity of sensory awareness spanning "sight, hearing, movement, touch, memory, imagination and anticipation."[39]

Site making occurred with growing diversity in the Song dynasty, during which it grew to involve religion, commerce, history, and aesthetics. Each chapter in this book discusses a specific aspect that contributed to or complicated specific locales at and around West Lake. The commodification and standardized treatment of these sites demonstrates how they became coordinates for collective memory and social engagement. For viewers, these sites were necessary landmarks for navigation within the natural environment; they were also sources of security during the political turmoil and historical changes at that time. Seeking, naming, and recoding scenic sites was itself an ordering, even a disciplining mechanism through which knowledge was constructed. Sightseeing evidenced an increasing engagement with geographical knowledge and an attempt to sort out the changing physical and social landscape.

Consequently, West Lake was not merely a sightseeing destination or a playground, but also a "re-creation space," both hosting recreational activities and re-creating those who toured around it. The association between human and place constitutes a vital source of identity, a point of departure from which people understand the world. Borrowing art historian W. J. T. Mitchell's distinction, this book looks into not only what West Lake "was" or "presented," but what it did to different groups of people.[40]

The lake had three layers of meaning. It was a *place* for sociocultural engagement; it was where the materiality of sight and sightseeing *took place* through numerous occurrences, including events, entertainment, dredging projects, and ecological changes; it was also where sightseers, including writers and painters, could be put "*in place*" with the passage of time and the growing body of knowledge. To grasp this three-layered meaning of West Lake, this book focuses on visiting, writing (in both literary and imaginal formats) about, and conceptualizing the lake.

West Lake at times was inconsistent, as the identity of a place varies with the intentions, personalities, and circumstances of those who experience it. The lake not only consisted of assemblages of conflicting and shifting landscapes but also acquired different identities. It functioned as a commercial market and as a water resource; it embodied literary tradition and political discourse; it served as a focus for artistic and religious pursuits. These different aspects share a similar geographical infrastructure and historical context. Time is part of people's experience of places, for these experiences are bound up with flux or continuity. Moreover, places themselves are the present expressions both of past experiences and of hopes for the future.

WRITTEN AND VISUAL SOURCES

Because sightseeing is shaped by a variety of social forces, its study draws on a wide range of sources. In the Song period, textual records about everyday life increased dramatically, and daily jottings, collections of anecdotes, tales, and local gazetteers offer "a mass of precise and picturesque details."[41] Notebooks (*biji*) and collected works (*wenji*) dating back to the eleventh century contain "observations about medicine, hydraulics, finance, astronomy, military strategy, carpentry, agriculture, and geology, including phenomena that the authors themselves could not explain but which they brought to the attention of more knowledgeable readers."[42] These sources include records of authors' travels, which tied together the practice of reading, touring, and writing. As Hargett argues, the diurnal chore of maintaining personal records and the more leisurely activity of reading others' diaries were common in Song literary culture.[43]

This book relies principally on "miscellanies," a type of *biji*.[44] These texts demonstrate the increasing attention to local knowledge, personal observation, and everyday life experiences.[45] Their "miscellaneous content, accommodative structure, and flexible form" make these sources challenging to use.[46] Miscellanies can be better interpreted as writings about *wenjian*, literally, "things heard and seen." These texts reflect a new emphasis on the role of hands-on personal experience.[47]

Sometimes the seeming casualness of *biji* compilers was intended to "show off" their modesty and prudence. This miscellaneous style demonstrated and encouraged a more versatile way of reading.[48] Equally important, these records were subjective books of remembrance and are unavoidably imbued with nostalgia. This book thus reads miscellanies as expressions of individual experience and political conviction, rather than as general records of universal conditions.

Four miscellanies, sometimes referred to as capital journals, on Southern Song Hangzhou are extant today, and they constitute the main body of primary sources used in this book. In roughly chronological order, the earliest of these miscellanies is *Record of the Splendor of the Metro Capital* (Ducheng jisheng), dated 1235. It was written by an author self-identified as the Codger Who Irrigates His Own Garden (Guanpu Naideweng). The second is the Old Man of West Lake's *Record of Multitudinous Splendors* (Fansheng lu), written in approximately 1250. Known for their use of colloquial language, these two works are relatively short compared to the next two lengthy miscellanies. The third is Wu Zimu's *Record of the Millet Dream* (Mengliang lu), possibly dated 1274.[49] The fourth book, *Old Affairs of the Martial Grove* (Wulin jiushi), the only one undoubtedly written by a literatus, Zhou Mi (1232–1298), was composed between 1280 and 1290.

This book is also informed by certain Ming dynasty works that preserve extensive records of the Song. These include *Gazetteer of Sightseeing around West Lake* (Xihu youlan zhi) and *Supplemented Gazetteer of Sightseeing around West Lake* (Xihu youlan zhiyu), both by Tian Rucheng (1503–1557), which provide detailed records of West Lake, and *Supplemented Old Affairs of the Martial Grove* (Zengbu Wulin jiushi) by Zhu Tinghuan (d. 1644), which offers a Ming analog to Zhou Mi's miscellany.

The new genre of the capital journal, which emerged in the Song dynasty, differs from other *biji* with its focus on one city and that city's unique organization. Before the Song dynasty, little was written about urban scenery, not even that of the grand metropolitan capital city of the Tang dynasty. Instead, poets prior to the Song dynasty concentrated mainly on the strictly natural sites such as urban gardens.[50] By the mid-Song dynasty, the city emerged as a literary topic, most famously in Meng Yuanlao's *The Eastern Capital: A Record of a Dream of Hua* (Dongjing meng hua lu), an account of the Northern Song capital, Kaifeng. Meng's book provided the model for the four capital journals on Hangzhou.[51] Despite their varied length, all four of these capital journals provide colorful and vivid pictures of a commercial cityscape with hidden dynastic power structures. Though usually written in a casual or informal style, these books are meticulous about all they detail, including shops and commercial goods, seasonal activities, temples, storytelling and theatrical performance in the entertainment quarters, and anecdotes about the city and its environs.[52]

These journals convey the centralizing of palace and imperial events, as well as the massive scale of the city and its profusion of commodities. On the one hand, the annual cycle of festivals that was coordinated with the rites of the imperial court remained a prominent organizing principle. On the other hand, however, writers also found topics that did not fit perfectly into this structure. Therefore, in the middle of the annual cycle recorded in *Old Affairs of the Martial Grove*, Zhou Mi suddenly moves to a general topographical depiction of West Lake. This break with the expected structure was an attempt to incorporate newly emerging information into the hierarchical, imperial-centered long-standing cosmology. As cultural historian Christian de Pee points out, capital journals "juxtapose the recent tropes of the city as an extension of nature with the organizing principles of older urban texts to create a semiotic replication of the disorienting sensory experience of the metropolis."[53]

This book also draws on travel diaries, a genre that encompasses other *biji* and literary works, especially poems. The Tang-Song period produced China's earliest travel diaries, but it was not until the twelfth century that they became established as an independent literary form with discernible conventions and characteristics.[54] Several factors contributed to their popularity in the Song: the development of land and water transportation, the frequency of official travel, and the literati's concern with everyday life. Throughout the Song dynasty, many literati were fond of compiling *ji*, or records. This was not an invention of the Song dynasty, but at that time, travel chronicles appeared in unprecedented numbers. This type of prose writing usually served as a literary testimonial marking a site or as a record of impressions during a brief excursion.

Most of the travel writings used in this book fall into the category of "day trip essays," each of which records a short trip to some particular destinations.[55] In other words, these writings focus on well-known landmarks. In the thirteenth century, the genre of day trip essays expanded to include poems about excursions to a particular place. Many poems were written on mundane themes pertaining to the sensual enjoyment of West Lake. More than one thousand song lyrics about West Lake written by about two hundred poets are included in Tang Guizhang's *Complete Compilation of Song Lyrics of the Song Dynasty* (Quan Song ci). Collected works of certain prominent historical figures, such as Su Shi and Lin Bu (967–1028), contain rich materials about their sightseeing experiences. These were reread and reconstructed during the Southern Song and helped shape the experience of later sightseers.

These day trip essays and poems contain rich historical references, literary allusions, and scholarly comments. The most significant value of these works lies in the intimate glimpse they afford of the daily mobility and taste, as well as the personal thoughts, of scholar-officials in Song China. The most productive approach to each of these travel accounts is to read them as a series of representational practices within specific contexts, rather than as verifiable experience.[56] Reading and analyzing these poems and literary essays demands caution due to their potential for distortion. It is necessary to remember that poems were partly governed by their particular genre and its conventions.

Local gazetteers are the best source on the engineering and construction of West Lake, as well as relevant government regulations. Three gazetteers survived the Southern Song, compiled during the Qiandao (1165–73), Chunyou (1241–52), and Xianchun reigns (1265–74). Three out of fifteen chapters in the first one survive, including the earliest information on the gardens added to the lake. Five out of fifty-two chapters in the second gazetteer survive, and these provide more-detailed records on scenic spots.[57] The last gazetteer includes the earliest extant sightseeing map of West Lake, complete with the notation of all the sightseeing spots mentioned (map I.2). This map is the primary source consulted by this book for spatial information about sightseeing routes and scenic spots.

MAP 1.2 Southern Song Map of West Lake, ca. 1268–1275, with important sites noted. Cartography by Bill Nelson, 2019, after Jiang Qingqing, *"Xianchun Lin'an zhi" Songban "jingcheng situ" fuyuan yanjiu* (originally based from Qian Yueyou, *Xianchun Lin'an zhi*, 1.9).

1. Imperial Street
2. (Lin'an) Prefectural Government
3. Qiantang Gate
4. Bodhi Monastery
5. Harvest and Comfort Gate (Golden Flood Gate)
6. Temple of Five Dragon Kings
7. Willow Temple
8. Boat Landing Pavilion
9. Harvest and Joy Tower
10. Assembled Scenery Garden
11. Clear Wave Gate
12. Qiantang Lake Gate
13. *wazi* (entertaiment quarter)
14. Imperial Phoenix Hill
15. Long Bridge
16. Clear Water Lock
17. Fang Family Valley Mountain
18. Altar of Heaven
19. Imperial Boat Lane
20. Leifeng Padoga
21. Purity and Compassion Monastery
22. Nanping Hill
23. Wine Warehouse
24. Paper Money Bureau
25. The First Bridge of the Southern Hills
26. The Second Bridge
27. Lake and Mountain Hall
28. The Third Bridge
29. Three Worthies Hall
30. The Fourth Bridge
31. Qu Winery
32. The Fifth Bridge
33. The Sixth Bridge
34. Tomb of King Yue
35. Four Guardians Temple
36. Solitary Mountain
37. Lin Bu's Tomb
38. Broken Bridge
39. Boat Landing Pavilion
40. Lake Dredging Bureau
41. Big Buddha Head
42. Virtue Growing Hall
43. Slip Water Bridge
44. Protecting Chu Pagoda
45. Agate Monastery
46. Mount Ge Hill
47. Mansion for the Manager of Affairs
48. Nine-li Pine
49. *wazi* (entertaiment quarter)
50. Hua Family Mountain
51. Big Wheat Hill
52. Small Wheat Hill
53. Southern Peak Route
54. Mist and Cloudy Cave
55. Southern Peak
56. Upper Tianzhu (Monastery)
57. Middle Tianzhu (Monastery)
58. Lower Tianzhu (Monastery)
59. Flying Hill
60. Cold Spring (Pavilion)
61. Soul's Retreat (Monastery)
62. Gathering Celebration Monastery
63. Northern Peak
64. Northern Outside Wine Warehouse
65. Wine Warehouse
66. (Grand) Canal

While local gazetteers were written from the perspective of the government and local elite, fictional stories and anecdotes provide crucial information about the popular viewpoint. Local legends that circulated and were widely accepted at the time, such as those in *Book of Hearsay* (Yijian zhi) by Hong Mai (1123–1202), provide insight into not only how the common people may have viewed West Lake but also how they appropriated the literati tradition it conveyed. This book's discussion of the sightseeing business and accommodations provided by temples also draws occasionally on fiction, especially Zhou Qingyuan's *Two Anthologies of West Lake* (Xihu erji). Although the stories were compiled during the Ming dynasty, some included in this work were already circulating orally during the Song and Yuan.[58]

Additionally, certain monasteries, such as the Soul's Retreat Monastery (Lingyinsi) and the Tianzhu Monasteries (Tianzhusi), preserved records of their interactions with the local community in the form of stone carvings, historical relics, and temple gazetteers. Though published after the Song, the temple gazetteers preserved detailed records of Song dynasty buildings, developments, and even anecdotes. The Japanese record of the Five Mountains and Ten Monasteries, which was made around 1248 by Japanese monks who had visited Hangzhou, also provides valuable material for reconstructing the physical appearance of important temples.[59] These sources also offer insights into the relationship between temple visits and excursions.

Though written records of paintings of West Lake date back to the Northern Song, the earliest extant painting of the lake was produced during the Southern Song dynasty. Court painters, such as Li Song (1166–1243), Chen Qingbo (ca. 1253–1258), and Xia Gui (ca. 1190–1230), produced most of the paintings of West Lake surviving from this era. One long hand scroll titled *Scenic Attractions of West Lake* depicts the scenery around the lake in clockwise order, focusing on various buildings, boats, and people along the lakeshore.[60] All these paintings play an essential role in this book's discussion of the material details of excursions and the aesthetic appreciation of natural scenery. It is worth noting that while landscape paintings provide straightforward evidence of how sightseeing influenced the way in which West Lake was depicted and appreciated, they were also highly colored by contemporary aesthetic standards. This book's analysis of painting aims at reconstructing a way of seeing that was determined by both personal experience and the aesthetic standards of the time.

This book's three parts focus respectively on how the lake was experienced, represented, and perceived. This structure reveals three aspects of one place: the physical, the symbolic, and the mental—an analytical tool borrowed from philosopher and sociologist Henri Lefebvre.[61] It explores the sophisticated sense of West Lake that emerged through physical construction and touring, the idealized representation of the lake in writing and painting, and the cultural conventions of the time.

PART 1

The Material Construction of Nature

CHAPTER ONE

LEISURE

Commercialized Sightseeing beyond the City Wall

VISITORS TO WEST LAKE DURING THE QINGMING FESTIVAL (THE beginning of the fourth solar month) near the end of the twelfth century encountered a prosperous and impressive scene of sightseeing activities. At that time, the presence of the imperial family was prominently evidenced by drums, dancing performances, and elaborately decorated dragon boats sporting colorful flags. The local government organized regattas offering lucrative prizes, and noble families distributed attractive knickknacks to the spectators. Residents of the capital, both men and women, gathered on the causeways and around the Three Worthies Hall (Sanxiantang). Literati paid homage inside, and the common people purchased souvenirs outside. In the afternoon, people flew kites, watched performances, or composed poems with their literati friends. Some visitors went directly to the entertainment quarters while others chose to visit a powerful family's garden open to the public on festival days. At both these kinds of destinations, performances and games were offered. Not until the evening did the tourists return to the city.[1]

This was the scene depicted by Zhou Mi and other contemporary scholars. Literati and noble families enjoyed sightseeing almost every day, and the common people would join them during festivals. Although West Lake was praised for its natural beauty, actual enjoyment of the lake was experienced through leisure activities and commercial offerings. These included, but were not limited to, boating, wine houses, restaurants, entertainment quarters, and souvenir booths. The joys and tribulations of excursions to West Lake intersected with commercial development, as revealed in material details of the structure of sightseeing activities that enabled the lake to mediate the relationship between state and society and facilitate social interaction.

Studies of leisure during the Song dynasty concentrate mainly on the Northern Song capital of Kaifeng. Scholars have argued that Kaifeng was the first capital to become a center of commerce.[2] During the Northern Song, leisure life was marked and advanced by the collapse of the walls between city wards, the moving of shops to the side of the street, and the extension of entertainment activities into the evening.[3] These features continued in Southern Song Hangzhou, which similarly grew into a thriving center of activity. The term *duren* (residents of the capital) was first coined by Meng Yuanlao in *The Eastern Capital* (Dongjing meng hua lu) and was later borrowed by official and nonofficial Southern Song literati in Hangzhou. Literary records reveal that "residents of the capital" emerged as a new group of consumers and participants in public events. Another relevant term was *youren* (sightseers), which was used to intentionally avoid reference to traditionally defined social classes. It emphasized the activities in which these people were engaged and their mobility.

While further developing the urban features inherited from Kaifeng, Hangzhou also exhibited new features that stemmed from its unique geographical setting. The surrounding rivers and mountains confined the city, which had to abandon the traditional layout for capital cities. As a natural landscape outside the city wall, West Lake altered the economic map of the city when this site became a setting for the daily, seasonal, and commercial activities of urban residents. The development of such a leisure zone outside the city proper represents a fluid public space that was conducive to complex commercial interactions and social pleasure.

Sightseeing activities can be viewed as examples of materiality and as an arena for interaction with the state order. Varying forms of material objects around the lake, including boats, food, drinks, and games, were documented in contemporary texts and paintings. Although these records reflect a romantic perspective on the capital city, the details they provide are essential in conceptualizing both the materiality of this space and an internal hierarchical structure. Regulation by the government and active participation by the imperial family incorporated the market commercialization in the city outskirts of West Lake into the urban administration and at the same time enhanced their ruling legitimacy. It was during this process that West Lake developed into a paradise for sightseers in the Southern Song.

HANGZHOU'S CULTURE OF CONSUMPTION

Commercialization in Song China has received extensive scholarly attention. The development of a commercial economy during the Song dynasty was reflected in two trends: more widespread consumption of luxury items and increasing variety in the items available for mass consumption.[4] Both were vividly apparent in the capital of Hangzhou, and the increasingly relaxed commercial regulation during the Song dynasty also allowed marketplaces to form spontaneously in the outskirts of the city and surrounding villages.

Hangzhou, in particular, benefited due to several factors: the rapid development of merchants' groups, the local culture of consumption, and the gathering of powerful and wealthy families. In general, contemporary accounts associate the people of Hangzhou with a mercantile mindset. They were described as "good at and eager to make a profit."[5] During the Song dynasty, 414 different kinds of businesses could be found in Hangzhou, and each one was comprised of many hundreds of households.[6] The growth of merchant families reflected the high level of urbanization and population congestion in the capital; it also evidenced a more flexible attitude toward social hierarchy. Although the social status of merchants was traditionally low, this gradually changed during the Song. A Jiading-period (1208–24) gazetteer stated that all four ranks of people—officials, farmers, artisans, and merchants—were equal parts of the foundation of society.[7]

Commercial development led to economic competition that fostered conspicuous consumption. Contemporary writers tended to believe that the ample resources in south China encouraged a hedonistic lifestyle among Hangzhou residents. City dwellers were said to have a strong passion for amusement and were depicted as grasping every opportunity to maximize their pleasure and comfort. As one local gazetteer recorded, "The people of the capital [Hangzhou] invited courtesans, and never stopped singing and drumming—a custom that has continued since olden times."[8] These portrayals and criticisms continued after the Song dynasty and even became a conventional interpretation of local culture in Hangzhou. As the Ming dynasty scholar Tian Rucheng commented, "The people of Hangzhou liked luxury and a relaxed lifestyle. . . . As for daily living, food, and drink, they preferred the most up-to-date and expensive items. They looked down upon anything priced even a little lower."[9]

Along with this growing desire for fashionable luxury and new objects, the production and circulation of commercial items also underwent unprecedented development. Hangzhou residents were fond of a kaleidoscopic mix of novelties, including those in this list from social and cultural historian Jacques Gernet: "Beauty products (ointments and perfumes, eyebrow-black, false hair), pet cats and fish for feeding them with, 'cat-nests,' crickets in cages and foodstuff for them, decorative fish, bath wraps, fishing tackle, darts for the game of 'narrow neck,' chessmen, oiled paper for windows, fumigating powder against mosquitoes."[10] The demand for exquisite handicrafts reflected an obsession with objects and collecting. During the Song dynasty, art collecting grew in popularity and undoubtedly influenced the consumption style of society as a whole.[11]

The obsession with material objects also influenced the excursion market. Boats were made in various sizes with different decorations and were given creative names. The government produced a variety of wines to attract consumers, and peddlers sold more than twenty varieties of colorful souvenirs. Materialism shaped the sightseeing experience and how the lake would be remembered. The wide array of entertainments and commodities fostered the emergence of a group of connoisseurs of boats and pleasure pursuits.

Extravagant entertainments and consumption aroused two types of discourse when these activities conflicted with moral values. On the one hand, period accounts usually frowned on the conspicuous consumption of the powerful families.[12] This was echoed in literati recommendations that Emperor Ningzong (1168–1224, r. 1194–1224) should refrain from undertaking numerous excursions. Notably, imperial sightseeing was abandoned during Ningzong's reign. As a poem by Huang Hong attested, "Most of the dragon boats disappeared from the lake; this was because the previous emperor [Ningzong] was very thrifty."[13] The emperor's own abstention also was interpreted through the framework of filial piety. An official once suggested that the emperor should not undertake lake excursions too often because the Empress Dowager Li (1144–1200) was buried beside West Lake. The emperor was said to have accepted this suggestion, thereafter dramatically decreasing his outings compared to rulers before and after him.

On the other hand, the government also rationalized its involvement and support for excursion businesses by emphasizing the moral responsibility of local government to nurture the livelihoods of the common people. In the year 1050, when the Wu region experienced a famine, the local manager Fan Zhongyan (989–1052) encouraged the people of Hangzhou to take excursions on the lake and hold boat races. He even encouraged the monasteries to launch several construction projects as "labor costs were low during the famine." Arguing against contemporary criticism, Fan said, "Banqueting, sightseeing, and construction are all means to collect the money of wealthy families and support the poor."[14] He believed that the more sightseers there were around the lake, the more opportunities there would be for small merchants and peddlers to do business. Hangzhou was the only city in the region to emerge economically unscathed from this challenging year. While both negative and positive attitudes toward consumption coexisted, this latter view seems to have been more dominant. The government's supportive or encouraging role in leisure activities was frequently apparent and proved to be essential to the continuation of the sightseeing market.

PLEASURE SEEKING: FROM THE URBAN CENTER TO THE OUTSKIRTS

Performances, games, and shopping experiences filled and enlivened sightseeing trips. Inside the city, entertainment was mainly confined to wine houses and the entertainment quarters called *wazi*. *Wazi* hosted more than ten different kinds of performances, including dramas, singing, storytelling, puppet shows, talk shows, and historical fictional stories.[15] Of the twenty-one *wazi* of Hangzhou, two were located close to West Lake: one outside the Qiantang Lake Gate (Qianhumen) and the other on the west bank of the lake (see map I.1). The locations of these two entertainment quarters were selected deliberately. The Qiantang Lake Gate, adjacent to the Harvest and Joy Tower (Fenglelou), was the main gate used by residents of the capital to reach the lake. The *wazi* on the west side of the lake was located close to major gardens owned by powerful officials and eunuchs and was also where the wine bureau and the paper money bureau were established (see map I.2).

While the state hoped to regulate commercial space by concentrating entertainment activities within the preset sphere of *wazi*, the reality was an increasing expansion and integration of entertainment activities. Providers of entertainment constantly demanded extra street space to attract more customers; peddlers also brought mobile commerce to every corner of city life. The expanded urban market spurred the development of the city's suburbs, and the area around West Lake offered an open space where entertainment providers were no longer confined to alleys and streets and a freer domain for merchants to thrive without challenging the state too directly.

CUSTOMER-CENTERED ENTERTAINMENTS

Many forms of entertainment were available around the lake. Zhou Mi listed nearly thirty types, including flute and zither concerts, dance, drama, drumming, a pot-shooting game, football, the art of tea drinking (*fencha*), singing, circuses, water puppet shows, Daoist magic, fireworks, and kite flying.[16] Many of them were not confined to a particular space, and some, such as fireworks and water puppet shows, required an open environment beside the water. A majority of these entertainments were portable and could offer mini theatrical experiences anywhere in the area. Providers of these entertainments were called "people who chase opportunity" (*ganchenren*). The name indicated that these performers were mobile and not bound to certain places or employers.

The structure of the lake market was different from that of the urban marketplaces; the relationship between customers and sellers moved further away from the kind inherent in traditional shops and entertainment quarters, with their fixed locations. There, customers came for services and performances; on the lake, the performers sought out sightseers. The "small-feet boats" (*xiaojiao chuan*) on the lake, whose name derived from their short length, further enhanced this free movement of entertainment. Guests could call for them and buy a song or the company of beautiful courtesans, who enjoyed the romantic label of "water immortals." Some of these boats provided equipment for games like pot shooting, and some carried special goods for people to buy as souvenirs or gifts. These boats were active sellers; they "pursued opportunities, chasing [customers] and seeking to sell [their performances]."[17] The active discovery of customers recast the commercial space by shifting the focus from shops to consumers. Traditional relations between buyers and sellers were reversed in this more interactive context.

Furthermore, while entertainment quarters offered mainly performances in which customers could be only spectators, the entertainments around West Lake provided more opportunities for active participation in games, such as soccer and kite flying. While elite women usually engaged in kite flying in their private gardens, the lake offered a domain close to the public gardens for those who could not afford a private terrace. *Guanpu*, a combination of selling goods and gambling, was one example of how, in preparing a fun activity, the foremost consideration was engaging audiences. The *guanpu* merchant displayed all his goods, or awards, and prepared up to eight coins. Customers competed for a prize by throwing the coins in a basin. The customer whose coins all faced up could take the award item right away. Otherwise, the customer lost some money. During the Northern Song, *guanpu* were permitted only during the Lantern Festival, the first day of winter, and the Cold Food Festival. But during the Southern Song, the government no longer restricted *guanpu*, and most city residents participated both as hosts and as players.[18] In many cases, the performing aspect of *guanpu* was expanded while the profit-making aspect was minimized. Participation was an essential element emphasized in these theatrical experiences, in which city residents could become both performers and interactive spectators.

BOAT RACING

Another major form of entertainment that took place on the lake was boat racing. On boat-racing days, more than ten dragon boats would gather on the lake amid scenery festive with colorful flags and the sound of drums. Boat racers who had been recognized by the Hangzhou governor, the highest bureaucratic official in charge of Hangzhou (similar to the mayor of a modern city), or the imperial house in previous events would dress up in embroidered clothes and decorated hats, "to be different from the others." Their emphasis on past acknowledgment by governors and emperors evidenced the effectiveness of hierarchical order on the popular mindset. The municipal government sponsored this event, and the capital governor himself would contribute certain types of prizes to encourage the participants. Imperial eunuchs and distinguished visitors would also contribute to the prizes that "could not be counted." These public events were dominated by competition among contestants for material prizes; written accounts of the races were positive in tone and departed from the traditional attitude of eschewing material pursuits. The large audiences in particular created a triumphal and celebratory atmosphere. As Zhou Mi recorded during the Chunxi reign (1174–89), "The people of the capital, both men and women, all gathered on the Su Causeway (Sudi) and the White Causeway (Baidi);[19] there was almost no place to stand. On the lake, the decorated boats, which resembled fish scales [because they were so numerous], there was no way for them to move."[20]

Although Zhou Mi's depiction may have been romanticized by nostalgia, his description of the essential elements in this event is plausible. The support of the government, the contributions of powerful families, the showmanship of the boat racers, the mass audience of Hangzhou citizens, and the abundance of colors and sounds all were essential in transforming a public event into a theatrical experience. There was a stage, and there were actors, directors, plots driven by abundant prizes, and an actively engaged audience. While the material prizes commercialized the whole scenario, the harmony of the scene was construed by the government as an expression of political authority.[21] This was both a hierarchical performance and a collective carnival.

The government sponsorship of boat racing might have been an attempt to lure people away from the "tidal bore" event on the Zhe River. It was a local custom to swim in the autumn high tide holding a small flag. While struggling against the fierce current, participants strove to ensure that the flag remained dry. Scholar-official Cai Xiang (1012–1067) during the Northern Song fulminated against such a practice, as it was thought to contravene Confucian warnings against risk-taking that would make their parents worry. But the large prize and the enthusiastic audience combined to fuel even greater interest in this event in the Southern Song. Encouraging a similar water-centered public spectacle on West Lake provided an alternative to satisfy sightseers' pursuit of a bustling environment.

PERIODICALLY OPENED PRIVATE GARDENS

In addition to the open space of the lake itself, entertainment could also be found in occasionally opened private gardens, which dominated much of the lakeshore. Elite families in the Southern Song were not only involved in conspicuous consumption but also engaged in the conspicuous offering of entertainment. Some private gardens in and outside the city, such as Eunuch Jiang's garden, opened as amusement parks on select days. Every year before the Cold Food Festival, various games and performances were held in the garden of Eunuch Jiang, who served as a park commissioner in the court. These performances included archery, football, and cockfighting, "in order to satisfy sightseers."[22] The open garden was not a commercial space, as Jiang did not intend to make money through these games. Instead, this was a form of conspicuous competition among the elite and the powerful families. Opening these gardens allowed a temporary creation of public space where government control was relaxed.

Nevertheless, while the boundary between public and private might collapse during an open-garden day, the inherent social hierarchy and power structure still remained unambiguously in force. As Zhou Mi explained the allure of these events for urban residents, "This garden resembles the forbidden [imperial] garden, similar in content yet smaller in scale."[23] The mimicking of the imperial garden on a smaller scale was a compromise between sumptuary regulations and the desire for conspicuous consumption. The imperial order was reflected in, and also virtually enhanced by, the high officials' mimicry and the visitors' curiosity.

SHOPPING FOR SOUVENIRS

Pleasure came not merely from performances and games, but also from the simple act of purchasing commodities. Consumption, a natural phenomenon in every prosperous market, functioned as a powerful source of pleasure. The joys of consumption are rooted in the imaginative processes of the self, whose internal emotions generate a sense of pleasure surrounding the meanings and anticipation associated with various objects and experiences. Indeed, many popular commodities available around West Lake resonated either with a specific feature of the place or with the memory of a pleasurable activity.

The most popular commodities sold at the lake were collectively termed "local products of the lake." This name indicated that these objects were seen as symbols of West Lake and were most likely sold only around the lake. These local products included particular fruits and vegetables, soups and wines, games, grass "suitable for boys" (*yinan,* meaning grass believed to be able to bless the woman who wore it with a baby boy), props for drama, ornamental plants, flower baskets, painted fans, colorful flags, sweet fish, rice-flour cakes, clay figurines, toys mounted on sticks, powder balls, seasonal flowers, and clay baby dolls.[24] These local products and souvenirs could be found on the imperial boat and the "small-feet boats" alike, in the private gardens opened to the public, and around religious sites, especially the Previous Worthies Hall (Xianxiantang), the Three Worthies Hall, and the Four Guardians Temple (Sishengguan), all of which were must-see spots that attracted many consumers.[25]

These commodities were regarded as souvenirs of outings to West Lake. Souvenir purchasing was associated with the desire to personalize and materialize the landscape and experiences with the lake's scenery.[26] Souvenirs made West Lake acquirable and transformed the excursion experience into goods. In addition, these local products let people hold on to passing moments.[27] After an excursion, Hangzhou residents reportedly returned home with little dragon boats, toys on sticks, and other local products to give their friends and relatives. Many of the local products reminded visitors of the performances they had watched and the food they had enjoyed on their excursions. Sweet fish was a snack made from flour and shaped like a fish. Colorful flags evoked memories of the boat races. Symbolizing West

Lake products, events, and games, these local souvenirs could help people describe their excursion experience to their friends. This was not only a way to share but also a way to show off. As Wu Zimu commented, "Hangzhou's local culture [was] competition for extravagance."[28] It was as important to be seen by others as visitors to the lake as it was satisfying for sightseers to cherish their memories through material legacies of their visit.

Fresh flowers and grass were regarded as local products, as the western suburb of Hangzhou was known for gardens that provided flowers to city residents.[29] While houses and shops occupied land inside Hangzhou city, the more open landscape around West Lake allowed for the growing of flowers. As poet Zhao Fan wrote during the Chunxi reign, "In the old days, people only grew grain and vegetables, not flowers. Only families around West Lake planted flowers."[30] Irrespective of age or wealth, Song women prized flowers for daily personal adornment.[31] The pervasiveness of this fashion for using flowers encouraged wealthy people to buy early-blooming and expensive flowers to differentiate themselves. In the sixth lunar month, when jasmine was the most expensive flower, women would wear as many as seven sprigs, despite the fact that this would cost several tens of *quan* (a type of paper currency, also known as *huizi*) and would last for only one day.[32] Plants were also widely used for home decoration. The garden located beside the Slip Water Bridge (Liushuiqiao) was known at the time for pine trees in strange shapes along with flowers of the four seasons; these flowers were sold daily.[33] The desire to bring natural elements into urban life was prominent in popularizing specific local products.

As the value of a particular commodity or practice was advertised by its use or adoption by high social classes, some simple toys became known as local products. For instance, the passion for baby dolls made from clay came from an anecdote about the sightseeing experiences of the family of the minister Han Tuozhou (1152–1207). During a spring excursion, the family was said to have made its own clay puppets. Family members tied cotton to the clay puppets' heads. The popularity of clay baby dolls, therefore, was closely associated with the example set by a powerful family. Toys on sticks also became popular due to the unique cachet created by the role-modeling of the imperial family. Documents recorded that emperors asked servants to affix these toys on sticks to the imperial dragon boats.[34] Interestingly, these items originated with peddlers who carried various toys hanging from sticks to attract buyers.[35]

The connection between imperial example and the leisure enjoyment of the common people reveals a cooperative integration of state power and market commercialization. One example was the process through which imperial calligraphy became a commodity in the urban market. *Compendium of Numerous Treasures and Rarities* (Baibao zongzhen ji), a merchant manual that circulated in Southern Song Hangzhou, provides instructions on how to evaluate various products, including imperial calligraphy. The manual comments on how to determine whether a particular example of calligraphy is an authentic piece from the court and which emperor's calligraphy is more likely to be authentic.[36] On the one hand, this was a playful use of imperial calligraphy: imperial power was appropriated and given new meaning in the commercial market. On the other hand, the criteria for determining authenticity show the desire for and value placed upon this quality. Although not all "imperial" calligraphy was indeed the emperor's own handwriting, these pieces still carried the emperor's seal and the value it embodied. The reciprocal relationship between imperial power and market commercialization allowed this product to benefit both the imperial family and the marketers.

PROFESSIONAL GUIDES

The practice of pleasure seeking involved all types of commodities, and sightseeing itself was also commoditized. The abundant offerings and numerous locations of entertainment at West Lake gave birth to a new career—that of professional guide. In the fourteenth-century scroll *Scenic Attractions of West Lake* preserved in the Freer Gallery of Art, an attendant with a parasol follows every gentleman. Some servants are shown carrying parasols and looking for sightseers (figure 1.1). Historical documents reveal that a group of excursion guides was called *xianren*, indicating that they were at leisure or lacked a set profession. This term has the negative connotation of idleness without accomplishment, but *xianren* were in high demand. These guides searched for the best places for pleasure seeking, decided what routes travelers should follow, and recommended activities for sightseers.[37] This new job emerged to meet the pleasure seekers' demand for local guidance. The guides were sellers of the West Lake entertainment market who sought to actively engage new consumers in this market. They were the product of a well-organized leisure realm in which the sightseeing experience itself could be designed by professionals and tailored for customers.

Most of the commodities and entertainments available around the lake were superfluous, not essential to everyday life. Bright colored, appealing to the senses, and often noisy, they were bought and sold in a manner that

FIGURE 1.1. Servants with parasols at West Lake. Detail from *Scenic Attractions of West Lake*, ca. fourteenth-century depiction of the scene in the mid-thirteenth century. Ink and color on paper, 33.3 × 1849.8 cm. Freer Gallery of Art, Smithsonian Institution, Washington, DC: Gift of Charles Lang Freer, F1911.209.

was competitive and conspicuous. From many perspectives, they were far removed from the simple water-ink landscape paintings and reclusive literary depictions of the lake. They evidenced both the preference of Hangzhou residents for amusing craftworks and the leisurely atmosphere sought after in sightseeing.

BOATING ON THE LAKE: FASHION AND CONSPICUOUS CONSUMPTION

As the hand scroll *Scenic Attractions of West Lake* is unrolled, the numerous boats that decorate the lake surface immediately catch the eye. Three kinds of crafts are meticulously depicted in the scroll (figure 1.2). The largest one, with more than six panels of windows that opened from the inside, could carry at least twelve people.[38] Four or five boatmen row the boat with long oars. There are almost sixty vessels like this; some are docked at the Boat Landing Pavilion (Shangchuanting) near the Qiantang Gate (Qiantangmen), while others are floating beside the dikes. Medium-sized boats were operated by one boatman and could carry three to four guests. Some of the medium-size boats have a small flag at the stern, advertising entertainment or goods offered on board. The hand scroll shows more than eighty boats

FIGURE 1.2. Large boats, medium-sized boats, and small boats. Detail from *Scenic Attractions of West Lake*. Freer Gallery of Art, Smithsonian Institution, Washington, DC: Gift of Charles Lang Freer, F1911.209.

of this size. Also, several tiny boats are depicted around the bigger boats, perhaps selling food and wine.

The flourishing of lake boats was made possible by major improvements in ship manufacturing and advances in water transportation. The growing overseas and interregional trade in southern China allowed Hangzhou to become a major port in the transportation system.[39] Conveniently located midway between the Yangzi River and the port cities in Fujian, Hangzhou attracted many big ship owners to establish there.[40] The use of watercraft within Hangzhou was more extensive than in other cities. The uneven surface of Hangzhou streets made the movement of carts through the city difficult, a problem that led to increased reliance on water transportation.[41] The continuing dredging of the rivers and waterways ensured that boats would play an essential role in the smooth operation of the city.[42]

Boating was the preferred way to enjoy the scenery of West Lake: floating on the lake offered a new perspective for the sightseer's gaze. Song sources frequently mentioned boating on the lake. More than 30 out of the 184 poems in the anthology *Bamboo Lyric Songs of West Lake* (Xihu zhuzhi ci) center on boating.[43] These poems depict the lake boat as both a favored vantage point for sightseers and a dynamic component of the lake scenery.[44]

DECORATION AND NAMES OF BOATS

Boating on the lake usually started with a festival during the second lunar month. *Record of Multitudinous Splendors* documents this scene on Boat Landing Day during Emperor Ningzong's reign period: "Around the Cold Food Festival, all of West Lake is filled with decorated boats, just like a floating bridge. Head boat, second boat, third boat, fourth boat, fifth boat, boats with railings, rowboats, paddle boats, melon-skin boats, small boats—more than five hundred in all. There are several dragon boats near the Northern and Southern [Routes]."[45] Later in the summer, boats would be in high demand when it was much cooler on the lake and under the shade of the willows.[46] Even during the winter, wealthy families would play "snow boats."[47]

Floating on the lake, the boats with their various colors and shapes added to the scenery. Jiang Kui (1155–1221) mentioned small red boats; a poem by Gao Xiaochou described a white boat with a beautiful red curtain.[48] The bright colors indicated that the lake boats were no longer considered as simply utilitarian transportation vessels but as pleasure boats. Owners decorated their boats not only to satisfy themselves but also to make a claim about their own character.

Boats attracted so much attention from capital residents that many boats were given literary names such as "Big Green," "Ten Types of Silk," "Hundreds of Flowers," and "Bright Jade."[49] Smaller boats had names like "Seven Treasures," "Golden Lion," "Gold Success," or just the family name of the owner.[50] Some names were elegant and well known among urban residents, such as "Floating Star Ferry," "Wind-Facing Ship," "Snow Roof," and "Cloud Cruiser."[51] Those who most frequently named boats were the so-called busybodies (*haoshi zhe*). The naming practice brought leisure boating into the literary conversation and further promoted boating as a fashion.

Boat-naming during the Song exerted long-lasting influence. The Yuan dynasty scholar Bai Tingyu mentioned boats in an essay about West Lake: "[There are] decorated boats and orchid ships, light cruisers, and big ferries. They have names, such as 'Bright Green' and 'Clear Floating.' *Gold Success* is small and fast; *Bright Jade* carries hundreds of guests; *Total Success* could carry four groups and use only half of its rooms."[52] Almost all these boat names were recorded in Southern Song texts and seem either to have continued into the Yuan dynasty or to have become standardized as names for specific types of boats. Ming scholar Wang Keyu (b. 1587) compared the Ming lake boats to the Song: "Talking about West Lake boats, today's [Ming dynasty] boats follow the Song tradition but are smaller . . . the craftsmanship of the boats is similar, the biggest one just adds an extra floor, and the decoration is extremely luxurious. But the names of the boats have become worse and worse."[53] Southern Song lake boats, and especially their names, were thus taken as standards for evaluating subsequent boats.

THE FASHION OF BOATING

The Southern Song fashion of boating started with the imperial family. As a public space, the lake offered a stage for the emperor and his family to demonstrate their prosperity and authority in front of the residents of the capital. In looking at the imperial family's use of boating, it is, therefore, difficult to separate a purely political purpose from an avocation for sightseeing. Emperor Xiaozong (1127–1194, r. 1162–89), for example, served the abdicated Emperor Gaozong (1107–1187, r. 1127–62) devotedly; he always took the imperial family to tour the lake on Gaozong's birthday. The imperial boat was extensively decorated, "covered with an embroidered curtain with pearl decorations, hanging on the boat were pearls, jades, [model] dragon boats, toys on sticks, and flower baskets." Xiaozong was an adopted son of Gaozong. He therefore had an even stronger-than-normal motivation to publicly demonstrate his loyalty to and care for Gaozong, in order to strengthen his legitimacy of ruling.[54] Zhou Mi also noted that such sightseeing demonstrated the emperor's merit. The spectacle of imperial boats attracted the attention of residents of the capital throughout the Southern Song. Sources documented in detail a boat commissioned by the Emperor Lizong (1205–1164, r. 1224–64). Constructed out of precious fragrant wood, this craft was so valuable that it was used only once, by the Zhouhanguo Princess.[55]

Wealthy and powerful families also had their own boats built, as a way to demonstrate their social status and wealth. There was no better platform for conspicuous consumption than the spacious surface of the lake; the wealthy in particular preferred to invest their wealth in fashionable things.[56] As Wu Zimu recorded, the "powerful families and wealthy households" would take their own boats for an excursion. Eunuchs and families of officials took small boats called "lotus-picking boats." Although Wu Zimu did not elaborate on what types of boats the powerful families built, he expressed his fondness for the lotus-picking boats, which were covered with dark green cloth and decorated exquisitely inside.[57] The sumptuary law was applied loosely, if at all, to boat making. The scholar Zhao Meishi, for example, had a large boat finished in black lacquer whose interior furniture was all made from decorated fragrant wood. Beneath the seating area was expensive *agila* wood. The enormous expenditure required to build this boat impressed even the high official Lü Shikui.[58] Furthermore, some self-designed boats, such as that of Jia Sidao (1213–1275), indicated the convenience of access to the court granted to their owners and symbolized the great privileges the court bestowed on them. Favored by the emperor, Jia used his boat to travel to court meetings directly from his lakeshore house. He commissioned a unique boat that was propelled not by oars but by a rope and mechanical apparatus and that traveled "as fast as flying."[59] Boat construction thus became an arena in which wealthy and powerful people could flaunt their resources and claim their special status.

RENTAL BOATS

Ordinary people hoped to mimic the activities of the rich but could not afford to build their own boats, and visitors from elsewhere in the country did not own lake boats. Boat rentals, therefore, became a popular business at West Lake, as the excerpts from the poems below illustrate:

> [I] urge you to rent a West Lake boat often.
> The rain pours on the roof of the boat; we will reach the flagged pavilion to enjoy wine.[60]

> In front of the Harvest and Joy Tower, outside of the Golden Flood Gate [Yongjinmen], [I] rent a small boat.[61]

> Rent a skiff to carry the bright moonlight;
> [I am] happy as the [noisy] flute and drum all the way back to the city.[62]

Renting boats was not restricted to daytime, and literati even preferred boating at night as a way to avoid noisy travelers. In Southern Song Hangzhou, the city gates closed at night to insulate the urban center from any disturbance occurring in the suburbs and to force urban residents to return home after dark.[63] However, this did not result in the closing down of boat rentals for the night. A story mentioned that a courtesan and a scholar rented a boat after the gate closed because they could not go back into the city.[64] The ongoing business of renting boats provided a backup plan for those unable or unwilling to return to the city at night. Night boating thus possibly reduced the significance of the nocturnal closure of the city gates.

FIGURE 1.3. Pier outside the Qiantang Gate. Detail from *Scenic Attractions of West Lake*. Freer Gallery of Art, Smithsonian Institution, Washington, DC: Gift of Charles Lang Freer, F1911.209.

Boats were available for rent near the Boat Landing Pavilion. The inscription of Li E (1692–1752) on *Scenic Attractions of West Lake*, which is based on his viewing of the painting and his reading of the Southern Song documents, mentions two public boat landings: one was outside the Qiantang Gate (figure 1.3), and the other was outside the Willow Temple (Liusi). All of the piers were located beside the city gate for the convenience of tourists coming from the city. Two private piers, one belonging to a powerful official's family beside Long Bridge (Changqiao) and the other belonging to Jia Sidao, accommodated the boats of the imperial family and the elites.

Renting a boat included amenities such as the provision of food and wine. Freed from the need to worry about supplies, passengers needed to bring only a tip. Renting a boat was popular year-round, and there were no closure days. Reservations were necessary on holidays, such as the eighth day of the second lunar month, the Cold Food Festival, and the Qingming Festival.[65] At these times, the big boats were first rented to noblemen and officials and only afterward made available to other city dwellers.[66] It is not clear whether this was a social custom to satisfy powerful people or whether it was due to the elite's connections with the boat businesses. The social hierarchy, though seemingly absent on ordinary days, was evident during festivals.

The high demand for boats during these festivals inflated the rental fee, which could reach about two or three hundred *quan*.[67] Since there were different issues of paper currency and the value fluctuated, it is impossible to calculate the exact value of this amount of money, but comparisons with other records suggest its purchasing power. *The [Official] History of the Song Dynasty* (Song shi) recorded that in 1260, the Hangzhou government once used fourteen million *huizi* to buy four hundred thousand *dan* of rice.[68] Two hundred units of paper currency were therefore equal to about six *dan* of rice. Social historian Cheng Minsheng estimates that the average amount of rice consumed daily by one person during the Song was one or two *sheng*; two hundred units of paper currency were therefore enough to feed three hundred people for one day or one person for almost a year.[69]

This is an extreme example of how expensive a boat rental fee could be; renting a boat during other times was possible for ordinary urban residents. The growing demand for boat rentals during festivals reflects the fact that the common people were willing to spend most of their savings on high-end pleasure activities.[70] Competition in lower-class consumption derived from the desire to follow the boating fashion of the elites and to attract attention while doing so. To imitate and thereby to differentiate oneself constituted a dualistic principle that underlay the pursuit of fashion in society.[71] While imitation was more commonly seen among the lower classes, those in the middle and upper classes were equally driven by a desire to be different.

Boating on the lake was a prominent and overt way to convey a message of distinctiveness. West Lake served as a public stage, and the activity of pleasure boating was not readily available within the city. This was a social theater, in which all social classes struggled to be seen and to attract attention. The emperor used these occasions to demonstrate his filial piety; high officials used boating to show off their privileges; literati wanted their customized boats to be noticed; and commoners could also participate in a show of fashion by renting a boat or familiarizing themselves with boats' names.

DRINKING AND EATING: HIDDEN POWER IN THE WATERING HOLE

Hangzhou was widely known for its advanced offerings of restaurants and wine houses. Zhou Mi recorded a long list of foods, divided into three categories, that were fashionable in Southern Song wine houses.[72] The first type was snacks and nuts, such as flavored green tangerine peel, almonds, pinellia tuber, round cardamom, ginger, olives, and mint. The second type, "home style" (*jiafeng*), included spiced deer meat, crab, sheep hooves, wine-flavored clams, squid, ground shrimp, and dried fish. The third type, "food to neutralize the effect of alcoholic drinks" (*xingjiu kouwei*), included river ray, oyster, squid, snail muscles, little yellow croaker, blood clams, and ground horseshoe crab meat.[73]

A few observations can be made based on this list. First, people's knowledge of and the presentation of food became more advanced and sophisticated during the Southern Song. The three categories of foods—snacks, main dishes, and small dishes with wine—were considered various stages of a meal. The practice of naming and listing foods, both in writing and in chanting while greeting guests, continued the Northern Song showmanship in food culture.[74] Second, the concept of drinking while eating was widely accepted; hence, certain foods were considered suitable to accompany the consumption of wine. Third, unlike in the Northern Song, seafood and fish were now dominant. Many types of edible seafood came from nearby counties.[75] While the main dishes intended to accompany wine presented a mixture of northern- and southern-style foods, the local southern seafood cuisine gradually came to dominate the popular small dishes.

The urban culture of the Song dynasty and the fondness of Hangzhou residents for luxury goods caused them to prefer eating out rather than preparing food at home. Favorite eating spots included restaurants, temples, and simple food stalls. Restaurants thrived due to this new clientele. Excursions to West Lake similarly presented opportunities to savor specialized foods offered on and around the lake.

WINE HOUSES AND RESTAURANTS

The most famous restaurant by the lake was the Harvest and Joy Tower outside the Golden Flood Gate, one of the more than ten official wine houses.[76] This wine house had the advantage of lake scenery and proximity to the city gate (figure 1.4). Customers who faced the lake could view it from a higher elevation. As Wu Zimu wrote: "Outside the gate, there is a wine house, called Harvest and Joy, which used to be called the Rising Emerald Tower (Songcuilou). Besides West Lake itself, one can see thousands of peaks around the vast pool of green water. Willow ponds and flower valleys can be seen through the railings. Floating boats and decorated ships that carry singers and performers all gather on the water beside the restaurant. This is the best spot for sightseeing."[77]

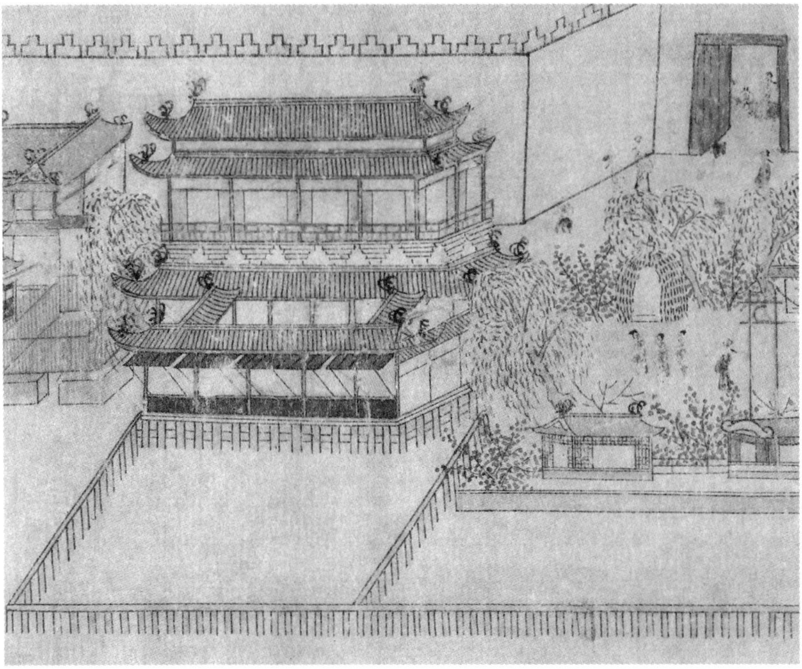

FIGURE 1.4. Harvest and Joy Tower. Detail from *Scenic Attractions of West Lake*. Freer Gallery of Art, Smithsonian Institution, Washington, DC: Gift of Charles Lang Freer, F1911.209.

With such a view of the lake, there was no better place to have a succulent meal during an excursion or to treat friends from afar to a welcoming dinner. Hong Mai recorded a story in which the Wutong Deity visits the Harvest and Joy Tower one evening.[78] This story highlights the luxury silverware used in this wine house. In popular mythology, the Wutong Deity was the god of money; the association of this deity with the wine house reflected its prosperity. Frequented by urban residents, this wine house was described as "filled with laughter and happy singing, day and night; the number of customers did not decrease, even on hot, rainy, windy, and snowy days."[79]

Wine houses offered a feast of sumptuous food as well as first-rate service, performances, and an opulent environment, as Wu Zimu recorded:

> Colorfully painted, the gate of the restaurant is called the Joyful Gate. Green and red fences stand in front of it. The curtains are made from green silk; the gardenia-shaped light is covered with red silk and gold powder. The courtyard and corridors are decorated with lush flowers and woods,

> with nice wine seats. Once a customer steps into this restaurant and takes about ten to twenty steps into the main corridor, it becomes two corridors, one on the south and one on the north. Along the halls are clean compartments and comfortable seats. During the night, the candles are bright and luminous, flickering up and down. Dozens of courtesans, who are wearing heavy makeup, gather in the main corridors. They are waiting for the guests to call them. They look like immortals gazing from afar.[80]

This account reveals a few characteristics common to Southern Song wine houses in Hangzhou. First, the setting and decoration were foremost features. The extensive and colorful decorations were all meant to attract attention. The show began with colorful fences that reached out to the street. Once the customers entered the wine house, the architecture was structured to guide their physical movement as well as to pique their curiosity. The process of parting curtains and moving along corridors resembled theater attendance. These wine houses offered not merely wine and food but also experiences.

Second, courtesans were the main attraction. Most of the houses had more than ten regular courtesans. There also were servant girls who would sing for the customers without being called, hoping for tips.[81] Most of the courtesans, especially the ones in major wine houses, were licensed and regulated by the government. To collect as much tax revenue from its wine monopoly as possible, the Song government encouraged wine consumption, and according to contemporary scholar Lü Zuqian (1137–1181), the government was "even afraid people wouldn't drink."[82] The government also performed a special ritual every year when the official wine bureau began to make new wine, hoping to attract many customers. During this process, leisure entertainment and state business became mutually reinforcing.

These wine houses were also known for their multiple services and differing interactions with the customers. The waiters would ask every customer about their needs and chant the names of special dishes. Small dishes offered before the wine were just for viewing (*kancai*), while the actual dishes for eating, which were better prepared, were served with the wine.[83] The aesthetics of food presentation were as much a concern as the actual taste. The intention was to entertain an audience of paying consumers. The intricate connection between food and performance, upon which later food culture was modeled, appeared in Kaifeng during the Northern Song.[84] Eating in these wine houses was more a social engagement than a simple

FIGURE 1.5. Restaurant banner. Detail from *Scenic Attractions of West Lake.* Freer Gallery of Art, Smithsonian Institution, Washington, DC: Gift of Charles Lang Freer, F1911.209.

opportunity to feed oneself. The money that diners spent also paid for various experiences after entering the wine house. Having a simple meal in a midsize restaurant in Hangzhou would cost about a hundred *wen,* which was about the daily cost of living of a lower-class city dweller. The price at a big wine house was much higher.

In addition to grand wine houses, numerous smaller pubs and food stalls surrounded the lake. Many of these shops hung banners advertising "good wine and fine food" (figure 1.5). These locations provided more affordable food and a casual environment for diverse contacts between people from different social and economic backgrounds. In contemporary documents, these small restaurants appeared frequently as the subject of gossip and strange happenings.[85] This was partly because people from different backgrounds mingled more beside the lake than in the city. Another reason was the desire of the elite to pursue simple activities outside the city wall. They would, therefore, sometimes choose small pubs over big wine houses while wandering around the lake.

Contact across classes sometimes occurred by means of wall writings in these pubs. It was not an unusual practice for these pubs to erect white screens or walls on which tipsy customers would write poems. These functioned as forums, where customers could enjoy and comment on each other's compositions. They also functioned as advertisements for the pubs. Through the process of transmitting these texts, the writing walls became recognized public places.[86] According to one anecdote, Emperor Gaozong once visited a small pub and commented on "Wind through the Pines" (Feng ru song), a poem by Yu Guobao, an ordinary literatus.[87] The emperor changed one word in Yu's poem as a clever game, showing off his own literary talent. Soon after returning from this excursion, the emperor summoned Yu and promoted him.[88]

The reason this story enjoyed wide circulation deserves further analysis. In anecdotes, it is not uncommon for emperors (or emperors in disguise) to go out among the common people, often to take the "pulse" of society. This story, like many others, humanized and naturalized imperial power by placing the emperor in an ordinary pub and by offering an alternative to the official practice of appointment. Meanwhile, such a dramatic encounter with the emperor, or an encounter imagined each time the story was retold, enhanced the prevalent imperial power. It reflected the expectation that the emperor would favor talented scholars, and it extended the penetration of the imperial order into small suburban pubs. While the lake and its little pubs existed outside the city, the presence and circulation of imperial encounters announced a hidden power structure.

FISH SOUP AND NORTHERN FOOD

The lake's little "melon-skin boats," named for their simplicity and lightness, provided a choice of small dishes for the convenience of passengers. These boats usually sold snails, jellyfish, and seasonal fruit, which were welcomed not only by urban residents and elite men and women but also by the imperial house. It was recorded that Emperor Gaozong once bought a bowl of fish soup made by Song Wusao (fifth sister-in-law of the Song family), a Kaifeng native who had immigrated from the north after the Northern Song. After tasting the fish soup and getting to know her family history, the emperor rewarded her with ten gold coins, a hundred silver coins, and ten bolts of silk.[89] Her fish soup was then sought after, and its popularity continued into later periods.[90] Gaozong's high evaluation of this soup was associated with his nostalgia for the old capital. Not only the food itself, but also the memory associated with it, moved the emperor and likely attracted other consumers. In valuing snacks and migrants from the old capital, both seen as symbols of the dynastic past, the emperor was claiming the legitimacy of the imperial house. Moreover, the emphasis on this proclivity in the urban journals glorified the image of the emperor and enhanced the connection between the Northern and the Southern Song.

Nostalgia associated with particular foods made northern-style cuisine popular. Kaifeng was a showplace of specific regional cuisines; restaurants there specialized in the cuisines of distant provinces and places.[91] However, the regional food system underwent changes during the Southern Song. Restaurants that were once categorized as offering southern dishes could no longer be described as such. Instead, a northern-style taste was now sought after (even if with some difficulty) and became more highly valued. In Zhou Mi's list of foods, two nonlocal types were spiced deer meat and sheep hooves. Similarly, lamb from Li Qi'er and milk from the Wang family were among the most prized snack brands in Hangzhou.[92]

All these foods originated in northern China and catered to northerners. After the Mongol invasion, immigrants from the north had flooded into Hangzhou, swelling its population to several times the original size.[93] These immigrants brought other practices with northern origins, such as the storage of ice.[94] Before the Shaoxing reign (1131–62), it was not common in the south to store ice. But in 1138, after a great snowfall, immigrants from the north saved ice in their cellars. From then on, this method of ice storage spread and was used to make iced drinks for sightseers during the summer.[95]

Benefiting from the massive migration after the Northern Song, Hangzhou began to offer a mixture of northern and southern cuisines. As Wu Zimu said, "In the two hundred years since the court moved to the south, people got used to the local environment. Food and drink mixed; north and south were no longer distinguished."[96] This commentary regarded the convergence of customs from different regions as progress and a sign of active cultural communication. Meanwhile, southern food, which former residents of the northern capital might once have considered exotic, acquired higher status as "local" and capital-city food.

SEAFOOD AND LOCAL CUISINE

Seafood played a major role in the urban cuisine of Hangzhou, and West Lake in particular was known for its ample supply of freshwater fish.[97] The government regulated but did not prohibit fishing in the lake.[98] Of the various lake fish, the carp was reputed to taste the best.[99] Fish from West Lake was not only available at the lake but also sold in large quantities in the city.[100] Song literati acknowledged that it was good to eat fish and freshwater crab from the lake in the lakeside restaurants, where it was fresher and cheaper than inside the city.[101] In his essay about crabs, Gao Sisun (1158–1231) declared West Lake crab the best in the country.[102] The Song government forbade fishing on the lake with long rods, which could disturb the underwater environment, so that the crabs reproduced peacefully.[103]

The abundant and varied offering of foods was accompanied by an emphasis on a food's origin, for this provided information about authenticity. As Zhou Mi recorded, during the summer, when the residents of the capital escaped to the lake in search of a cooler environment, small boats offered a wide choice of seasonal fruits and summer desserts. These included lotus roots from the Assembled Scenery Garden (Jujingyuan), lychees and plums from Fujian, waxberries from Fenghua County, and other refreshing treats. Not all the fruits and snacks were associated with a specific place, but Zhou provided sources where possible.[104] The connection between place and food evidenced the discerning attitude of urban residents about what they ate and these consumers' pursuit of the best food. This increased attention on various places in the south, and their local products reflected the Southern Song interest in exploring the region's resources. The sections on local products in the newly compiled gazetteers for the southern provinces evidenced this interest.

Northern foods and the memories associated with them, along with local foods from various southern cities and provinces, made up the diverse culinary repertoire available at West Lake. The broad offerings of wine and the opportunities to taste food from different places added to the allure of sightseeing at the lake. Meanwhile, the complex and varied origins of visitors to the lake determined the mixed offerings of northern and southern foods. The discourses about food and wine, for example, were not merely about taste. This mélange of food traditions offered at the lake helped enhance Hangzhou as a capital that represented different regions and embodied a memory of the Northern Song.

CONCLUSION: PUBLIC SPACE AND STATE ORDER

Taken together, these components of the excursion market at West Lake constituted a public space that was characterized by flexibility of location, open hours, and consumption that was relatively leniently regulated by sumptuary laws. Visitors could rent a boat at several boat landings or enjoy a drink in any restaurant, teahouse, or wine house. Sightseers could enjoy entertainment and purchase various commodities on the boats, in the wine houses, and on the dikes. The expansion of commercial space into the less-regulated natural landscape tempted purveyors and consumers to embrace the fluidity of conspicuous consumption. The sightseeing experience was thus concretized, commoditized, and theatricalized.

By providing city dwellers with consumption-oriented places to seek pleasure, sightseeing experiences at West Lake created a seemingly shared space. This space functioned as a sort of "watering hole" that allowed people to interact with others from different social groups. New social interactions emerged, such as relationships between buyers and sellers, sightseers and guides, and fashion leaders and followers. Almost everyone, from the imperial family down to commoners, found ways to enjoy the lake. Sometimes class divisions seemed to blur for a while, when wealthy people and commoners enjoyed the same scenery, when they encountered each other in the same pub, or when they viewed or participated in similar entertainment.

Nevertheless, with the joys of drinking and eating came reminders of hierarchical power, hidden yet persistent. Different choices, ranging from the most to least extravagant, were available for all types of consumption, and the choices made demonstrated the power of a visitor's wealth. More importantly, the social hierarchy was displayed through fashion. Boating was made available to commoners via rental services, and specific local products carried meaning as souvenirs. West Lake was sometimes depicted as a stage, where sightseeing undertaken by the members of the imperial court and noble families was observed, discussed, and copied by ordinary people. Conspicuous consumption thus became widespread due to the desire to demonstrate taste and wealth.

The state participated in the development of commercial sightseeing through basic regulation of the city outskirts, such as the night curfew of the city gate, and it restrained those who harmed the order of the market. The development of entertainments gave rise to market scams and brawls, such as using beauties to seduce young men and cheating in the *guanpu* game.[105] For instance, Hong Mai described a kidnapping case that occurred at the lake, in which the perpetrators were eventually punished after a careful investigation by the government.[106] Only talented and tough officials were assigned to take charge of public order. In addition to the Bureau of Military Affairs, several thousand watchmen and special policemen were responsible for specific areas in the city.

On the other hand, the government did not restrict West Lake's commercial activities. There were no time restrictions on excursions and no strict regulations on the small business that prospered around the lake.

Instead, the government was supportive of the emergence of this suburban retail space. Zhou Mi reported, "Sightseeing and commercial activities were not prohibited."[107] On special occasions when a large number of visitors gathered on the lake, the emperor would even delay the closure of the city gates to reduce the risk of people in the crowds injuring each other in a rush to return to the city.[108] Moreover, the municipal government exerted its influence mainly through hosting the boat race that opened the sightseeing season and through its monopoly on wine making and the issuing of wine permits. Sources describing the vibrancy and abundance of the sightseeing market usually referenced the imperial ruling. For instance, Zhou Mi attributed the relaxation found in sightseeing activities to the peace and prosperity during the Southern Song.[109] Given the harassment from the northern dynasty and the Southern Song desire to recover the north, Zhou Mi's words were more an encomium to the court than an accurate depiction of reality.

Moreover, imperial spectacle dominated sightseeing entertainment. The imperial house loved to make a public show of its sightseeing and to engage with the common people, from scholars to sellers of fish soup. In the anecdotes about imperial engagement with West Lake, the emperor himself becomes a consumer, a sightseer, and a connoisseur of the enjoyments found there. His participation in leisure activities constituted a type of spectacle, less formalized yet more accessible to commoners. The lake therefore blended imperial space and commercial space.[110]

The convergence between the desire of the capital residents for pleasure and enjoyment and the desire of the state to offer a public space as both an outlet and a stage for imperial order enabled the lake to become a leisure zone for Hangzhou. This leisure zone hosted dazzling entertainments and conspicuous consumption, and it expanded social interaction, popular culture, and the engagement of the state and the imperial house. It was both a commercialized and a politicized space. Architecture historian Jianfei Zhu has shown that suburban and rural space in Beijing was used as a supplement permitting social life to thrive without challenging the state head-on.[111] Similarly, the formation of West Lake as a leisure zone outside the city proper redefined the relations between urbanites and suburbanites.

Commercial activities permeated the city and West Lake, each of which provided goods to the other: lake products, such as fish and cultivated plants, were widely sold in the city, and diverse foods from different places arrived at the lake through the Hangzhou market. While sightseeing was intended to offer enjoyment of the scenic beauty of West Lake, the majority of the joys these capital residents sought at the lake were aesthetically the opposite of natural beauty. Ironically, the lake's location outside the city made it a public domain that attracted interwoven social engagements. But it was also West Lake's increasing economic exchanges with the city and the public performances of power at the lake that blurred the line between the city and its suburb.

CHAPTER TWO

URBANIZATION

Water Management at West Lake

IN 1079, WHEN SU SHI SERVED AS THE GOVERNOR OF HANGZHOU, he proposed to the imperial court a dredging project, noting that "West Lake is as important to Hangzhou as the eyebrows and eyes are to a person. Neither can ever be dispensed with"—a metaphor that conveyed both the practical and the aesthetic significance of the lake to the city. Hangzhou was sandwiched between the Zhe River and West Lake. The river water ran rapidly and carried a significant amount of silt, and the groundwater in the area was salty and undrinkable. Consequently, West Lake provided water for Hangzhou throughout imperial history. The construction of irrigation canals also supplied lake water to surrounding farmland and provided water transportation. As map 2.1 indicates, Hangzhou during the Southern Song resembled today's Venice or Delft. Through the city ran more than ten waterways, many of which connected with the lake. These waterways allowed for faster, more convenient travel within the city.[1]

The water network connection between West Lake and the city of Hangzhou has long attracted academic attention. Scholars of urban history discuss engineering projects at the lake in their studies of Song dynasty Hangzhou;[2] economic historians evaluate the lake's significance in Hangzhou's economic map from the perspectives of irrigation and transportation.[3] These scholarly analyses connect the lake to the broader urban context, but they depict West Lake as less important than the city of Hangzhou.

West Lake's complicated ecological role influenced the government's ongoing physical interventions and maintenance. The efforts of the government during the Song dynasty to regulate West Lake represented an enduring attempt to reconcile competing desires for economic profit and resource sustainability. The government consistently sought to balance

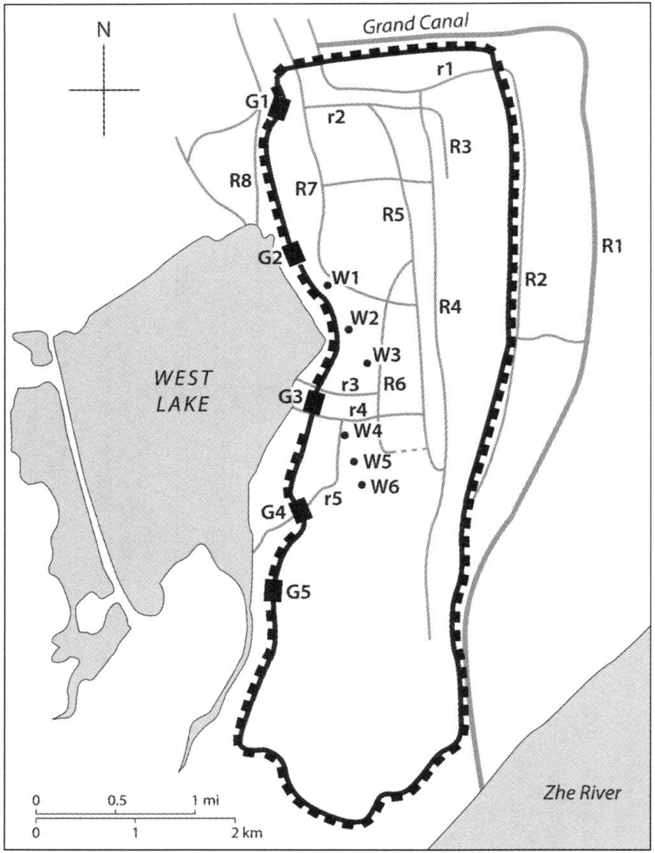

MAP 2.1. Waterways, wells, and gates in Southern Song Hangzhou, ca. thirteenth century. Cartography by Bill Nelson, 2019, after Zhang Huiru, "NanSong Hangzhou shuihuanjing yu chengshi fazhan hudong guanxi yanjiu," 38.

City Wall of Lin'an

G **City Gate**

- G1 Yuhang Gate (Yuhangmen)
- G2 Qiantang Gate (Qiantangmen)
- G3 Harvest and Comfort Gate (Fengyumen)
- G4 Clear Wave Gate (Qingbomen)
- G5 Qiantang Lake Gate (Qianhumen)

• W **Six Wells Constructed by Li Bi**

- W1 Small Square Well (Xiaofangjing)
- W2 White Turtle Well (Baiguijing)
- W3 Prime Minister Well (Xiangguojing)
- W4 Square Well (Fangjing)
- W5 Golden Ox Well (Jinniujing)
- W6 West Well (Xijing)

R **Waterways running from north to south**

- R1 Outer Sand River (Waishahe)
- R2 Vegetable Market River (Caishihe)
- R3 Mount Mao River (Maoshanhe)
- R4 Salt Bridge Canal (Yanqiao yunhe)
- R5 Market River (Shihe)
- R6 Golden Flood Pond River (Yongjinchi hedao)
- R7 Clear Lake River (Qinghuhe)
- R8 Peach Blossom River (Taohuahe)

r **Waterways running from west to east**

- r1 White Ocean Pond River (Baiyang chihe)
- r2 Market River (Shihe)
- r3 Water Gate River (Shuimen hedao) *
- r4 Golden Flood Pond River (Yongjinchi hedao)*
- r5 Clear Lake River (Qinghuhe)*

* r3–5 comes from the lake

short-term tax benefits and long-term economic development. The rise of leisure sightseeing activities during the Southern Song further complicated and positively influenced the practical usages of the lake. This interweaving of environmental protection, financial profiteering, and the desire for sightseeing made the lake space and the urban space of Hangzhou more interdependent.

Over time, West Lake became an increasingly important focus of administrative government. As the health of the lake became linked to the sustainability of Hangzhou, the lake was ecologically transformed and spatially incorporated into the city. It thus became an example of "urbanized nature." Practical parameters were required for the hydraulic management of the lake, and this generated unprecedented conflicts. Unlike urban spaces, where property divisions and ownership were usually clearly defined, the physical space around the lake could be claimed by multiple groups. This issue came to the fore in the Southern Song when the majority of powerful families from the old capital moved to Hangzhou and started to build private gardens around West Lake.[4] Water management thereafter had to be negotiated by the municipal government and these families. Hence, increasing privatization of the lakeside landscape generated conflict between privileged interests and the state's attempts at regulation as well as between private enjoyment and public benefit.

THE INITIATION OF LAKE DREDGING DURING THE TANG AND NORTHERN SONG DYNASTIES

Dredging West Lake to better support Hangzhou's needs for water began in the Tang dynasty. Public officials carried out the most famous and influential dredging projects during the Tang and Northern Song dynasties, even though hydraulic management was not part of their classical training. They emphasized the financially sustainable and healthy daily operation of the lake, but they also interfered with the natural environment. West Lake became a focus for both hydraulic management and political contention.

The lake's main sources of water are underground springs and surface creeks that flow from the surrounding mountains. Four streams sustain the level of the water in the lake (figure 2.1). Despite Hangzhou's rainy climate, the availability of water for the city fluctuates from season to season and from year to year. The relatively dry years in the second half of the Southern Song made the water situation worse.[5] West Lake experienced several periods of drought; in the 1240s, its water receded, and grass grew on much of

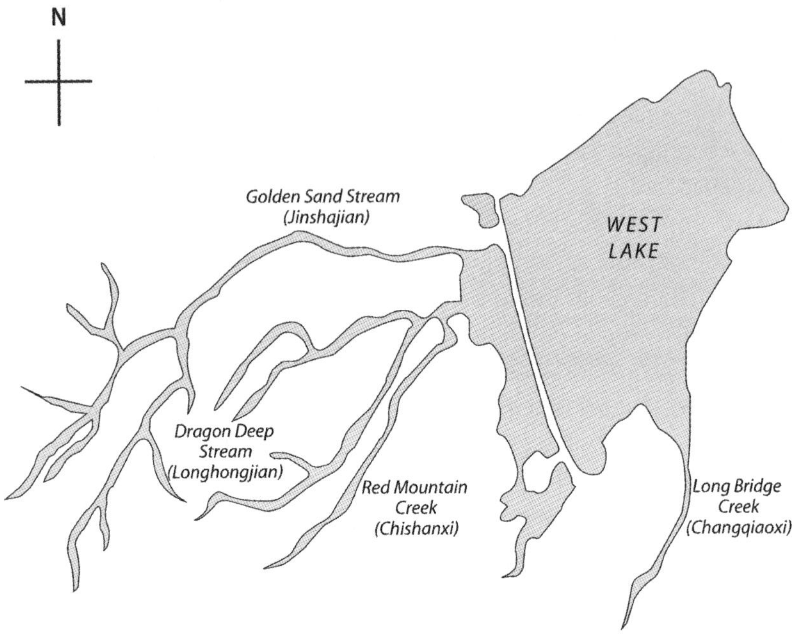

FIGURE 2.1. Water sources for West Lake. Figure by Bill Nelson, 2019, based on the illustration displayed in West Lake Museum, Hangzhou.

the lakebed. The local government prayed unsuccessfully for rain, and people wrote satirical poetry contrasting the beautiful lake scenery of the past with the contemporary drought-stricken landscape.[6] Even when the streams were sufficient to maintain the lake water and rainfall was significant, West Lake was often plagued by excessive mud and pollution.

The survival of the lake was due in large part to ongoing dredging projects. Most of the islands and causeways that adorn the lake today were built during the Tang and Song dynasties. In this sense, the lake was human made, though its formation was also a long-term natural process, and it has long been extolled by literati as an example of pure nature. West Lake was also only one part of a more extensive water system established over many centuries. Waterways were dug from the lake for transportation, culverts were constructed to supply drinking water, and floodgates were built to facilitate irrigation. In its role as part of a water management system, West Lake was viewed more as a dynamic component of the city than a natural environment outside the urban sphere.

In the long tradition of lake dredging, a comparatively large amount took place during the Tang and Song dynasties. Wu Nongxiang (1632–1708),

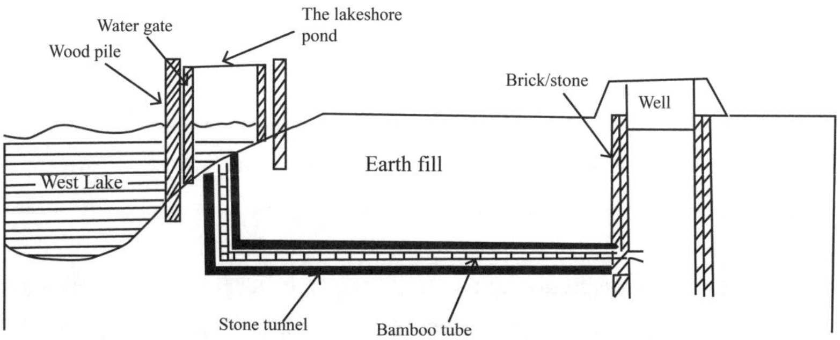

FIGURE 2.2. Structure of Li Bi's six wells, and of most of the later wells, which served Hangzhou's water needs (ca. eighth century); the stone channel improvements were added in the early eleventh century. Figure by Bill Nelson, 2019, based on the illustration displayed in West Lake Museum, Hangzhou.

a Qing scholar who compiled a book documenting the water management of West Lake, focused especially on these two dynasties. He commented that the local counties benefited from a lake with a better and more stable quality of water.[7]

The earliest record of engineering involving the lake was a description of the six wells dug under the leadership of regional inspector Li Bi (722–789). Before Li ordered workers to tap these wells, the low-quality water in the city was dirty, salty, and unsuitable for drinking. The six wells were connected via conduits to lakeside ponds (figure 2.2). Li added grass and other filters to bamboo tubes to clean the water before it entered each well. These wells continued to function as primary sources of drinking water at least into the Song dynasty. The Prime Minister Well, which survives today, is named after Li's official position.

The most important water management project during the Tang dynasty was undertaken by Bai Juyi. During his term as the local governor, Bai noticed that Hangzhou experienced rain during the spring but usually had droughts in the summer and fall.[8] He decided to add a causeway from the Yuhang Gate to the Qiantang Lake Gate, near the edge of the city, to enlarge the capacity of the lake. Local officials rejected Bai's proposal at first because they were concerned that using lake water for farmland irrigation would reduce the water level and eventually hurt the fish and water plants. Bai argued that the survival of fish could not be compared with the survival of human beings and that benefiting water plants could not compare with benefiting farmland. The disagreement in the discussion of this project foreshadowed a series of conflicts in later dynasties, in which Bai's human-centered philosophy was echoed regarding the management of West Lake.[9]

Bai finally arranged for the construction of a new causeway that divided the lake in two. The west side is today's lake, and the east side is the lower lake. When drought hit the farmland region, the government would open the water gate (along the city wall, connecting the lake and rivers inside the city) to let water from the lower lake flow into the affected lands. After finishing the lake causeway, Bai wrote "Stone Cabinet Records on Qiantang Lake" (Qiantang hu shihan ji) to describe the function and preservation of the causeway, as well as the operation of the water gate. In it, he commented, "Every *cun* [about 1.3 inches] of lake water could water over fifteen *mu* of land [about 2.47 acres]; every *chi* [about 1.09 feet] could sustain over fifty *mu* [about 8.2 acres]. If we repair the causeway following these rules and let the water flow out according to schedule, then over one thousand *mu* of land [about 164 acres] can avoid bad years."[10]

Bai also set up several rules in "Stone Cabinet Records on Qiantang Lake" to tackle potential corruption and conflicts in the administration of the lake. First, when drought hit, the common people could report to Hangzhou Prefecture without going through Qiantang County. Second, some private land would emerge only when the water receded, so Bai emphasized that the water gates were to remain closed unless there was a direct order. This was aimed at preventing the unnecessary release of water. Third, he put a marker next to the lake; when the water level exceeded this line by one *chi*, the government had to release lake water.

The combination of these three rules revealed several difficulties in managing West Lake. The water level and the decision whether or not to release water were relevant to individuals' economic concerns. Those who owned farmland beside the lake preferred a lower water level so they could use their property for agricultural purposes; however, those who owned gardens stretching to the lakeshore preferred not to release water because they needed it for scenic beauty and possible fishing. The decision as to whether or not to release water was not an easy one for local governors, so the marker served as a strict and impartial criterion for decision-making.

During the Five Dynasties, Qian Liu (852–932), the king of Qiantang, arranged lake-dredging soldiers (*liaohubing*) to manage the lake. He rejected a proposal to turn the lake into farmland but created the Golden Flood Pond to the south of the Golden Flood Gate to transmit lake water farther into the farmland. Fishing was allowed during Qian's reign, but required a tax payment.[11]

TABLE 2.1. Northern Song lake-dredging projects

Date	Official	Method(s) of water management
1007	Wang Ji (952–1010)	Added a water gate on the lakeshore to prevent the overflow of water
1016	Wang Qinruo (962–1025)	Prohibited fishing
1060	Shen Gou	Dug another well for Hangzhou residents
1041	Zheng Jian (992–1049)	Opened *fengtian* (diked or floating paddies)
1073	Chen Xiang (1017–1080)	Invited talented monks to repair the six wells
1071–1090	Su Shi	1. Dredged the lake and built the Su Causeway 2. Repaired the six wells 3. Set the boundaries for *fengtian*

Around six dredging projects took place during the Northern Song, all initiated by Hangzhou governors (table 2.1). Su Shi's projects lasted from 1071 to 1090, and his proposal to the court in 1079 most fully articulated the rationale for lake dredging. Later officials widely cited this document. Su Shi began by stating the importance of engineering for water management: "The revitalization or abandoning of such things as pools, lakes, rivers, and ditches are associated with the fortunes of the state."[12] Su urged the imperial court to take action in managing the lake because he observed diked or floating paddies (*fengtian*) consuming excessive amounts of lake water. It was common practice among those living in areas adjacent to the water to use wooden frames and mud to create floating fields, allowing them to grow water plants such as water chestnuts on the muddy land along the shore. Though this use of ponds and lakes was more prevalent in southern China than in the north, this type of aquaculture was usually not regarded by local governments as a standard practice and thus often escaped the government's financial regulation. As Su observed, *fengtian* covered only 20 to 30 percent of the lake when he first took charge of Hangzhou, but after sixteen to seventeen years, half of the lake was covered by these floating paddies. He concluded, "In another twenty years, West Lake will no longer exist."[13]

Su continued by discussing five essential functions of West Lake.[14] These were: serving as a "life-releasing pond" that accumulated merit for the state, providing drinking water for Hangzhou residents, offering irrigation for nearby farmlands, supporting the canals that ran through the city of Hangzhou, and accruing profit for the government by providing water used to brew rice wine. Although Su framed the first function in Buddhist terms in an attempt to cater to the imperial family, the other four were pragmatic. The second function brought to mind a popular saying of the time: Hangzhou relied on "vegetables from the east gate, water from the west gate, firewood from the south gate, and rice from the north gate."[15]

Su's third and fourth functions—the lake as a source of water for irrigation and canals—are evident in map 2.1. The lake contributed to at least three waterways in the city's environs (r3, r4, and r5), and these three rivers connected to another two rivers (R5 and R6) that ran from north to south. Locks connecting the lake and the waterways were located at the Clear Wave Gate, the Qiantang Lake Gate, and the water gate to the north of the Clear Wave Gate. Beginning in the Northern Song, whenever the management of West Lake fell into arrears, waterways within the city, especially the Salt Bridge Canal (R4), would become dependent on the Zhe River and the Grand Canal instead of the lake. The sand and mud carried by these two waterways would gradually accumulate and block the water channels passing through the city. Dredging these water channels forced city residents to cope with muddy water flowing everywhere. The presence of a troop of laborers charged with dredging also disturbed the city's order and safety.

To manage the five functions of the lake, Su Shi came up with a four-part project: building a causeway with mud dredged from the bottom of the lake, repairing the six wells, setting up boundaries for land to be irrigated with lake water, and issuing new rules for taxes related to lake management. These components addressed the major concerns of lake management: maintaining water capacity, providing drinking water, limiting the growth of water plants, and setting up a self-sustaining mechanism to manage the lake. Before Su started the dredging work, there were more than 250,000 *zhang* of floating paddies (*fengtian*) on the lake.[16] He estimated that it would take about two hundred thousand workers to remove the floating paddies, and he was able to hire half that number with funds from the municipal government. He then requested that the imperial court fund the rest. Su started the work at the end of the fourth lunar month, the beginning of the rainy season, when precipitation loosened the water plants' roots, facilitating the task of removing them. The workers excavated the lake, making it significantly deeper and broader, and they then used the mud they had dug up to construct a causeway connecting Solitary Mountain (Gushan) and Northern Hills (Beishan). Su added willow and peach trees to the dike; their extensive roots helped to hold the soil together.

After removing the resulting mud and overgrown water plants, Su constructed three pagodas in the middle of the lake to mark the boundary allowed for diked paddies. The tax on water plants, approximately 454 *guan* a year, initially went to Hangzhou Prefecture.[17] Su subsequently ordered Qiantang County to retain this tax revenue as additional funding for lake dredging. On behalf of the government, he also hired farmers to plant some water chestnuts. The fees collected from the cultivation and sale of the water chestnuts were retained for lake management.[18]

To provide sufficient clean drinking water for urban residents of Hangzhou, Su repaired Li Bi's six wells with the help of four monks.[19] These monks were first recruited to repair the wells by Chen Xiang when he served as the Hangzhou governor. At the time, Su was the administrative assistant, and he recorded the details of the methods Chen used to orchestrate the work on the six wells. When Su became the governor and the six wells dried up again in 1090, drinking water became overpriced. Once again, Su sought the services of the four monks to reopen the wells. Zigui, the only one who was then still alive, undertook the project and this time replaced the bamboo tubes with tiles and covered them with a stone channel. A few other new wells were also opened at the same time. After this project, Su proposed that the imperial court should honor Zigui with the title *huiqian* (lit., "benefiting relocation").[20]

The planning and rationale for Su's dredging project demonstrates how the maintenance of a vast clear lake was typically discussed within the contexts of imperial virtue and political benevolence. Su persuaded the imperial court to assist by claiming that after the municipal government started the project, the common people thought "the emperor . . . [had] benefited [future] generations by allowing thousands of people to make a living by themselves." Su used this type of rhetoric to exaggerate the reaction of the people, some of whom, he claimed, "were so moved [by the benevolent policies] that they burst into tears."[21] His emphases on public benefits and on accumulating merit for the imperial house were familiar moral discourses to eleventh-century literati. This proposal led to increasing efforts during the late eleventh and the twelfth centuries to interpret and manipulate nature in the context of a universal moral pattern.[22] Large-scale rearrangements of the natural environment now could be rationalized and promoted by invoking these familiar frameworks.

Emphasis on the benevolence of the imperial court dovetailed with the need to dredge the lake in order to maintain it as a site for the "life-releasing ritual" that would accumulate merit for the dynasty.[23] As Su Shi put it, if the lake dried up, "the dragons, fishes, and turtles would start dying in the dry pond; how could an official bear this?"[24] Thus, he connected the condition of the lake with the success of China's rulers. Later officials carried on this strategy of associating economic benefits (or potential losses) and state rulership to legitimize ecological improvements. When the Ming dynasty official Yang Mengying (1459–1518) proposed more lake dredging, he reiterated the rationale offered during the Song and claimed, "If West Lake were taken or blocked, the advantageous positioning [*xingsheng*] would be harmed, and reproduction [of fish and aquaculture] would not continue."[25] Ecological concerns were thereby further politicized.

A profitable, ecologically sound economic operation that would benefit the Hangzhou government also was the focus of the arguments Su made to support his lake-management projects. He presented a carefully evaluated and detailed proposal that covered the necessary labor and money involved. But aside from the cost-effectiveness of maintenance, another reason to protect the lake was the wine business. Su not only noted that the tax collected from the wine business brought in more than 200,000 *min* (equal to *guan*) annually, but also mentioned the costly result of not maintaining lake water that was clean and clear. He argued, "If the lake does not have sufficient water, then [the government] will need to hire people to carry mountain spring water from afar. Annually, this would involve the cost of hiring over two hundred thousand laborers."[26] His policies to ensure sustainable funding sources for lake dredging, and especially his allocation of a water-plant tax to the water management fund, reflected his emphasis on sound, sustainable financial administration.

Although the aims of Su's proposal were more practical (involving hydraulics) than aesthetic, his introduction of West Lake at the beginning of the document is artistic and even emotional. He compared the importance of the lake for Hangzhou to the importance of eyes and eyebrows to a person. His lake-dredging project, and the many similar ones that followed, entailed prominent improvements of the lake's scenery. The well-constructed lake causeway soon became a new sightseeing attraction because it afforded a fresh perspective on the landscape and allowed tourists to cross the lake. Three pagodas that Su used to mark the boundary for the cultivation of water plants soon became one of the ten "must-see" vistas, and they are still there today.[27] Su's extensive poems about the lake also enhanced the aesthetic tradition relating to this natural environment.

Likewise, later officials of the Southern Song not only dredged the lake to maintain a sufficient water supply for consumption and multiple economic purposes, but also added dikes, pavilions, and plants to the lake, for both excursive and decorative purposes. After Emperor Xiaozong rebuilt and extended the Su Causeway to connect the Southern and Northern Hills, sightseers found that the boat route along the eastern embankment of the new causeway did not quite reach the Northern Hills. The government consequently added two higher bridges to connect the Northern Hills and the Big Buddha Head (Dafotou), so that sightseeing boats could pass through smoothly.[28] The increasing attention devoted to the needs of sightseers during the Southern Song was the result of the interest of the imperial family and powerful families residing around the lake. Their involvement was a major factor in promoting water management at West Lake as a national initiative during the thirteenth century.

INSTITUTIONALIZING LAKE DREDGING DURING THE SOUTHERN SONG

Throughout the 150 years of the Southern Song, West Lake became increasingly important because of its proximity to the imperial capital in Hangzhou. During that time, almost all dredging projects struggled with how to restrict the cultivation of water plants and to stabilize the water management system. While water management efforts during the Tang and Northern Song dynasties were still nascent and relied on the vision and efforts of individuals (such as Bai and Su), these projects became more systematic and came increasingly under governmental aegis during the Southern Song. Lake dredging experience was considered a criterion relevant to decisions concerning promotion of officials, and local gazetteers became more informative about human interventions around the lake. These developments made West Lake an essential component of the capital city and caused people to view the lake in ways very different from its original role as part of the natural environment.

The historical records on West Lake dredging during the Southern Song are more detailed and reveal more government sponsorship than those of earlier dynasties. The attitude in these records toward newly acquired knowledge, such as water-management expertise, was mixed. The scholar-officials who produced these records were aware of the importance of recording this knowledge for future reference, but in so doing, they often used the moral language of traditional literary writing.

Institutionalized management during the Southern Song started with Zhang Cheng's appointment of a Qiantang Prefectural District Defender to supervise the overall water project and his special allocation of two hundred soldiers to work on lake dredging (table 2.2).[29] Zhang Cheng also proposed to Emperor Gaozong that the government undertake the dredging of urban

TABLE 2.2. Southern Song lake-dredging projects

Year	Official	Method(s) of water management
1137	Zhang Cheng (d. 1143)	1. Appointed a Xiantang Prefectural District Defender to take charge 2. Allocated 200 more soldiers for lake dredging 3. Forbade the creation of diked paddies and the use of fertilizer
1148	Tang Pengju (1088–1165)	1. Dredged the lake 2. Repaired the six wells 3. Added locks between the lake and the water tunnels entering the city 4. Added an additional construction foreman in charge of daily inspection; made this a long-term project 5. Forbade future hydroculture
1169	Zhou Cong	1. Focused on pollution from garbage and waste 2. Rebuilt the six wells 3. Added another 100 soldiers (of the previous 200 soldiers, only 35 remained) 4. Added yet another construction foreman in charge of lake dredging 5. Continued to restrict the cultivation of water plants
1173	Shen Du	Reiterated the importance of prohibiting hydroculture and diked paddies, particularly on the southwestern side of the lake
1189	Zhang Zhuo	1. Repaired the six wells and the three water gates 2. Punished a powerful eunuch who built a pavilion on land cultivated with lake water
1247	Zhao Yuchou	1. Enlarged the lake water storage capacity 2. Repaired the six wells 3. Rebuilt the water transportation infrastructure 4. Removed water plants growing along the city gates 5. Dredged all the mud next to the lake bank and causeway to level the bottom
1268	Qian Yueyou (1216–1288)	1. Inspected and cleaned up the mud next to the Harvest and Joy Tower and Jade Lotus Hall (Yuliantang) 2. Cleaned up the water gate next to the Clear Wave Gate and added a water gate next to Long Bridge to prevent silt accumulating in the lake 3. Designed a new drinking-water system

waterways to improve transportation, but this suggestion was at first rejected due to other officials' concerns about the project's massive cost. When Zhang brought this up again in 1138, he argued, "Nowadays, Hangzhou is the home of the imperial family, and both public and private boats carry commodities worth over one hundred times the value of the goods before. What really matter to everyday life are the two major rivers in the city. I am not asking [the court] to dredge all the waterways. With about one thousand soldiers from the county and the imperial guards, we could finish the project within half a year."[30]

The allocation of soldiers for dredging projects, which Zhang mentions, was the norm during the Southern Song. Lake-dredging projects usually required between two hundred and one thousand soldiers. When Tang Pengju undertook a comprehensive water project, he prepared boats and equipment to remove excessive water plants; Zhou Cong added another construction foreman (*haozhaiguan*) to oversee lake dredging.[31] These institutional improvements were the results of accumulated experience gained in dredging the lake and were made possible by increased material support available for the capital city.

Qian Yueyou's water system was one of the best examples of Southern Song government efforts to manage drinking water. It was efficient and ecologically informed. Before turning to the water system within the city, Qian and his assistants found it necessary to assure that the lake water was clean. One issue they tackled was that during the rainy season, the rain washed silt into the lake, especially close to the Qiantang Lake Gate. Qian ordered the construction of a water tunnel next to the gate to guide the flow of water through the Clear Water Lock (Chengshuizha) next to Long Bridge. The government then had laborers construct several stone water conduits to guide water from the lake into the city. These conduits had been made of bamboo, and later Zigui used tiles instead. During the term of Zhou Cong, the channel was reported to be broken and thus made the Benefiting Relocation Well (Huiqianjing), which was named after Zigui, dysfunctional. The stone water channel rebuilt by Qian Yueyou and his team was much deeper and wider than before, with an approximate length of 1,700 *chi*. Along this channel, a small water storage was dug every 50 *chi* for the purpose of draining and filtering. The conduit reached to the Benefiting Relocation Well. Large stones covered the well, with four shafts from which people could retrieve water. To the south of the well, a ditch was dug to reach the river where Golden Text Bridge (Jinwenqiao) was located. The water that flowed through this ditch was for merchants to use; they transported and sold the water in other parts of the city. Next to the Benefiting Relocation Well, the government built a new shrine and stationed guards to prevent pollution of the water by city dwellers. A drainage pipe for sewage was placed on the north side of the road, at a safe distance from the drinking water.[32] The system as a whole fulfilled the requirements for filtering, transporting, and discarding water. It also attempted to use engineering, along with religious and administrative means, to prevent damage to the system and pollution of the water. From the time that Li Bi first opened the six wells during 781

TABLE 2.3. Titles of officials in charge of lake-dredging projects

Year	Hangzhou governor	Title before dredging project*	Promotion after dredging project*
1139	Zhang Cheng	Edict Attendant in the Cabinet of Brilliant Strategies (4b)	Vice Director of the Ministry of Revenue (3b)
1144		Academician in the Hall of the Dragon Diagram (3a)	Military Commissioner (2b)
1148	Tang Pengju	Auxiliary in the Hall for the Diffusion of Literature (7b)	Chief Minister of the Court for the National Granaries (4b)
1169	Zhou Cong	Auxiliary in the Hall of the Dragon Diagram (7a)	Compiler of the Imperial Archive (6b)
1173	Shen Du	Vice Minister in the Bureau of Military Personnel (4a)	Minister in the Bureau of Military Personnel (3a)
1189	Zhang Zhuo	Auxiliary in the Hall of the Dragon Diagram (7a)	Vice Minister in the Bureau of Military Personnel (4b)
1247	Zhao Yuchou	Chief Minister of the Court for the National Granaries (4b)	Vice Director of the Ministry of Revenue (3b); Academician in the Hall for Aid in Governance (3a)
1268	Qian Yueyou	Vice Director of Directorate for Armaments (6b)	State Founding Baron (5b)

Sources: Wu Zimu, *Mengliang lu*, 12.216–20; Tuotuo, et al., *Song shi*, 283.9562, 292.9767, 361.11312, 390.11958; *Jingkou qijiu zhuan*, 8.3b. Translation from Hucker, *A Dictionary of Official Titles in Imperial China.*

* The number and letter in parentheses indicate the rank of each official title. Ranks range from lowest (7b) to highest (1a).

to 784, the local government gained experience in improving this advanced system for providing drinking water.

Another important difference between Northern and Southern Song water management was the change in status of the official in charge. The Northern Song officials Su Shi, Wang Qinruo, and Zheng Jian were all demoted to positions in Hangzhou after falling out of favor with the emperor or the chief minister.[33] Wang Qinruo was assigned to supervise Hangzhou as the "Grand Guardian of the Heir Apparent," a grandiose title that was nonetheless a demotion. During the Southern Song, on the other hand, nearly all officials who took charge of Hangzhou had already held high positions or been previously awarded titles (table 2.3). Half of them, including Zhou Cong, Zhang Zhuo, and Qian Yueyou, simultaneously held the title of Vice Fiscal Commissioner of the Two Zhe Region while serving as Hangzhou governor.[34] Given Hangzhou's status as the capital of the Southern Song, it is not surprising that the position of Hangzhou governor became associated with prestige and potential. These officials received further acknowledgments and promotions after they undertook dredging and water-management projects.

In both the Tang and the Song dynasties, dredging the lake was a routine duty for the Hangzhou governor. In the Southern Song, it became a significant event in the political careers of those officials and earned them political capital. Bai Juyi noted that lake dredging was the first and foremost responsibility he assumed during his term. When he left Hangzhou, he wrote to the common people, "I left only lake water, to save you during years of drought."[35] Furthermore, as table 2.3 indicates, most of the relevant Southern Song officials were acknowledged and rewarded by the imperial court for their efforts to preserve the lake, and many were promoted to higher positions. Zhang Cheng's dredging project was the only achievement recorded for his six-year tenure in Hangzhou in the official history, and yet he soon rose to become the Vice Director of the Ministry of Revenue.[36] Tang Pengju, after successfully carrying out a preservation plan, became the Chief Minister of the Court for the National Granaries.[37]

Lake dredging required professional knowledge and management expertise. Consequently, those with experience, such as the four monks in the Northern Song and later Southern Song lake-dredging soldiers, were repeatedly appointed to undertake similar tasks. Officials with lake-management experience, such as Zhang Cheng and Zhang Zhuo, usually were entrusted with repeat terms as Hangzhou governor. Practically speaking, the continuation in office of those with knowledge of and experience with lake dredging ensured the effective and consistent maintenance of the lake. But historical documents placed more emphasis on benevolent governance than hydraulic expertise in recording the local activities of these officials. For example, Ming scholar Tian Rucheng commented, "Dredging West Lake not only involves a tremendous amount of work but also involves huge costs. One cannot accomplish [a dredging project] without a personality that is honest, determined, and open minded."[38]

Official documents about the history of water management in China commonly equated technical skills with moral attributes. Practical expertise was recognized under the heading of character traits relating to general statecraft ability.[39] Officials' successes were attributed to "education, dedication, and administrative capability."[40] Official historical records of West Lake water management emphasized the officials' dedication to work and compassion for the common people as well as vaguely categorizing skills in managing hydraulics as "administrative capabilities."

These recording practices are also reflected in local gazetteers of Hangzhou. *The Gazetteer of Hangzhou during the Xianchun Reign* (Xianchun Lin'an zhi), for instance, chronicled water management under the section "Mountains and Rivers."[41] Both the geographical setting of the lake and physical projects pertaining to the lake were listed to underscore the distinctive features of the Hangzhou region. However, the technical information provided typically was sparse. The most detailed technical project related to the infrastructure for maintaining drinking water was overseen by Qian Yueyou, whose leadership was recorded in a gazetteer. The gazetteers were intended more for demonstrating the capabilities and political merits of contemporary officials than for documenting technical knowledge.

Technically informative treatises were produced mainly by officials who were personally involved in these projects, echoed the literati trend during the Song dynasty of incorporating observations about and uses of hydraulic innovations and other practical knowledge in their miscellaneous writings. These records document the governors' contributions and provide instructions for later officials. Their achievements in addressing real-world problems, including building effective dikes, tackling hydraulic issues, and increasing tax income without creating social antagonism or hardship evidenced the extent to which their classical education also permitted them to consider both sociological and ecological issues.

In retrospect, lake management during the Tang and Song dynasties was successful. Wu Nongxiang commented on the outcome of the Tang-Song dredging endeavors at West Lake: "After the Tang and the Song, the salted and silted land became fertile farmlands; the muddy water plants vanished. Lands that surrounded the lake could provide several *zhong* of grain in a one-year harvest. Therefore, people used two out of ten tracts of land for the construction of Buddhist monasteries and Daoist palaces and another three [out of ten] for tombs and gardens. Furthermore, 40 percent of the area was separated by causeways to become ponds and shoals."[42] Wu's standard for proper water management was twofold: the water had to be clear of mud and the lakeshore land had to be suitable for farming.

These two concerns stood at the center of a dozen lake-dredging projects that spanned almost five hundred years. Wu chronicled how, over time, people undertook different types of construction projects on the land after a successful dredging. High crop yields allowed and encouraged the allocation of some of the land for other, nonagricultural purposes: monks and priests incorporated more land into their properties to support temples, and noblemen built their gardens on this new land. The outcomes of the lake-dredging projects were complicated and sometimes led to misuse. What stood out over time was a conflict between personal economic benefit and the resource needs of the city as a whole. Consequently, negotiations to find a balance between the protection of private property and the preservation of public space framed the government's decisions concerning diked paddies and the wine business.

FENGTIAN: THE CONFLICT BETWEEN ECOLOGICAL AND ECONOMIC CONCERNS

The lakeshore land, as Wu Nongxiang recorded, was fertile and therefore suitable for farming. This land was ideal for the cultivation of water chestnuts and Zizania, a form of wild rice. Repeated regulations issued to prevent the excessive cultivation of water plants during the Song dynasty reflected the conflict between collecting profits from private cultivation of the paddies and sustaining sufficient water storage capacity for the entire city. While the government always placed the maintenance of sustainable public resources above private economic profits, governmental policies usually proved ineffective. Conflicts between the government and powerful families revealed a divergence between public interest and private desires. Amid this tension between public and private, what both sides cared about was no longer the lake itself, but the benefits it could generate.

West Lake was known for the cultivation of several unique and rare water plants that were renowned for their exceptional flavors and profitability. Contemporary documents recorded meticulously and with great enthusiasm the various types of water plants that were grown as popular treats. Water chestnuts especially stood out. A red variety was fresh and sweet, while the cheaper black kind was dusty and bitter tasting. Water bamboo, which was usually harvested elsewhere only in the autumn, was available throughout the year on West Lake. The profits that accrued from planting this crop on the lake could be ten times greater than the investment.[43]

Moreover, lotus also appeared on the Southern Song menu. The red lotus from West Lake was famous for its seedpod, while the white lotus grew roots under water. The red variety from the Assembled Scenery Garden was called "embroidered lotus" and was known in the market for its sweet roots. Since the Assembled Scenery Garden was an imperial garden, this raises the question of how a product intended for the emperor's family ended up in the public market. It is unclear whether merchants bought lotus roots from the Imperial Administration Bureau or got permits to pick this delicacy directly from the imperial garden. Either possibility indicates that the imperial palace was involved in the marketing of water plants and likely profited by selling these products. The leisure activities available in Hangzhou and around West Lake at the time led to a high demand for these delicacies. Furthermore, some water plants, especially the lotus flower, were essential elements that contributed to the natural beauty of the lake. Their blossoms are featured in thousands of poems about sightseeing.[44]

Regardless of the economic benefits of the water plants, their cultivation was always controlled and sometimes even forbidden. Farmers were not allowed to grow them anywhere. Planting water chestnuts and water bamboo encroached upon the lakeshore and thus reduced the amount of water the lake could hold. Five out of seven water-management projects during the Southern Song dealt directly with water plants, and the other two indirectly tackled this issue. The frequency of bans on the cultivation of water plants, however, only speaks to the ineffectiveness of such policies.

Driven by high profits and the aesthetic desire for lotus flowers, wealthy and influential families that lived at the southwestern corner of the lake continued to plant water chestnuts and lotus flowers. A poem noted this in a satirical tone:

> Ten miles of beautiful lake scenery with ten miles of fences for diked paddies,
> Those who made the farming frames are all wealthy and powerful families.
> Only after ten years, when those families' official terms come to an end,
> Can people then see the lake scenery without the fences.[45]

This poem was collected in a Ming dynasty record, but its date of composition remains unclear. Regardless of when this poem first circulated, it is emblematic of social tensions regarding water plants. Unlike the literary glorification of lotus flowers and the commercial celebration of selling water chestnuts, this author regarded water fences as a disturbance of the lake scenery. The poem also suggests that the powerful position of lakeshore families prevented the complete removal of these water plants. The spread of diked paddies along the lake banks meant less access for ordinary urban residents.

Official documents also revealed the difficulties faced by the local governor in dealing with excessive diked-paddy cultivation by powerful families. The boundary set by Su Shi lapsed during the transitional period between the Northern Song and the Southern Song. An increasing number of immigrants only exacerbated the situation, with more people inhabiting land on the lake and more powerful families gradually taking advantage of the fertile lands around the lake for their gardens. Soon after the capital moved to Hangzhou, Zhang Cheng first issued his ban on aquaculture. He especially emphasized the harmful consequences of using aquatic fertilizers.

Within ten years, this ban already seemed to be failing. Emperor Gaozong complained that the water in West Lake was turgid and the lake surface had shrunk, and he asked the local government to remedy the problem. The emperor's concern was twofold: safeguarding the quality of the water for human consumption and preserving the scenic attractions. Emperor Gaozong himself was fond of touring the lake. In response, the Hangzhou governor at the time, Tang Pengju, issued a regulation prohibiting the rental of space for cultivating lotus flowers.[46] However, Tang banned only the prominent families' practice of hiring people to work on diked paddies; he did not ban the existence of paddies owned by ordinary households, as these plots were essential to the livelihoods of a large number of peasants. This new issue for the Southern Song government resulted from an expansion in the forms of agricultural production. During previous dynasties, agriculture was mainly confined to conventional dry-farmland cultivation, but now, immigration to the water resource–enriched south led to increasing interest in and better conditions for hydroculture.

Although Tang's order seemed strict and was prompted by a request from the emperor, it was not effective in practice. The government reiterated this policy in 1169, 1173, and 1189. In 1247, the cultivation of water plants became such a concern that the government purchased the lotus flowers and water chestnuts cultivated on the side of the lake adjacent to the city for 30,000 strings of cash—an amount equal to the commercial tax income of a middle-sized city at the time.[47] Spending this much on something that had been repeatedly prohibited was likely the result of a government desire not to offend the cultivators. The excavated water plants were from the lake area between the Golden Flood Gate and the Qiantang Lake Gate, near the Assembled Scenery Garden and other gardens.[48] The owners of these large areas of water-plant cultivation were members of the imperial family or noblemen. Yet this area also included six water gates along the city wall, so the water plants posed a threat to the water channel.

The use of the physical landscape generated conflicts between privilege and regulation, and between private enjoyment and public benefit. Powerful officials and eunuchs wrote most of the recorded cases about polluted lake water and damage to the appearance of the lake. While almost all of the constructed edifices and vacant spaces within the city were clearly labeled as someone's property, the space on the periphery or outside the city wall seemed to have fewer defined owners.

In most of the cases, government regulations and ecological concerns trumped privilege. For instance, the official Bao Du once criticized the eunuch Liu Gongzheng for building houses immediately adjacent to the shrine for Prime Minister Li. Bao not only denounced the eunuch for being disrespectful, but also for using lake water to wash horses and clothes at a spot where the common people retrieved their drinking water. Bao also criticized the eunuch Chen Minxian for polluting the water. Chen built houses on the pond in front of the Sacred Fungus Monastery (Lingzhisi) and had a kitchen right on the water. Bao argued that this was the precise area from which the official winery obtained its water, so the pollution generated by Chen would "endanger the offerings to heaven and the ancestors." Although modern concepts of hygiene were then unknown in China, the concern for water quality reveals an environmental consciousness concerning cleanness and pollution. Upon receiving Bao's report, the government punished and demoted both eunuchs.[49]

The winemaking mentioned by Bao was one of the five essential functions of West Lake listed in Su Shi's proposal as evidence for the necessity of dredging the lake. The wine business was crucial for two reasons: wine offerings were essential in the rituals associated with ancestor and heaven worship, and the imperial court levied commercial taxes on the production of wine. In the case of water-plant cultivation, economic and ecological concerns conflicted, but in the case of the wine business, economic and ecological considerations effectively bolstered the court's support. Winemaking further complicated the interconnections among sightseeing, lake management, and economic profit.

THE WINE BUSINESS

West Lake was essential to the business of winemaking. It provided spring water of better quality than other places and functioned as a massive market for selling wine. The Northern Song official Zhou Zizhi (1082–1155) once argued against a proposal to move the winery away from the lake, suggesting that the lake water was "pure and sweet."[50] With the development of sightseeing and entertainments around the lake, more and more visitors were consumers of wine. The wine business wove together the sightseeing market and the need for high-quality water resources. This interconnection contributed to the convergence of desires for revenue and sustainable resources.

During the Song dynasty, the government controlled the making and selling of wine. The Song government imposed nationwide taxes on wine consumption in government-operated wine houses, on private wine sales by means of permits, and on wine contractors.[51] Taxes on the making and consumption of wine contributed significantly to government income; the revenue was second only to land and salt taxes.[52] According to Zhou Zizhi, the profit made from wineries was also enormous, more than 300,000 *min* in the year 1064.[53] The principal government-owned winery was located on the north side of the lake, close to the rivers; a few other government wine facilities were found on the northeast lakeshore, next to the Boat Landing Pavilion (map I.1). One was called Qiantang Official Warehouse (Qiantang Zhengku).[54] Another was situated at the foot of Nanping Hill, close to the south end of the Su Causeway. The government constantly created new types of wines; more than seventy varieties were developed during the Southern Song. Every year the government performed a particular ritual when it began to make new wine.[55] This ceremony would attract a large audience and became an ideal occasion to sell wine.

The government had more than a dozen major wine houses spread throughout the city. Two were at the lake. One was in the Harvest and Joy Tower on the east side of the lake, and the other, West Creek Wine House (Xixi ku), was on the west side of the lake.[56] While the Harvest and Joy Tower served mainly day-trippers from Hangzhou, West Creek Wine House was designed primarily for those who were lodged in the temples on the west side of the lake.[57] Aside from the government-owned wine houses, smaller private inns could also sell wine as long as they purchased state permits.

Wine was a major attraction for visitors, and many poems mentioned wine along with the lake's scenery and sightseeing activities.[58] Southern Song artists even regarded the government winery together with the lotus flowers around it as one of the Ten Views, made especially memorable by the aroma of wine and the fragrance of lotus blossoms. During some festivals, crowds at the lake overflowed the inns, and people brought wine to the nearby teahouses.[59] These teahouses also sold plum wine in the summer in addition to rice wine.[60] Those who sold wine in restaurants and wine houses were called Masters of Wine Measuring (Liangjiu Boshi).[61] Originally used to refer to court academicians or learned scholars, the title "master" (*boshi*) reflected the importance of wine in everyday life.

Wine also benefited efforts to preserve West Lake by generating commercial tax revenue. Every year after the Lantern Festival (the fifteenth day of the first lunar month), the Hangzhou government allocated 200,000 units of paper currency from the Wine Bureau to repair public facilities, such as dikes, gardens, bridges, and roads. The Wine Bureau paid the government to hire laborers to undertake repair and maintenance work on the Southern Hills (Nanshan) and the Northern Hills, work that included painting the buildings around the lake and adding different varieties of flowers to plantings, all of which was meant to "reflect the lake scenery and to provide convenience for sightseers."[62] The Wine Bureau funded these projects in order to attract more consumers to the lake. Government officials also supported this allocation of funds because wine revenues both solved the problem of replenishing the dredging fund and improved the appearance of the lake, thus showcasing their prowess in governing. Moreover, this arrangement offered a justification for the government-operated businesses around the lake: profits made from the lake were used to improve conditions around the lake, and the improvement of public facilities could potentially ease the moral concerns about the government making commercial profits from the people. Just as the Hangzhou government worked to institutionalize water management, Song officials paid equal attention to the maintenance of funding sources. They wanted lake management to be both self-sustaining and intricately woven into existing urban administration.

The principle used to allocate the wine tax embodied the traditional attitude toward money and finance in good governance. As early as the Han dynasty (206 BCE–220 CE), discussions about the government's monopoly of salt and iron led to the concept of balancing commercial profit from the sale of these commodities with political responsibility. The Northern Song literati officials agreed that the ruler should use the wealth from tax revenues to serve the public good, as well as to stimulate trade. They agreed that wealth was essential to upholding common welfare and the public interest. Su Shi's proposal to the court, with its precise calculations pertaining to labor and money, its consideration for the common people, and its appeal to imperial virtue, exemplifies this line of thinking. This principle was further developed during the Southern Song. Due to the immigration to southern China, commercial taxes and government monopolies became equally significant and even surpassed tax revenue from traditional agricultural products. The allocation of wine-tax funds to the construction of public infrastructure

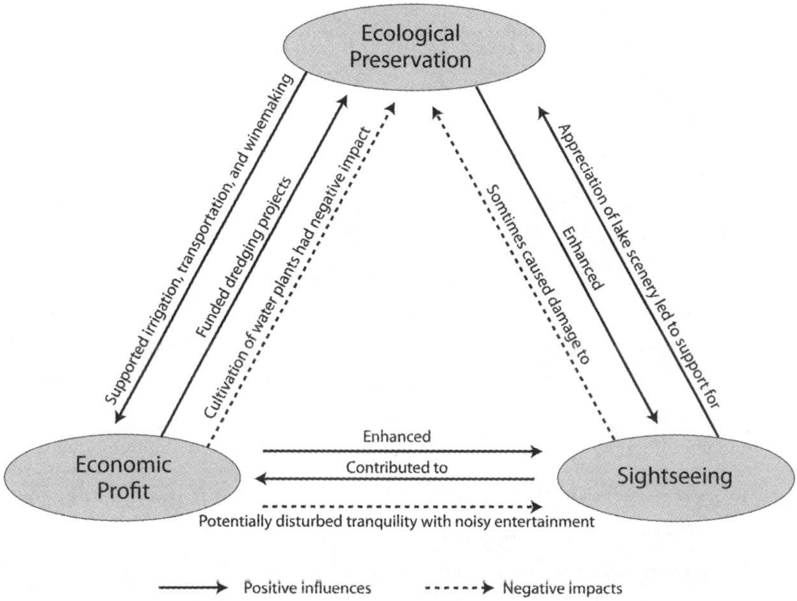

FIGURE 2.3. Interrelationships among ecological preservation, economic profit, and sightseeing around West Lake. Illustration by Bill Nelson, 2019.

was rationalized with the new idea of combining the profit-driven commodity economy with the welfare-directed moral economy.

Winemaking burnished the lake's status as a special place. West Lake was a wine-producing center, a major sightseeing market, and the recipient of landscape improvements funded by proceeds from the wine tax. Meanwhile, winemaking also transformed the lake into a vehicle for articulating political morality and made it part of the financial web of the city of Hangzhou.

CONCLUSION: URBANIZED NATURE

The intricate relationship between West Lake and the city of Hangzhou derived from and affected the interactions of economic profits, ecological preservation, and sightseeing activities. These three aspects worked together: they both improved and hindered one another, making the lake space and the urban space interdependent. As is shown in figure 2.3, a sustainable lake that supported irrigation, farming, and the wine business was essential for economic development, and the quanlity and amount of water in the lake were crucial factors in the beautification of the lake's scenery. Dredging projects enhanced the landscape by adding garden-like designs and features. The profits made from the lake were used to engineer the lake and improve the facilities for sightseeing. Travel activities, in turn, promoted economic benefits around the lake.

On the other hand, conflicts were common and were one of the main reasons that lake dredging projects took place only every ten or twenty years. The growing boom in sightseeing sometimes harmed the lake, and wealthy families erected illegal construction projects on the lake and polluted the water. The desire for economic profits from water plants also had an adverse impact on the lake's ecology and the sightseeing experience. Nevertheless, despite the continuing conflicts among these three aspects, environmental concerns stood at the top of the government's priority list. Although the government celebrated sightseeing for both commercial and symbolic reasons, it regulated and even sacrificed water plants and other tourist attractions to guarantee Hangzhou's water supply.

Ecologically sustainable projects on the lake and the pragmatic utilization of the lake water were essential components of the place-making process. The lake was regarded as a source of water resources and a place for wine consumption. From the pre-Tang period to the present, the lake's physical existence has been incorporated into the urban development of Hangzhou, and West Lake still plays a crucial role in the lives of Hangzhou's urban residents. The lake offers an excellent example of the essential and dynamic role that a feature of the natural landscape—no matter how human altered—can play in government decision-making. West Lake was not merely a suburban region that provided resources but a dynamic component of the city's development.

The interplay of economic profitmaking, ecological preservation concerns, and sightseeing activities did not allow West Lake to remain a "natural" environment, despite portrayals to the contrary in literature and gazetteers. West Lake could not exist or be fully understood without the context of Hangzhou. Neither could it operate as it did by itself. While ecological work projects sustained West Lake as a physical place, the meaning of that place developed in accordance with the economic support it provided to the city. Most of the time, people saw West Lake not as a natural environment but primarily as a place for winemaking and/or water-plant cultivation and consumption, or as a reservoir. The lake posed unprecedented challenges to government administration, and the government's water-management efforts were viewed through the lenses of morality and political benevolence. When urban management became essential for the preservation of the lake, and when the scenic beauty of the lake was enhanced by human projects, the lake itself became an urbanized landscape.

The urbanized landscape redefined the interactions between leisure and nature. The physical construction of the lake served the needs of the city of Hangzhou and allowed a better lake view for the majority of the population. This development relied on and resulted in increased leisure activities. Meanwhile, the encounters of noblemen and powerful families with the lake were evaluated and regulated within the framework of the lake's function in an urban context. West Lake encouraged leisure activities in nature, but these encounters were designed to be sustainable for both the city and the lake.

Although West Lake played a complex and essential role in the daily life of Hangzhou, people's concept of the lake extended beyond its everyday practical functions. Part 2 (chapters 3 and 4) looks into textual and visual idealization of this natural landscape. Literary and artistic depictions of West Lake turned place making into creating an idealized identity in a place. Many of these depictions embodied new genres or styles, evidencing a changing engagement with geography.

PART II

The Idealized Representation of Nature

CHAPTER THREE

SEEKING IDENTITY IN PLACE

Writing and Reading West Lake

WHEN ZHOU MI WROTE ABOUT WEST LAKE SHORTLY AFTER THE fall of the Southern Song, he highlighted the convergence of scenic beauty and sociocultural integration that made it into a primary cultural landmark of the Song era:

> West Lake has the foremost scenery in the realm, perfect in the morning and the evening, in bright weather and in rain, and in all four seasons. . . . Here one may see the inhabitants of the capital contract marriages or celebrate the end of the year, gather with their families or send off the dead to be buried, discuss sutras or sacrifice to the gods. One may see arrangements made for an appointment to an official post or for a bestowal of imperial grace, commissions [granted] by the imperial court or by the central government, noble eunuchs and prominent officials, great merchants and powerful personages, a companion bought for a thousand pieces of gold and gamblers staking a million. One may even see smitten lads and lovesick girls, and secret assignations and illicit gatherings.[1]

The increasing number of scholars attracted to the lake led to an extensive literary legacy, including but not limited to poems, miscellanies, and gazetteers. These visitors included officials and noblemen who moved from the Northern Song capital, examination takers, and local officials who reported to the central government annually and at the end of their terms. The civil service examinations occurring every three years filled Hangzhou with educated people on a regular basis. These examination takers usually visited West Lake to enjoy the scenery and consult fortune-tellers in the lakeside temples. Those who passed the examination would either serve in the central government or receive appointments to serve in another province. For the former group, visiting West Lake continued to be a popular activity on days off.[2] When members of the latter group of officials finished a term, they had to return to the capital to wait for their next appointments. These officials often revisited West Lake every time they were in Hangzhou and wrote poems comparing what they saw with the scenery they remembered from earlier visits.[3]

The practice of writing, traveling, and reading transformed the space around West Lake into a collection of sites. These locations were thus not merely physical places but instead were built into a framework and a vocabulary with which West Lake could be understood and narrated. These writings were responses to the emerging social environment in Southern Song Hangzhou: the changing dynastic history and the feeling of insecurity it provoked, as well as the burgeoning city life and its expansion into the natural landscape. The relocation of the capital from Kaifeng to Hangzhou and the threat from the northern dynasties generated psychological pressure that influenced all types of writing. Moreover, by the early Song dynasty, writers had begun to perceive and record natural and daily rhythms in the life of cities,[4] and writing about urban space during the eleventh century explored universal moral patterns.[5]

The attempts to understand the surrounding environment and the rich information these texts contained endowed West Lake with multilayered meaning. These diverse literatures attempted to make sense of a changing period and increasing contact with the natural landscape by evoking different pursuits of desires and concerns. West Lake is thus a good example of how a place enabled visitors to claim and reinforce their diverse identities. The lake functioned as an anchor for writers and readers seeking identity through literary tradition and political lineage; it also revealed the outlines of the system of knowledge with which Song people navigated the new capital and the new dynastic history. Written records are both products of the Song sociocultural environment and the means by which people conceptualized the natural landscape.

Flower appreciation in Luoyang during the Tang dynasty and its relationship to the record of famous gardens written by Li Gefei (ca. 1045–1105) offers an earlier example of how a particular place was built out of and in turn enriched the literary tradition.[6] During the Song dynasty, the connections between place and literature were further strengthened. This was due to the development of print technology, the spread of literacy, and the convenient transportation system that allowed quick access to any destination. Literati were fond of traveling to confirm what they read,[7] and scholar-officials' travel and writings helped to shape the cultural traditions of famous sites.[8] Writing was a crucial place-making factor, and place functioned as inspiration and anchor for accumulated writing. Cataloging sites could serve the political needs of claiming control over nature and provide a mainstay of cultural identity.

Writings on West Lake all demonstrated, diversely yet vividly, the desire to record or deploy the iconic place. This interest could be represented as an inquiry into the origins of place names, the documentation of past visitors to famous places, a meticulous record of geographical features, or a playful use of anecdotes about the place in the literary tradition. These writings usually embodied two aspects of place. Each text in its own way is a process of reengagement with a place and a re-creation of the intimacy between the writer and the materiality of a city.[9] These writings created a multilayered place for writers and readers to interpret their surroundings. They allowed literati to understand their relations to the lake in the context of the cultural lineage, enabled officials to make political claims, and defined the common people's perception of their living space.

These writings both constructed the place as an iconic location and demonstrated awareness of historical time. The writers looked back to the cultural tradition and forward to an uncertain future. This might appear as nostalgia for the past, as sensitivity to the vicissitudes of the moment, or even as an ambivalent anticipation of the arrival of the future. These writings embodied an awareness of passing time, which both reflected and shaped the Southern Song sense of history. Meanwhile, the desire to establish something eternal or to understand the unstable environment motivated writers to shift the way they recorded information.

In this regard, four types of writing are of particular interest: records about historical literary figures, depictions of the lake as a state symbol, documentation of sites as local history, and fanciful stories that reflect urban residents' concerns. This typology does not imply that all pieces of writing can be neatly sorted into one of these four categories. A single piece of writing can easily carry multiple meanings, and one scholar could write about West Lake in many different ways in the course of his life or even during one trip. Nevertheless, this typology provides a useful way to approach and discuss a large body of writings. It indicates possible ways people interpreted West Lake, and each type of writing reveals a specific function of West Lake in Song culture. Together, they represent the complexity and contradictory views of West Lake.

WEST LAKE AS ENSHRINED IN LITERARY TRADITION

Hangzhou's literary fame preceded its political status. The renowned literati who visited and lived in Hangzhou created West Lake's significance among intellectuals. The famous poets Bai Juyi and Su Shi both reshaped the physical appearance of the lake as governors of Hangzhou and at the same time wrote poetry about it. Another scholar, Lin Bu, was famously associated with West Lake through his accounts of his reclusive life there. The literary works of these famous figures inspired later literati to continue their cultural lineage.

The fame of Tang and Northern Song intellectuals reached its zenith during the Southern Song when a large number of literati moved to the new capital. They found in earlier literati a familiar connection on which they could draw and thus consistently referred to these earlier figures. For instance, in 1203 Xin Qiji (1140–1207) invited Liu Guo (1154–1206) to visit Shaoxing. Liu, who at the time resided in Hangzhou and could not make the journey to meet his friend, responded with the poem below. In it, Liu created an imaginary scenario to explain why he could not leave Hangzhou: he had to tour West Lake with Bai Juyi, Lin Bu, and Su Shi.

> However, I was stopped by Fragrance Mountain Kulapati [Bai Juyi], who invited Lin Hejing [Lin Bu] and the Old Immortal Dongpo [Su Shi].
> Dongpo says, "West Lake can be best compared to the Lady of the West, who approaches the altar with lightly or thickly layered powder."
> The other two, turning away and disregarding Su's words, pass their wine cups.
> White clouds wander back and forth near the Tianzhu Monasteries as we observe the grand gold and green buildings.
> Wide open and spacious, towers and palaces are spread out east and west of the two creeks;
> Water flows around the southern and northern hills, which pierce the clouds.
> [Lin] Bu says, "Speaking of the wafting of subtle fragrance, [nowhere else] can compare to Solitary Mountain.
> Let us visit the plums first, [since we] can only do this on sunny days.
> It will not be too late to visit Jiaxuan [Xin Qiji] after that; let us stay and linger here."[10]

This humorous reply made the imagined invitation plausible by directly citing from the literary classics written by these historical figures, including Su's metaphor of the Lady of the West. The invitation seemed impossible to refuse due to the prominence of the three figures.

Bai Juyi, who served as the prefectural governor of Hangzhou from 821 to 824, was among the first group who wrote about the beauty of West Lake:

> On the north of Solitary Mountain Monastery [Gushansi], west of the
> Jia Pavilion [Jiating],
> The lake surface climbs up to meet the low clouds.
>
> I savor the east side of the lake the most and will never tire of roaming
> there,
> The White Sand Causeway lies in the shadow of the green willows.[11]

This poem serves as a mini travelogue with its references to specific geographic locations. Those familiar with the lake through personal experience or reading could easily picture his travels or even replicate them.

Like Bai Juyi, Su Shi also helped spread the fame of West Lake through his famous poems.[12] Southern Song records concisely captured Su Shi's connection with West Lake:

> When Su Shi took charge of Hangzhou, he sometimes went sightseeing on West Lake. He often asked the attendants with banners and flags to go out through the Qiantang Gate, and he crossed the lake by boat from the Golden Flood Gate with one or two old soldiers. He would have a meal in the Universal Peace Monastery [Pu'ansi] and travel around the Tianzhu and Soul's Retreat Monasteries. He brought the necessary paperwork with him and passed judgments at his desk in the Cold Spring Pavilion [Lengquanting]. He wrote as quickly as the wind and rain to pass judgments on the lawsuits. Cases could be solved with ease while he was laughing and chatting. After finishing his business, he drank with colleagues and subordinates and went back to the city by horse at dusk. Along the street, people in the city watched him, the grand administrator.[13]

In this account, two types of place names tie the story together and add credibility. Gate names are location references, and names of monasteries and the pavilion are places of interest. They provide a real-world setting for the legendary story.

The interplay between people and place is prominent in stories about Lin Bu, who was known for his reclusive lifestyle. Later records mentioned his affinity for cranes and plum blossoms, regarding him as a model hermit: "Lin Bu lived in seclusion on Hangzhou's Solitary Mountain. He raised two cranes, which when released, would launch themselves into the sky and fly around for a long time, finally coming back to their cage. Lin Bu often visited the temples around the lake by boat. When a guest arrived at his house, Lin's young attendant would receive him and open the cage to set the cranes free. Later, Lin Bu would return by boat, because the flight of the cranes was a signal [that a guest had come]."[14] His unhurried manner stood in contrast to busy life in the city. Lin was later referred to as the West Lake Hermit.[15]

Having long lived around West Lake, all three literati were national figures yet remained deeply rooted in local memories. Their writings about their local outings were already in circulation during their lifetimes and gained more influence with the passing of time, as later writers projected admiration onto the place that inspired and hosted these legends. The reaffirmation of historical figures in writings was fundamental in traditional Chinese literature.[16] In the prose piece "Records of Traveling the Dragon Well" (You Longjing ji), Cheng Mi (1164–1242) recorded his reading of lake touring by Qin Guan (1049–1100) during the Northern Song and his own trip to the lake. This piece of travel writing detailed all the sites he had read about in Qin Guan's writing and the ones he himself saw. Cheng also emphasized his viewing of portraits of famous figures from the Northern Song, including Venerable Biancai (1011–1091), Fan Zhongyan, and Su Shi. He concluded by lamenting the 130 years that had passed between his excursion and Qin Guan's, noting that "the people have changed so much, while the scenery resembles the past." [17] He also said that he recorded his impressions as "a report to future travelers," manifesting an awareness of the continuation of the literary tradition. Reading about earlier sightseeing experiences and seeing the lake through the eyes of these famous people, later literati participated in a form of communion with the virtues and cultural values embodied by these past worthies.

Remembrance was demonstrated not only in writing but also in following the steps of the historical figures and constructing new places in memory of them. Visiting such landscapes, as Ellen Cong Zhang observes, "allowed scholars to claim that they had established the most intimate emotional connection with their cultural past via physical traces left by former worthies."[18] Through the visits of revered historical figures, certain places, such as the Cold Spring Pavilion in the anecdote about Su Shi,

FIGURE 3.1. Three Worthies Hall. Detail from *Scenic Attractions of West Lake*, ca. fourteenth century. Ink and color on paper, 33.3 × 1849.8 cm. Freer Gallery of Art, Smithsonian Institution, Washington, DC: Gift of Charles Lang Freer, F1911.209.

became landmarks and even must-see spots for scholars.[19] Furthermore, new sites such as the Three Worthies Hall were added to the lakeshore in memory of Bai Juyi, Su Shi, and Lin Bu during the twelfth century (figure 3.1). Famous figures and famous places mutually supported each other.

West Lake of the Northern Song became a cultural ideal for the Southern Song literati, who sought a sense of belonging after the turmoil of the dynasty's transitional period. Their construction of a new identity connected to Hangzhou served to reconcile their feelings of being exiled from the cultural center in northern China. The cultural tradition of West Lake imbued with historical figures provided a vehicle for the emotions and desires of these displaced literati. Nostalgia for the Northern Song thus pervaded the writing about historical figures. The idealized lives of Bai, Su, and Lin embodied the Confucian value of doing good deeds for the state and the Buddhist and Daoist value of living quiet and reclusive lives. Even though these values were considered desirable, it was difficult to live according to them in the turmoil of the Southern Song. Writings about these figures or the places mentioned in their poems, or inventing imaginary conversations with them, enabled Southern Song literati to inscribe themselves into the cultural lineage.

Many of these Southern Song writings circulated at regular gatherings on West Lake, and these activities served to create and confirm membership in literati circles. Zhou Mi's description of West Lake cited at the beginning of this chapter refers to it as a "watering hole" for social engagement. Among these social activities, poetry clubs stood out. Local literati or those who sojourned in Hangzhou followed the literary tradition of holding poetry gatherings on spring days at which they went boating and played poetry-rhyming games. Poetry clubs even compiled anthologies of their members' works and had them published.[20] The most famous poetry club had "West Lake" in its name, and Wu Zimu held a very high opinion of it: "[It] is composed of officials in the capital and visiting Confucian scholars from all around the country. Their poems, which project mood and feeling, are widely circulated."[21]

Yang Zan and Zhou Mi organized one of these clubs, and Zhou described one such gathering: "In the summer of 1264, Xiaweng [Yang Zan] met friends in the poetry club in the Encircling Green Garden [Huanbiyuan] near West Lake to escape the heat. Supplied with zithers, wine cups, pens and ink-stones, wearing short clothes made of coarse hemp and kerchiefs made with sackcloth, we drifted among the deep lotus and thick willows. As for the shadow of dancing and the dust of singing, we kept them from our eyes and ears. . . . Enjoying the wine, we picked lotus leaves and searched for poetry topics."[22] Poetry club excursions like this blurred the boundary between Hangzhou locals and immigrants and between officials who served the court and those who sojourned in Hangzhou.[23] The lake scenery with its assortment of specific places known through past and contemporary writings was an anchor to which these scholars attached their identities as literati.

The relationship between landscape and literary writing was one of reciprocal enhancement: the landscape served as a lasting reminder of the history it had witnessed, and the writing imbued these scenes with fame and rich meaning. Places, both in literary and physical forms, not only served as geographical indicators in writings but also bridged the literati tradition between here and there, now and then. The place and the historical figures formed an entity and became a type of trope for the culture centered on Hangzhou.

Appeal to literary tradition was by no means the only element that contributed to the reputation of West Lake; its status in history also benefitted from writing that regarded West Lake as a political symbol.

WEST LAKE AS THE SYMBOL OF THE STATE

The relocation of the court to Hangzhou and the residence of the imperial family among the southeastern hills encouraged new interpretations of the lake. People believed that the city's spectacular landscape of mountains and rivers imbued the city with royal *qi* (energy), making it inherently a place of great political significance.[24] Such political symbolism accorded to natural landscape was evident in Southern Song writings on West Lake, due to the desire for "dynastic revival" among scholars. This political significance was also demonstrated through the depiction of sightseeing as a sign of benevolent and peaceful rule.

The relative stability of the period between 1141 and 1234 encouraged the depiction of the beautiful scenery and elegant sightseeing around the lake. It was not until 1141 when the Song court signed a peace treaty with the Jin court that the imperial family seriously considered settling down in Hangzhou. The court constructed imperial palaces among the southern mountains and expanded the urban infrastructure. Meanwhile, in contemporary writings, the sense of danger that had permeated earlier works subsided, and people began to shift their attention temporarily from military crisis to their pleasant surroundings. Writings from these years sang the praises of the central government by depicting West Lake as a mirror of the general prosperity of the country. The Southern Song literati appropriated West Lake as a symbol of state revival. This was an attempt to incorporate the new living environment into the familiar literati discourse.

The connection between the lake and the state was not unfamiliar to the Southern Song literati. The Northern Song Hangzhou governor usually saw the role of West Lake as a "life-releasing pond," which accumulated blessings for the throne.[25] After the fall of the Northern Song, nostalgic writers further enhanced the connection between the lake and the state. In 1145, when the official Zhou Zizhi visited West Lake after an absence of approximately forty years, he was startled by the run-down scenery. He found that fewer than one-fifth of the scenic spots he had been to before had survived the war. Zhou wrote with frustration on the loss of north China to the Jurchens: "When Qiantang [an old name for Hangzhou] was at its peak, I could not find the opportunity to travel around the lake. . . . Only now, after the war is over, do I have the opportunity to look at the lake from dawn to dark. This is indeed regrettable."[26] In this lament, Zhou used the past grandeur of Hangzhou and West Lake to represent the Northern Song. Among people like Zhou who had been to Hangzhou before the fall of the Northern Song, its postwar condition aroused nostalgia for the way the lake used to be. These people would find solace when prosperous scenery gradually returned to the lake.

The emphasis placed on West Lake during the Southern Song grew out of the desire to prove that Hangzhou was qualified to serve as the new capital. The debate at the beginning of the Southern Song between Hangzhou and Nanjing encouraged Hangzhou supporters to convince dissenting scholars and officials. While Hangzhou was seen as a safe and expedient site for preserving the imperial house, Nanjing was supported due to the expectation that it would become a mighty frontier fortress.[27] One disadvantage of Hangzhou was its deviation from the traditional standard layout for capitals: the cityscape was not square, but elongated in shape, squeezed between the lake and the river. Also, adherence to past dynasties' convention of placing an array of sacrificial altars to the south of the capital proved to be unrealistic in Hangzhou: the southern part of the city was mostly mountainous.[28] Some officials also saw West Lake as a disadvantage for Hangzhou. Xin Qiji, for example, commented that Hangzhou was strategically problematic: if enemies opened the embankment of West Lake, it would inundate the city.[29] The supporters of Hangzhou as the capital, therefore, needed to find new evidence of heavenly blessings.

Praising West Lake's sacredness served to counter any criticism of this place. Scholar-officials projected their yearning for a home onto their writings about Hangzhou and West Lake in particular. It did not take long before West Lake acquired a high position in Southern Song political discourse. For instance, one official wrote this:

> Southeast of Wu Mountain,
> The imperial city is blanketed in luxuriant green.
> West Lake lies at its feet,
> The waves are permeated by the imperial spirit.[30]

In this poem, the author promoted the status of West Lake by highlighting its geographical proximity to the imperial city. West Lake was connected with and even blessed by the *qi* of the imperial house.

Undoubtedly the new court welcomed this metaphor. The government, which was dominated by the chief minister Qin Gui (1091–1155) and his followers, aspired to regard the prosperous lake scenes as the results of maintaining peace with the Jurchens, as well as signs of the new court's legitimacy. The theoretical roots of these beliefs came from the Confucian teaching that the emperor as the "the son of heaven" could influence the natural environment through his rule: effective and benevolent governance resulted in national peace while cruel and futile rule generated natural disasters. Zhu Dunru (1081–1159), the judicial commissioner of the East Route in the Zhe Region, praised the court in his depiction of the lake:

> Nowadays the true environment around West Lake,
> Is based on the revitalization of sage rulership.
> One only needs to listen to the music and watch the dancing;
> The fragrances linger, and deep cups are filled with wine.
> Celebrating the good years and the peace that pervades the country
> is the best of all.[31]

This poem begins with praise for the restoration and ends by identifying the period as a peaceful time. Similar celebratory feeling infused many poems about West Lake. The word "*zhongxing*," meaning "restoration," embodied the wishes of the Southern Song court to regain the strength of the Northern Song. This term functioned as political propaganda and continuously appeared in Southern Song documents to reaffirm the legitimacy of the throne.

The literati took people's enjoyment of the lake as an illustration of the country's potential for recovery; comparing the new capital with the old one was an essential aspect of this. The preface of *Record of the Splendor of the Metro Capital*, for instance, comments that "After Emperor Gaozong halted his carriage at Hangzhou, the city—because of the bright elegance of the landscape and the peaceful prosperity of the people—was perceived to surpass the capital [of the Northern Song] tenfold."[32] This account equated the prosperity of the lake with the well-being of the new dynasty. The comparison with the old capital also arose out of the feeling of nostalgia prevalent during the Southern Song. Writers deployed descriptions of the prosperous scenery and compared it to the old capital to reconfirm the qualifications of Hangzhou to serve as the new capital and to illustrate the restoration discourse.

Emphasizing the emperor's sightseeing on the lake was a standard lens through which Southern Song literati organized their narratives of the city and the lake. Zhou Mi began *Old Affairs of the Martial Grove* with an admiring description of an imperial visit during the Chunxi reign.[33] The court organized grand annual processions to certain palaces and temples, especially those in which new protective deities were said to reside.[34] From the imperial perspective, these events served a function similar to the ritual and processions in the Northern Song.[35] The acknowledgment of and emphasis on the imperial presence on the lake exemplified the politicization of this place.

The desire to promote Hangzhou as a flourishing capital also motivated the compilation of local gazetteers. During the Southern Song, the local gazetteers were compiled within an imperial context and in the language of the authorities. Cartographic discourse and the production of empire mutually supported each other.[36] In the three gazetteers about Hangzhou, poems that eulogized the government were often included. Many of these poems emphasized and even romanticized the lake's historical tradition, the surrounding expansion of the cityscape, and the entertainment-oriented sightseeing. For example, in one poem, the local scholar Lin Yede wrote this:

> No dust [for the ruler] in the government and the people, this is the right time to enjoy pleasure with the people;
> Lake and mountains resemble paintings; usually, people project their emotions onto the scenery.
> Luxuriant is the old capital of Qiantang; grand is the new government in Lin'an.
> Three thousand alleys are filled with flowers and willows that compete for beauty;
> Tens of thousands of households lay out silk to show off.
> Flutes and songs are the best in the whole country; the scenery astonishes the whole human world.
> Since ancient times, traditions have been prominent in the two Zhe areas;
> So much prosperity, all gather on West Lake,
> . . . It is lucky that peaceful and secure days have lasted for so long; it is proper to share pleasure with commoners.[37]

Using flamboyant words and parallel sentences, Lin conveyed the delights of Hangzhou, showing how much it deserved its status as the new capital of the recently revived dynasty. The account begins with a comparison between peaceful court politics and the beautiful natural landscape. It then emphasizes the historical tradition of this region and the grandeur of the new capital. Following this come details of the cityscape, with Lin exaggerating the number of roads and households. The poem then turns to entertainments and to West Lake as a significant symbol of prosperity. In the end, Lin praised the practice of sharing pleasure with the common people. He attributed the splendid scene to the political achievements of the government. This conclusion revealed that the poem was more a propaganda document than a literary record.

The theme of rulers sharing pleasure with the common people, a Confucian ideal promoted by Mencius, was essential to the concept of restoring the Song. In 1227, Cheng Mi and other scholars gathered on the lake to celebrate the Double Third festival. Cheng later recorded the event, emphasizing the harmony between officials and the common people: "The vendors sold congee near the municipal governor, and pleasure boats provided music and dance unsolicited. This was due to the benevolence of the municipal governor and his harmony with the urban residents, which replicated the peaceful scenery. . . . However, my peers and I should not be satisfied by such a view. Instead, we should recover the lost land and guard the emperor on his return to the capital of Kaifeng."[38] The first half of this account attributed the sightseeing scenery to benevolent governance, and the second half expressed the motivation to recover the north and return to the old capital.

Connecting the lake and the political lineage was an effort to make sense of and appropriate the new settings of the capital for political purposes. The literati interpreted the new capital's proximity to a natural landscape and the state's growing engagement with this place in the context of royal *qi* and in the framework of benevolent politics. The pervasive appropriation of nostalgia for the Northern Song supported the state's efforts to maintain its power and credibility. Nostalgic discourses thus promoted continued loyalty to the imperial family. The appropriation of nostalgia might also have helped maintain the Han cultural lineage, which was then under threat from the northern dynasties' military strength.

In addition to viewing West Lake from an imperial perspective, the capital journals and gazetteers also included meticulous records of different sites. The viewpoints of these writings are a hybrid of state legacy and local history. The records of West Lake as local history constructed a new category of knowledge and evoked a different type of nostalgia.

WEST LAKE AS BUILT INTO THE LOCAL HISTORY

The Song dynasty witnessed a growing interest in geographical knowledge. Scholars have studied in depth the proliferation of geography books and demonstrated that the writing of these local histories promoted local pride as well as systematized new knowledge.[39] In the Southern Song, due to the increasing popularity of excursions around West Lake, the local government invested substantial sums in constructing sightseeing-related projects. In the process, local elites gained growing geographical knowledge that they wanted to record.

Local gazetteers' documentation of West Lake demonstrated a commitment to local sites, a departure from the Northern Song model of the nationally focused gazetteer such as *Overall Documentary of Geography* (Fangyu shenglan) and *The Record of Scenic Spots Across the Country* (Yudi jisheng).[40] The Southern Song changes revealed both the transitional nature of the system for compiling gazetteers and the changing format of circulating information. During the Southern Song, literati scholars and local officials started to participate in gazetteer compilation projects, with local officials supervising the compilation work of local scholars.[41] Some gazetteer compilers had gained reputations for writing about local scenery and products from their previously published manuals, such as Chen Renyu (b. 1212), one of the compilers of the *The Gazetteer of Hangzhou during the Chunyou Reign* (Chunyou Lin'an zhi).[42] In addition, the political crisis at the end of the Northern Song enabled literati to become the primary producers and consumers of these texts relating to history and current affairs.[43]

Of the three extant gazetteers from the Southern Song, *The Gazetteer of Hangzhou during the Xianchun Reign* was the most informative. Compiled and published by Qian Yueyou between 1268 and 1273, this gazetteer included West Lake in the chapter titled "Mountains and Rivers" and provided geographical and historical information about surrounding places. The records in this and the other local gazetteers not only provided accurate information to readers who would never be able to see these places but also functioned as proto-guidebooks telling visitors what to see. This was in response to the expanded readership of gazetteers: they were read by local officials as part of their clerical training and now also by other literati who were interested in local affairs.[44]

The Gazetteer of Hangzhou during the Xianchun Reign provided detailed information on government-sponsored projects, including newly constructed and repaired scenic sites. Indeed, more projects were undertaken during the Xianchun reign than before. The following record is a typical example of the detailed information in the gazetteer:

> Small New Causeway [Xiaoxindi]: In 1242, Commissioner Zhao constructed a causeway connecting the Second Bridge [Di'erqiao] of Northern Hills and the Qu Winery [Quyuan]. Along the banks of the causeway, willows were planted as on the Su Causeway. [This causeway] reaches to the Soul's Retreat and Tianzhu Monasteries. Halfway across the causeway [the government] built a hall that opens in four directions and also three pavilions in which tourists can rest. In 1269, the local government launched another renovation project, piling earth on the causeway, increasing the height by more than two *chi* [a bit over two feet]. The length is approximately 250 *zhang* [about half a mile], and the width is about 25 *chi* [about 27 feet]. All the funding was provided by the court.[45]

A few features of this excerpt are worth noting. First, the Small New Causeway was carefully placed in its geographical setting. The references to the Second Bridge, the Qu Winery (the official brewery during the Southern Song), the Soul's Retreat and Tianzhu Monasteries, and the Four Faces Hall (Simiantang) provided the necessary geographic markers to locate the causeway. This was the gazetteer convention of visually showcasing the relative locations with words. Second, this record emphasized the purpose of the causeway as a project: to provide sightseers with a place to rest and to connect the lake sites to the monasteries located deep in the mountain. This causeway could significantly cut travel time for pilgrims. Third and last, this document revealed the imperial court as the funding source for the causeway project. The previous discussion of West Lake as a state symbol analyzed the court's motivation for funding projects like this. While continuing the tradition of earlier official records in its focus on contemporary political accomplishments, this gazetteer also differed from previous ones in its attention to physical sites and their histories. The new characteristic evidences the beginning of place-oriented history writing.

The meticulous recording and multifaceted presentation of scenic sites attests to a new literati interest in geography and also represents a standard format for categorizing local history.[46] The Southern Song gazetteer established the model for contemporary and later accounts of the lake. Its characteristics were a clear historical awareness and spatial logic, as well as the convergence of a state view and a local perspective.

The attention to physical sites and the use of the space-time structure was evident in the four capital journals.[47] Prefaces for both *Record of the Splendor of the Metro Capital* and *Record of Multitudinous Splendors* reveal the authors' strong motivations for recording the splendor of the city. Prompted by the growing sense that Hangzhou was in jeopardy, both authors began to record the histories of their surroundings. The sense of nostalgia in Wu Zimu's preface to *Record of the Millet Dream* was even more prominent: "With the passing of time things change. The wealth of cities and gardens, the splendor of the customs and the people: how could they all be preserved as they were?"[48] Wu not only borrowed the word "*meng*" (dream) from *The Eastern Capital* but also roughly followed the organization of Meng's work.[49] *Record of the Millet Dream* unfolds in ten chapters (*juan*), each of which has many subdivisions with headings. Wu's journal can be divided roughly into two parts, one on the geographical layout of the city and the surrounding landscape, the other on the city's annual calendar and special events. In this space-time structure, Wu meticulously recorded every detail of the daily life of Hangzhou residents. In Zhou Mi's *Old Affairs of the Martial Grove*, the preface also stated plaintively, "As time passes and things change, [I] have drifted around plagued by hardship. Thinking of past travels, it all seems like a dream and therefore is tied to my laments."[50]

Zhou Mi's book testifies to the importance of the circulation of knowledge regarding the physical sites and the recognition of its value. Although *Old Affairs of the Martial Grove* was compiled shortly after the fall of the Southern Song, the geographical information it recorded circulated during Zhou Mi's early years (the last three decades before the fall of the dynasty in 1279). Zhou devoted a whole chapter, "Scenic Lake and Mountain Spots," to the detailed documentation of sites. While other chapters included beautiful and even exaggerated descriptions of urban life and imperial events, in this chapter Zhou Mi adopted a style more common in gazetteers to list about 454 sites, with notations on particular smaller sites housed within specific palaces or temples. Most of these sites are also found in the gazetteer map (see map I.2). Zhou organized these sites into nine different routes, each with its own features, roughly sketched in figure 3.2. The Northern Mountain Route, the Southern Mountain Route, the Fang Family Valley Route, the Small Wheat Hill Route, the Big Wheat Hill Route, the Three Tianzhu Route, and the Ge Hill Route all featured religious sites, while the Three Causeways Route and the Solitary Mountain Route focused on natural scenery and famous historical figures.[51]

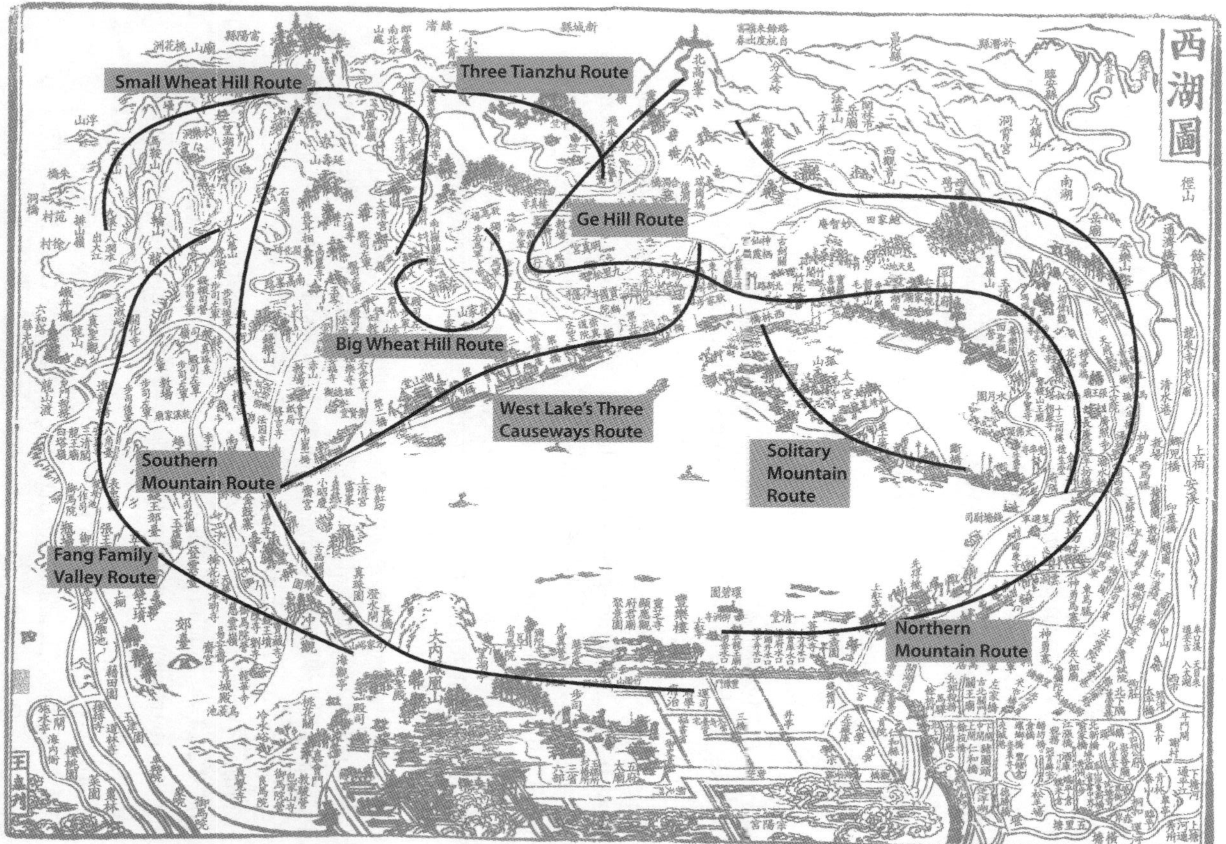

FIGURE 3.2. Sketch of Zhou Mi's nine sightseeing routes around West Lake, ca. thirteenth century. Illustration by the author, after *Wulin jiushi*, 377–403.

The different writing styles in *Old Affairs of the Martial Grove*, especially the stylistic inconsistency between the descriptive records of sightseeing around West Lake and the gazetteer language used in listing the sites, represent a transitional phase in documenting newly expanding knowledge. Zhou's book was either informed by officials' historical documents on imperial life or by encyclopedic records of knowledge about the city. Chapters in *Old Affairs of the Martial Grove* exhibit huge variations in subject matter. For example, *juan* 2 and 3 recorded annual celebrations; *juan* 7 was entirely devoted to anecdotes of how Emperor Xiaozong served Emperor Gaozong; and *juan* 10 focused on the culture of drama, a personal interest of Zhou Mi.

Similar inconsistencies also appeared in *Record of Multitudinous Splendors*. While this capital journal was known for recording the luxury of urban life in colloquial language, the author occasionally switched to gazetteer-style language that emphasized geographic facts to provide information on scenic sites in a particular place. For example, in recording an imperial visit to the lake, the book described the emperor visiting the Four Guardians Temple while boating on the lake. While the account as a whole followed the style of travel writings, the author included a traditionally styled, one-sentence listing of scenic spots inside the Four Guardians Temple: "Scenic sites in the garden include: Agate Hillside (Ma'naopo), Qin Dynasty Junipers (Qinchaogui), Six One Spring (Liuyiquan), and Lin Bu's Tomb."[52]

The geographical setting was not the only common concern of these journal writings. Attention to the annual calendar also figured prominently, a feature that first appeared in *The Eastern Capital*. In *juan* 3 of *Old Affairs of the Martial Grove,* Zhou Mi recorded all important events throughout the year, including imperial leisure such as "enjoying the coolness in the imperial palace," religious festivals such as the Ghost Festival (the fifteenth day of the seventh lunar month), and sightseeing activities such as the "welcoming the wine" event. More than half the events listed took place around West Lake. Such records reflected an attempt to incorporate newly emerging urban leisure activities into the long-standing imperial-centered cosmology.

Gazetteer-style writing also influenced poetry. The poet Dong Sigao (ca. 1260–1276) used a similar format in compiling his *One Hundred Poems of West Lake* (Xihu baiyong). In the preface to this work, Dong Sigao, a Hangzhou local scholar, openly expressed his consciousness of living during the capital's "peak of prosperity." He defined his motivation for writing as the desire to provide an authentic experience, and he placed particular emphasis on the authority of firsthand geographic knowledge. Indeed, his writing demonstrates a clear consciousness of sites and the history they embodied. Dong provided a brief history of each site and then elaborated on its natural beauty and historical background in one poem. His collection drew on the local gazetteers' structural conventions to emphasize specific places.[53] In contrast to his Northern Song peers, such as Yang Pan (ca. 1017–1106) and Guo Xiangzheng (1035–1113), who also composed hundred-poem collections on West Lake, Dong's compilation followed a sequence that resembled a counterclockwise tour around the lake. Dong's annotation of different sites was distinguished by his attention to relative positioning. The anthology also functioned as a catalog of sites visited, with observations focused on the process of recognition.

Dong hoped to preserve local knowledge and memory of Hangzhou that were at risk of dying out. In the preface, he noted that one of his motivations was to keep a record of local terms based on their original meanings, since his contemporaries were gradually forgetting them. An example he provided was a site near the lake known in Hangzhou dialect as *xiama* ("toad," usually referring to a street performance in which several toads answered each other). It was later mistakenly referred to as *xiama ling* (hill for dismounting horses), a term usually applied to a place where visitors needed to dismount from their horses to show respect. The name change was very likely the result of Hangzhou becoming the capital.[54] Here, Dong placed the importance of local knowledge on a par with Hangzhou's position as the capital. He shared the Old Man of West Lake's concern with the local dialect, which was threatened by the huge wave of immigrants spreading the official northern Chinese language. This attention to dying local knowledge reflected the perceived urgency of preserving Hangzhou's disappearing past during its transition to a capital city.

Detailed records on sites manifested not only unprecedented mastery and awareness of geographical locations but also the extent to which knowledge was shared within the community. During the Southern Song, these written records reflected and generated conversations about local scenic sites. They not only contributed to writers' and the readers' self-identifications as members of the local community, but also encouraged them to display their knowledge of the historical and literary traditions associated with these local sites, a talent that was culturally valued. When Ellen Cong Zhang investigates the making of sites during the Northern Song, she finds that the fame of certain sites was both established and expanded through the efforts of elites from other places.[55] During the Southern Song, however, as seen from the example of West Lake, it was local elites who contributed the most to the recording of local history.

These writings were also unavoidably colored by the unending vicissitudes of dynastic history. By the end of the Southern Song, people were especially sensitive to the similarities between their current situation and past experiences. This recollection of memory scared many people.[56] The most disturbing time probably came shortly after 1234, when Mongol armies swept northern China and ended the rule of the Jin dynasty. It might not be purely coincidental that the first capital journal came out in 1235. Although it was not until several years later that the Mongols started their military expedition into south China, the end of the peace treaty between the Jin and the Southern Song led to widespread insecurity. The sense of peril reminded people of the trauma at the end of the Northern Song that they had heard about from their parents or grandparents, and it strengthened the tendency to look on West Lake with nostalgia.

Subliminal fear about the limited lives of dynasties generated a sense of "preemptive nostalgia" in most of the writings about West Lake. Here, nostalgia is used in a sense broader than the traditionally defined one of lamenting something that has disappeared. Instead, it refers to missing things before they cease to exist. In other words, the unconscious impression that the beauty of West Lake was as vulnerable as the fate of the dynasty would never entirely disappear. As a result, many works focused on specific sites in an effort to convey to later generations how unique the city had been.

WEST LAKE AS A PLACE OF ANXIETY

While most of the writings discussed above conveyed a sense of West Lake as a place of particular importance, functioning as an anchor for identity, the lake was by no means a coherent place in the Song dynasty writings. It was subject to controversy and open to playful and satirized use. Two types of writing that depicted the lake alternatively were poetry of patriotic sentiments and anecdotes in *Book of Hearsay* (Yijian zhi), compiled by Hong Mai.

Not all the literati during the Southern Song celebrated the scenery of and opportunities to tour the lake. For example, as Xinda Lian points out, Xin Qiji and several other scholars, including Li Qingzhao (1084–1155), avoided West Lake as a topic in their productive lives as poets. Lian argues that these literati regarded the feminine lake as inadequate to support their patriotic sentiment.[57] Ever since Su Shi's comparison of West Lake to the Lady of the West, the lake was seen as gendered due its softness and misty beauty. Compared to north China's grand mountains, the southern mountains and lakes were softer, gentler, and mistier. Chen Renjie (1218–1243) recorded a poem written by his friends, which circulated widely. One of its lines is particularly powerful: "Southeastern China's seductiveness makes men become effeminate."[58]

Other scholars criticized sightseeing around the lake as a pleasure-driven lifestyle. For example, Wen Jiweng (ca. 1123–1175) lamented in one poem, "The ladle of West Lake water, since we crossed the rivers, [has seen] a hundred years of singing and dancing . . . nobody is ever again seen shedding tears at the New Pavilion."[59] Wen continued the poem, concentrating on the contrast with the war raging at the end of the Northern Song. His reflection spurred him to express a deep-rooted sense of crisis and an implicit critique of the Southern Song's peace-seeking policy. At the end of the poem, referring to the popular discourse about Lin Bu, Wen implicitly criticized the reclusive leisure attitude. In this poem Lin Bu, no longer the symbol of idealized literati life, exemplified those who wandered near the lake and remained ignorant about contemporary politics.

Literature scholars have analyzed in detail similar poems that depicted the scenic beauty as a way to express deep concerns about the dynasty.[60] These works associated the landscape and the pleasure seeking in it with the downfall of the dynasty. West Lake was taken as a scapegoat for the government's lack of commitment to fight against the northern enemies. For Southern Song literati, the move to Hangzhou not only placed them in the middle of natural beauty but also stirred in them conflicting feelings. They struggled to integrate their political concern with their appreciation of natural scenery.[61] To them, writing was a way to convey this struggle and to understand both the natural and the political environments. Similar to the writing of local history discussed in the above section, these writers too associated the lake with the fate of the dynasty, but from a critical perspective.

Nevertheless, the lake's political implications were rarely a concern in *Book of Hearsay* tales. The difference between these stories and other literary works was in part a function of differences in their readership.[62] Hangzhou was the place where Hong Mai began working on *Book of Hearsay*, and it was also one of the four primary publishing locations in the country. So ordinary Hangzhou residents were familiar with stories in *Book of Hearsay*, either by reading widely accessible print sources or by word of mouth from friends and storytellers.[63] While the literati culture was inclined to interpret the natural environment aesthetically and politically, for ordinary city dwellers the hustle and bustle of urban life created anxious feeling among residents and thus served as a stage for suspenseful stories. Therefore, some of the *Book of Hearsay* stories of Hangzhou revealed potential dangers in the capital life.[64] The mountains around the lake that were not fully explored further enhanced the sense of wildness.

Scholars have discussed at length the value of *Book of Hearsay* for studies of Song perceptions of the supernatural world and the social environment.[65] Although their subject matter is usually far from reality, these stories are important in that they reveal how knowledge could be creatively interpreted. Place names were of often little importance to the plots of these stories, except for adding credibility;[66] however, in some stories such as those discussed below, place names play a more complex role, reflecting West Lake's geographical position and the associated literary conventions.

In the first story, "The Nun from the West Lake Convent" (Xihu an'ni), West Lake is a liminal space that embodies potential danger to the protagonists when they cross the physical boundary of the city wall.[67] This story is about a young man who bribes a nun in order to take advantage of an official's wife. The nun tricks the wife with a temple feast and puts her in the same chamber with the young man. After he gets what he wants, he dies suddenly, and it takes a full year to resolve the resulting legal case. This story testifies to contemporary anxiety about close interactions between elite women and nuns and the increasing mobility acquired by women.[68]

Though the story of kidnapping could easily have taken place in or outside any large city, the inclusion of West Lake as a specific location made the choice of protagonist more plausible. The lake was known as the location of many religious sites, and visiting temples was a widely accepted reason for women to leave their homes. However, the geographical context of West Lake made it both a busy place and a wild landscape, thus enhancing the strangeness. Another *Book of Hearsay* story claimed that three out of ten of the people living in Hangzhou were non-human beings.[69] Moreover, visiting the lake involved crossing the city boundary to enter the less-cultivated natural space, an important element in the accounts of anomalies.[70] Although literati had visited West Lake during the Northern Song, the surrounding mountains were still largely unexplored in the early decades of the Southern Song. For example, Yuan Jiong complained during the early years of the Southern Song that life in the hills surrounding West Lake was quite hard and unpleasant.[71] The wildness associated with this suburb became the context of some eerie stories involving encounters between scholars visiting the lake and beauties who had been transformed from "the demons of grass and wood."[72]

The second story "The West Lake Administrative Assistant" (Xihu panguan) echoes an elaboration of literary allusions, and West Lake is central to such interreferentiality.[73] This is a retribution story with a didactic purpose: the sons of a military official mistakenly eat a crab that turns out to be the incarnation of the West Lake administrative assistant, and the sons all die. The story's reference to West Lake's identity as a "life-releasing pond" adds to its sense of veracity.

A local literary allusion explains why the crab refers to itself as the West Lake administrative assistant. Qian Kun, a Hangzhou native during Song times, once jokingly replied when asked where he wanted to pursue a position: "Anywhere with crabs but without a controller-general."[74] During the Song dynasty, the controller-general was appointed as a delegate of the central government to monitor local county governors and usually had a bad reputation among officials. From then on, people referred to the West Lake administrative assistant as a crab. *Tongpan* (controller-general) is transformed into *panguan* (administrative assistant) here to add familiarity by referencing the more colloquial title.

It was the place names in this story that later led to its inclusion in gazetteers. One place mentioned in the story was the Qiantang Lake Gate, where the military official catches the crab. The story misspelled the name of the gate, using the character for *qian*, "front." But later, when gazetteers cited this story, the name was corrected. In *Examination of the Historical Sites of the Southern Song* (Nan Song guji kao), Qing scholar Zhu Peng (1731–1803) quoted this tale to annotate the entry for "Qiantang Lake Gate," revealing Zhu Peng's purpose to preserve local history from the Song era.[75]

The last story, "Spiritual Travel around West Lake" (Shenyou Xihu), further incorporates physical and spiritual visits to West Lake as textual devices to enhance the familiarity and playfulness of the tale.[76] In this story, an immortal general, who is later revealed to be a disease demon, orders Chen Wu, a recently deceased villager and the narrator of the tale, to take him to West Lake, saying, "I hear that the scenery at West Lake is magnificent, but I regret that I have never been there. Now, since I have the chance to travel and inspect things, I want to go sightseeing around the lake. I would like you to be my guide. Once I have seen the lake, I will send you back." After several days of travel, Chen states that they arrived in Hangzhou and "went sightseeing on the lake. The Tianzhu and Soul's Retreat Monasteries, the market and gardens, we visited them all one by one, except that the deity dared not enter the Daoist palaces."

In this story, West Lake as a place helps to structure Chen's experience in his afterlife, adding to the playful elaboration of the general's identity. Even without explicit contextualization, readers would not have been surprised that the demon-general wanted to visit the lake or that Chen Wu referred to the places of interest around the lake as common knowledge. In real life, sightseeing at West Lake was a cultural pilgrimage for literati and a leisure amusement for the imperial family and ordinary city dwellers. In the story, ironically, the disease demon follows this fashion because he has heard that the scenery is exceptional, but his excursion causes the further spread of disease.

All three stories depict West Lake as a liminal place where boundary crossing was possible. The boundaries include those between the city and the suburb, between the supernatural and real life, and between life and death. Meanwhile, these stories were also informed by place-related literary conventions, which the stories deconstructed by twisting the textual conventions about West Lake and its status as a cultural landmark. Literary allusions collapsed in the playful association with supernatural beings.

These writings do not provide a perfect or homogenous picture of West Lake, but they convey concerns and anxiety about this place. They suggest alternative responses to the growing interaction with the natural landscape during the transitional period. In contrast to the stable, positive, and coherent writings discussed in the above three sections—writings that emphasize the permanence of local places and historical consciousness—these writings are fleeting, satirical, and impermanent, based on the dangers of pleasure seeking and boundary crossing.

CONCLUSION: WRITING IN PLACE AND TIME

West Lake accumulated its cultural significance through reading, writing, and touring. Traveling to the lake and especially paying visits to its well-documented sites, scholars participated in a virtual conversation with historical figures and thus acquired a sense of belonging to a cultural community. During and after the Jurchen invasion, state officials regarded the emerging sightseeing activities around the lake as a symbol of empire-wide revival and the consolidation of the new regime's power. During the last decades of the Southern Song, the local gentry sought to mitigate the feeling of political instability by compiling gazetteers and journals to record information on this "eternal" natural landscape.

West Lake functioned as an anchoring cultural landmark and also embodied the criticism and uncertainty of the expanding urban life in Hangzhou. Writings on West Lake constructed it as a prominent place. In their attempts to faithfully and precisely record various locations with cultural and political significance, literati grasped at stable elements in the spatial environment. This environment had a natural and cultural history of its own, different from the temporal changes then occurring. During this process, the lake functioned as an anchor for identity, through which visitors and commentators expressed their affection for and sought identification with literary traditions and local history and through which they grappled with their concerns for the fate of the dynasty. Nevertheless, West Lake did not always function as an anchor. Some scholars criticized its natural beauty and the sightseeing activities for distracting the court; some anecdotes generalized it as a less explored natural environment or transformed it into a playful entertainment.

Taken together, these writings encompassed the dynastic transition at the end of the Northern Song, the shifting of urban life in Hangzhou, and concern with the fate of the dynasty. Nostalgic feeling shaped almost all types of writings: accounts about historical figures and state symbols were inspired by nostalgia for tradition; local historical records demonstrated preemptive nostalgia; and tales of the supernatural conveyed a yearning for the familiar past. Distilling nostalgia into writing on West Lake both incorporated the place into complex historical developments and revealed the influential role of place in understanding these historical changes. Nostalgia appeared more candidly after the collapse of the Southern Song, when West Lake became a universal symbol for a bygone era.

Overall, despite their different vocabularies, styles, and audiences, these writings represented efforts to capture and interpret the natural landscape around West Lake, especially the increasing mobility between the city and the lake. It was not until the Ming dynasty that Tian Rucheng came up with a new descriptive gazetteer style to categorize information about West Lake more systematically. Tian published two books: *Gazetteer of Sightseeing around West Lake* and *Supplemented Gazetteer of Sightseeing around West Lake.* The first, more like the Southern Song gazetteer, was organized according to the different sightseeing routes recorded in Zhou Mi's *Old*

Affairs of the Martial Grove. Under each route, Tian included introductions to places of interest.[77] The second work included records that were more miscellaneous. It began with accounts of the imperial capital, Southern Song politics, and the run-down scenery after the fall of the Song court. It then moved to literary traditions, including stories of historical figures and literary works, as well as stories about prominent monks. Following this were records about famous craftsmen and sightseeing activities. It ended with anecdotes and supernatural stories. The format used in this account neatly gathered the information that was once scattered across Southern Song gazetteers, poems, urban journals, and tales. The diverse and incoherent accounts written during the Song dynasty were finally synthesized.

CHAPTER FOUR

A TOPOGRAPHIC AND AFFECTIVE PLACE

Landscape through the Sightseer's Eyes

ON FIRST SEEING WEST LAKE, A THIRTEENTH-CENTURY SCHOLAR exclaimed, "So beautiful! Unique! Green water is surrounded by blue mountains. Golden and green buildings rise from the natural setting, as in a colorful landscape painting. The east side of the lake, which is not surrounded by mountains, has city walls that touch the clouds and tens of thousands of roof tiles laid out like the scales of a fish. This scenery is like heaven on earth."[1] Zhou Mi, commenting on Zhang's statement notes, "Despite his less-than-refined words, the scenery of West Lake is [clearly] depicted." Comparing West Lake to a landscape painting suggests that the lush scenery of the lake, with water backed by mountains, was considered an inspiration and an ideal theme for such art.

The connection drawn between the real scenery of the lake and landscape painting was not a Southern Song invention. As early as the Tang dynasty, Bai Juyi began one of his poems on West Lake with the words "Now that spring is here, the lake seems a painted picture."[2] During the Northern Song, as Su Shi and several other monks drank wine and gazed at the lakeside scenery, Su wrote: "Whose talented brush could capture the scene on a three-hundred-foot canvas of silk? Such a painting would be unique throughout the realm as it is the image of West Lake." Then Su asked his friends to continue the poem, and the monk Zhongshu wrote, "No matter how much ink and color you waste, these beauties cannot be painted."[3] The comparison between painting and scenery was deployed naturally as a way to communicate the beauty of the lake. The growing popularity of landscape paintings among literati provided them with an apt tool for metaphor.

Landscape painting has been one of the most esteemed genres in Chinese visual culture for more than a millennium. A variety of landscape images,

TABLE 4.1. Extant Southern Song paintings and maps of West Lake

Title	Format	Painter	Approximate date	Current location or source
Painting of West Lake	hand scroll	Li Song	late 12th–early 13th century	Shanghai Museum, Shanghai
Willows and Boats on West Lake	hanging scroll	Xia Gui	early 13th century	National Palace Museum, Taipei
Clear Summer among the Lotus	hand scroll	Ma Lin	mid-13th century	Liaoning Museum, Shenyang
Painting of Spring Dawn at the Lake and Mountains	fan painting	Chen Qingbo	mid-13th century	Palace Museum, Beijing
Ten Views of West Lake	album paintings	Ye Xiaoyan	mid- to late 13th century	National Palace Museum, Taipei
Spring Dawn at West Lake	fan painting	Anonymous	13th century	Palace Museum, Beijing
West Lake map	printed map	Unknown; engraved by Wang Yao	1268–75	*The Gazetteer of Hangzhou during the Xianchun Reign*

including paintings, prints, and gazetteer maps, emerged as a result of experiencing and observing nature. These visual representations of the natural landscape were closely associated with cultural perceptions of the surrounding natural world. While artists wielded their brushes to reflect society's current environmental aesthetics, the conventions of visual culture also offered ideas about and perspectives on how to view and experience the natural landscape.

Landscape paintings could reflect both the artistic tradition of the time and human interaction with the landscape. Both nature and landscape images changed in response to the changing sociocultural context. Physical alterations to the natural landscape and developments in artistic styles of landscape images, however, did not always go hand in hand. It might seem that early landscape paintings could give us full insight into the natural environment and the landscape aesthetics of a previous era. However, the evidence provided by paintings is far too complicated to yield an easy interpretation. What the artist chose to depict or leave out was determined not only by the artist's knowledge of certain schools of painting but also by the demands of the existing cultural framework.

Southern Song painters, such as Liu Songnian (ca. 1155–1218), Chen Qingbo (ca. 1253–1258), and Ma Lin (ca. 1180–1256), produced a great many paintings of West Lake.[4] Four extant Southern Song paintings include "West Lake" in their titles, and a few others are also considered depictions of West

Lake scenery, although their titles do not explicitly mention this location (table 4.1). The earliest maps of West Lake also emerged during the Southern Song. Maps and paintings are different facets of visual culture, and both facets reflect contemporary geographical knowledge and aesthetics.

Paintings of West Lake continued to develop after the Song dynasty, reflecting continuous evolution in artistic styles and cultural taste. Some essential elements and standards remained more or less the same. Compared to later paintings, those of the Southern Song reveal remarkable artistic skill, including attention to depicting physical features, accuracy in representing seasonal elements, and mastery in rendering the misty environment. According to the Ming dynasty scholar Yuan Hongdao (1568–1610), when people thought about West Lake scenery, they automatically recalled Song paintings because of the similarities between the natural features and Song artistic styles.[5]

Art historians have long studied Southern Song landscape paintings of West Lake.[6] These paintings are viewed as representative examples of Southern Song art that can be mined for valuable geographical and cultural insights, and the development of West Lake paintings coincided with a crucial stage in landscape painting.[7] West Lake imagery and the depiction of real scenery in late imperial China exemplify how spatial imagination and physical experience interacted and conversed visually.[8]

Investigating the characteristics and development of visual representations of West Lake can establish a history of how West Lake was depicted and visualized, as well as how people interpreted and incorporated this particular landscape into their leisure lives and cultural conceptuality. West Lake images are not only representations of accumulated knowledge about the physical environment but also art that mediated the way people experienced nature. Due to the circulation of topographic knowledge and aesthetic sensitivities regarding sightseeing, Southern Song paintings of West Lake developed a unique artistic style and left a significant imprint—by defining pictorial style and subject matter—on the later appreciation and visual representations of West Lake.

LANDSCAPE PAINTING AND SIGHTSEEING

Its geographical setting and the development of leisure activities made West Lake a unique subject for landscape painting. Compared to other mountains and sightseeing destinations, its location allowed painters to observe it from close range. Depictions of West Lake were different from Northern Song monumental landscape paintings because artists were able to as well as motivated to incorporate their West Lake excursion experience into their art.

This intimate exposure of painters to the landscape and their depiction of real scenery could be both advantageous and disadvantageous. Ming scholar Tian Rucheng commented, "West Lake is rarely depicted well in writing or painting. If painters stick to the actual landscape, they are at risk of being rigid, but if they move too far away from the real scenery, the painting might lose its grounding."[9] So paintings of West Lake as a real site were required to be both realistic and artistic. Depictions of the landscape had to inspire the correct apprehension of the actual scenery in an artistic and even philosophical way.

The concepts of traveling through the scene and through romantic daydreaming had long been built into the visualizing tradition. Early in the fourth century, Zong Bing (375–443) in his "Introduction to Painting Landscape" (Hua shanshui xu) regarded the landscape as a site of human wandering by introducing the idea of "armchair traveling." This refers to the act of traveling or sightseeing in which observers did not (or could not) visit a site being described or painted. Instead, while reading a text or looking at a painting, they engaged in an imaginative journey to the site. Zong Bing also acknowledged that those who had experienced the landscape through actual travel were in a better position to capture its essence and represent it by brush.[10]

Song dynasty literature on reading about and viewing mountains and water also enhanced such associations between viewing and touring. Viewing and visiting the scene were interchangeable and mutually dependent in Song writings. Poems by Song literati described how seeing a landscape screen painting could be as engaging as the real landscape itself.[11] This viewing practice constituted congruent physical interactions with the landscape and thus profoundly shaped the definition and subject matter of landscape paintings.

Landscape paintings before the Northern Song were primarily depictions of imaginary landscapes conjured up by artists rather than representations of specific places. It was unlikely that the target audiences had ever visited the site ostensibly represented in a painting, and even the painter might never have visited it. For example, although Jing Hao (b. ca. 850) produced a famous painting of Mount Lu (Lushan), the historical records indicate that he never went there. His painting was based solely on impressions from literary descriptions of the mountain and possibly also observations of other mountains that he had visited. Other famous paintings from the Northern Song, such as *Early Spring* by Guo Xi (ca. 1023–1085) and *Traveling amid Mountains and Gorge* by Fan Kuan (ca. 950–1032), do not refer to specific mountains but merely depict general scenery that one might see in many mountains. These landscape paintings were abstract: general representations rather than ones based on actual experiences with real mountains, although the travelers and roads on which they traveled were carefully depicted to demonstrate the theme of movement.[12]

Paintings of West Lake, however, relied on painters' actual observations of and travel experience around the lake. Most of the artists who depicted West Lake were either natives of Hangzhou, such as Liu Songnian, or served in the Southern Song painting academy, which was situated near the River-Watching Gate (Wangjiangmen), on the lake's east bank.[13] Even after the Southern Song, when painters widely depicted other specific places, West Lake was still unique because of its accessibility. Unlike other places of interest, such as Mount Lu, Mount Fuchun (Fuchunshan), and Yellow Mountain (Huangshan), West Lake is situated right beside the center of an important regional city, and transportation around Hangzhou was convenient. It was a much more manageable destination for potential painters and mapmakers to visit.

The accessibility of West Lake contributed significantly to the development of visual representations of it, not only because the actual travel experiences encouraged artists to pick up their paintbrushes, but also because there were potential audiences who had seen the lake. The creation of Song dynasty imperial paintings included a process of interactive discussion. This involved other painters and feedback on draft sketches by imperial viewers, who might provide input multiple times and whose expectations were archived.[14] This communication shaped how painters and mapmakers wielded their brushes in depicting the lake. While it was mainly the imperial family and high-level literati who had access to most of the landscape paintings and gazetteer maps, documents also indicate that copies of imperial paintings and guide maps of Hangzhou were available for purchase in regular markets and street booths.[15] Though these images were not as commercialized as wood-block prints were in the Ming dynasty, the Southern Song audiences were not confined to a small group of officials.

TOPOGRAPHICAL RECORDS IN MAPS

Landscape images were not only, or even mainly, aesthetic. Instead, landscape served as a significant component of knowledge. This desire for landscape knowledge energized a realistic depiction of West Lake. The earliest extant map of West Lake is found in *The Gazetteer of Hangzhou during the Xianchun Reign* (edited ca. 1268–1273). At the beginning of the gazetteer, four maps were devoted to the prefecture, the capital, the imperial palace, and West Lake. The inclusion of these four maps demonstrated a layered spatial logic and the importance of documenting the natural landscape. The map of West Lake was the work of the engraver Wang Yao, who was highly esteemed in Southern Song Hangzhou.[16] This map labels 497 famous sites, including pavilions, wine houses, pleasure quarters, mountains, creeks, religious places, and official warehouses. The density of the place names on all four maps created challenges for the engraver. To fit all the characters within the landscape lines, Wang made words as small as six millimeters tall and sometimes even used simplified Chinese characters.[17]

The map's primary function was to preserve and spread geographic knowledge. Most of the 497 sites on the map also appeared in *Old Affairs of the Martial Grove,* showing that some knowledge was already circulating and being shared, at least among scholars. Such maps would have helped keep visitors from inadvertently missing a must-see scene. Among the site names on all four maps in *The Gazetteer of Hangzhou during the Xianchun Reign*, the map of West Lake included the most complete information,[18] indicating a demand for detailed geographical information about the lake and its surroundings, which arose from the nascent desire to explore West Lake. It also reveals how the map of a natural landscape functioned as a significant arena for the sorting of information on the natural environment.

The coding of places in maps followed encyclopedic and spatial logic. The map of West Lake in *The Gazetteer of Hangzhou during the Xianchun Reign* contained simple lines to indicate significant mountains and roads. Bridges were depicted in simplistic notations pinpointing the locations of causeways. This map also deployed the painting techniques of synecdoche, using a partial image to convey a more extensive structure.[19] The hint of distant peaks in the map might call to mind a series of hills, and the sketch of trees might signify a forest. The whole map was filled with place names. This concern with accuracy in spatial rendering and the linking of sites visually across Hangzhou's urban space reflects the logic of Song dynasty map-reading practices.

The differences between the map of the city and the map of the natural environment in the local gazetteer stem from the extent to which these maps were influenced by landscape painting. The city map is two dimensional, while the map of the lake attempts to present a three-dimensional space. Distant mountains are placed close to the upper frame of the map, indicating their height. Although the map is much shorter than a hand-scroll painting, it depicts a distance that ranged from the southernmost end of the mountains near West Lake to the north end.

The importance of maps depends on the degree to which they are accessible to their audiences. The earliest surviving maps of China date to the twelfth and thirteenth centuries; they appeared either on large stone steles or in printed books such as gazetteers. Both media facilitated the mass production of maps.[20] Beginning in the twelfth century, advances in print technology made geographic knowledge and the practice of map reading available to a larger audience. This map of West Lake and many other gazetteer maps emerged as instructional and reference tools for the government. The appearance of this map coincided with the compilation and printing of various kinds of instructional and reference works. The map and other documents such as the gazetteers and capital journal that included similar information for sites were both products of and instruments for the acquisition and circulation of geographic knowledge. Mapping and reading places that were recorded in a neat spatial structure required mapmakers to display a talent for abstraction and symbolization in coding nature; readers were expected to know how to decode the image by translating the lines and complex dots into the real geographical settings.[21] Maps became for the first time in Chinese history part of the repertoire of tools to convey and safeguard the collective memory.

The reorganization of knowledge in maps imbued those who used them with an imagined sense of order.[22] The extensive labeling of various places around West Lake on the one hand demonstrated the manifold construction and development in the new landscape, while on the other hand it also implied a new mastery of the surrounding environment. Meanwhile, the map also conveyed a power structure by the simultaneous use of different scales. The sites relevant to this power structure are labeled with larger characters, while the surrounding unrelated sites were indicated in smaller characters. This feature made them more direction indicators than actual locations. Examples of prominent places included the house of Prime Minister Jia Sidao, of whom the gazetteer compiler Qian Yueyou was a loyal follower (figure 4.1). In addition, the sites around West Lake and the ones that could be seen from the lake were much larger and more detailed than the ones hidden among the mountains.

Maps like this were used to guide visitors. It was recorded that during the Southern Song, travelers who visited Hangzhou always purchased a guide

FIGURE 4.1. Jia Sidao's residence, labeled "Mansion for the Manager of Affairs" (Pingzhang Fu) in large framed characters. Detail from map of West Lake by engraver Wang Yao in *The Gazetteer of Hangzhou during the Xianchun Reign*, compiled by Qian Yueyou, ca. 1268–75. From Jiang Qingqing, *"Xianchun Lin'an zhi" Songban "jingcheng situ" fuyuan yanjiu.*

map (*dijing*) of the city near the White Pagoda (Baita).[23] This structure is located on the south side of the lake, along the northern bank of the Zhe River, which during the Song was the main waterway used to access the city of Hangzhou. Purchasing this type of map was considered de rigueur for scholars. The maps available for public purchase were probably not the gazetteer map, but they were also printed and became so popular that a poem was written on the wall of the pagoda satirizing the buyers and sellers of the maps for caring more about touring Hangzhou than returning to the lost northern capital. These maps, which identified different types of lodgings as well as the distance between various sites and travel stations, not only constituted visual aids to help people imagine Hangzhou and what it could offer, but also included topographical information to facilitate their actual visits. The geographic information contained in these maps circulated among itinerant travelers, including officials, merchants, and scholars who traveled to and from the capital. Furthermore, the readers' appropriation of the information in guide maps for their use in urban journals and the vernacular literature served to circulate daily traveling experiences and also reminded people of the relations between the capital and other parts of the empire.[24] These maps conveyed both practical geographical knowledge and the geopolitical configuration of the state.

Maps met the demand for knowledge about the general outline of a place and functioned as encyclopedic sources for visitors. But maps were not enough for those who wanted to know what the scenery really looked like or for those who wanted to undertake armchair traveling. Their needs were met by landscape paintings.

PANORAMIC REPRESENTATION IN HAND-SCROLL PAINTINGS

Li Song's *Painting of West Lake* is possibly the most famous Southern Song depiction of the lake.[25] Taking a bird's-eye view, Li Song depicted a broad and realistic vista of the lake and surrounding mountains. At the center is the lake with several boats floating on its surface. Close inspection reveals that they contain tiny but carefully depicted figures, most likely fishermen. In the lower left corner is Phoenix Hill (Fenghuangshan), the site of the imperial palace.[26] The prominent structure nearby is Leifeng Pagoda, one of the geographical icons of West Lake. The distant mountains are rendered with faded ink wash. The long causeway, punctuated by six bridges, is the one built by Su Shi. Near the other end of the Su Causeway is Solitary Mountain. It is connected with another causeway built by Bai Juyi, in the middle of which is the famous Broken Bridge (Duanqiao). On the right-hand side of the painting is Precious Stone Hill (Baoshishan) topped by Protecting Chu Pagoda (Baochuta). Along the lower edge of the painting are roofs of buildings and gates, indicating that this is the side of the lake bordering the city of Hangzhou.

Although Li Song's painting and the gazetteer map of West Lake were both produced in the thirteenth century, they look different on first glance. While the primary concern of the mapmaker was to represent all the places around the lake in a standardized manner, Li Song concentrated on several iconic spots. The landscape was more flattened in the map, whereas Li Song was able to represent depth more skillfully. While the map functioned as a source of geographical information, the scroll led viewers into the landscape by emphasizing the landmarks.

However, the gazetteer map shared essential similarities with the Southern Song hand scroll. Both images represented the entire lake landscape from a high and distant viewpoint, which allowed the eyes of the artist, the mapmaker, and the viewers to move freely across this space. Hand-scroll paintings were artistic but also topographic; they were "planimetric" rather than "painterly," to use art historian Hui-shu Lee's words.[27] Just as copies of maps were available on the Southern Song market as guidance for visitors to the capital, copies of Li Song's painting probably also circulated on the market as more fleshed-out guidance. A fresh pictorial conception created by one of the major imperial painters would spread outward through copies and imitations in response to market demand.[28]

These topographic images shared an imperial view. The map was included in the gazetteer by the government to claim order for the natural landscape, and the painting by Li Song revealed the imperial court's desire to demonstrate the grandeur of the landscape it ruled. The mapmaker highlighted the imperial palace and essential government bureaus. Nature was shown within a hierarchical structure and in a controlled way, and the imperial palace was depicted with clouds to highlight the superiority and sacredness of the architecture. The imperial influence on the painting can also be inferred from the depiction of gardens owned by the imperial family or high officials around the lake. Comparing the painting with the map of West Lake, the large garden on the west side of the Su Causeway can be identified as the Qu Winery, the one controlled by the Hangzhou government. The private garden of Lu Yunsheng (ca. 1224–1264), an influential eunuch during the reign of the Emperor Lizong, is visible on the southwest corner of the lake.

Neither the painting nor the map uses the traditional approach of placing the north side of the landscape at the top of the image. Instead, both place the west side at the top. This perspective was the viewpoint from the imperial palace.[29] The desire to adopt the imperial viewpoint, however, may not be the only reason that depictions of West Lake placed it west side up. After the Southern Song, Hangzhou never again served as the capital, yet nearly all panoramic paintings adopted the same perspective. The geographical relationship between the city of Hangzhou and West Lake also informed later painters' and mapmakers' decisions to situate the lake west side up. The daily perspective of city dwellers may have been even more influential than considerations about the imperial view, especially as more city dwellers became potential painters and viewers of art during the Ming and Qing dynasties.

THE POST-SONG VIEWING AND PAINTING OF WEST LAKE SCROLLS

The hand-scroll model of topographic painting continued to appear after the Southern Song and exhibited further connections with mapping and emphasis on specific locations. This was due to an increase in visits to West Lake by painters and further accumulation of geographic knowledge about the lake. Most of those who viewed Li Song's painting would, consciously or not, try to identify each part of the painting with a physical location. For example, when Pang Yuanji (1864–1949) viewed Li Song's painting, he wrote, "Dimly discernible are the mountains; in the drizzling rain are the misty trees. The six bridges connect with each other, just like a belt; the Leifeng and Protecting Chu Pagodas face each other. Various Buddhist monasteries sit among the trees, while many boats go back and forth on the lake. The scenery of West Lake appears in front of my eyes."[30] Lu Shen (1477–1544) also noted in his inscription that the painting depicts the Su Causeway but not the Tomb of King Yue. These comments concentrated on iconic sites, implying that these viewers had visited West Lake and were familiar with the scenery. When they looked at the painting, they automatically called upon their own travels to confirm the construction of their experience. For instance, Lu said that viewing depictions of West Lake made him feel as if he had gone back to the lakeside.[31] Lu's experience enabled him to appreciate the scroll in ways that those without this personal observation could not.

The identifiability of the landscape depicted in West Lake paintings helped create and strengthen viewers' feelings of familiarity with the site, a key component that contributed to the affective bond a viewer could have with a physical environment. The growing feelings of familiarity tied viewers not only to the natural environment depicted but also to its artistic history and conventions. When Lu Shen and Pang Yuanji viewed the painting, their actual sightseeing experience and the depiction in the painting became interchangeable and cross-referenced. The Southern Song gaze remained solid and inspiring for the later personal gaze.

The Southern Song's convention of realistic depiction and the era's techniques for rendering depth set the standard for later panoramic representations of West Lake. Although later artists depicted small scenes expressively and emotionally, they appeared to be more objective and topographic in their panoramic paintings. Many later painters, including those from Japan, also adopted the composition seen in both Li Song's painting and the gazetteer map, placing special emphasis on Li Song's choice of pagodas as bookends for their depictions and including place names as the map did.[32] These later painters combined an artistic rendering of the natural landscape with the realistic style of the gazetteer map. *Painting of West Lake* by Xie Shichen (1487–ca. 1567) is an example of reading, identifying, and copying images with gazetteer-like techniques.[33] The artist was very likely copying the section depicting West Lake in *Painting of Places of Interest in Zhejiang* by Dai Jin (1368–1462).[34] Based on the arrangement and depiction of landscape in Dai's painting, Xie added light color and labeled essential locations. Dai Jin's extremely long hand scroll does not clearly depict the details of West Lake and in fact presents a puzzle when compared to other panoramic paintings such as Li Song's. Xie Shichen might have been confused when viewing Dai's painting while becoming especially interested in the section that includes West Lake. Xie therefore copied that section and labeled geographical signposts to make the painting easier to read. Xie's practice of copying only the West Lake portion from another long hand scroll and adding place names reveals the crucial function that signposts played as anchors for viewing and creating a painting.

THE *SCENIC ATTRACTIONS OF WEST LAKE* SCROLL

Historical records indicate that Li Song painted at least another three scrolls of West Lake.[35] As they all had the same title, it is difficult to determine whether or not any paintings by him other than the one we can see today in the Shanghai Museum circulated at the same time; nearly all the surviving descriptions of Li Song's *Painting of West Lake* closely resemble the extant work. The only exception is the description by Emperor Taizu of the Ming (Zhu Yuanzhang, 1328–1398, r. 1368–98): "One day, I looked through Li Song's paintings and discovered *Painting of West Lake.* In this painting, Li Song depicted the mountains and water with textured brushwork and drew the buildings in fine lines with the aid of a ruler. He painted human figures in the boats, raising the oar and lifting the paddle, hanging the sail and arranging the nets, throwing out the line and tossing the fishhook. Singers were singing, dancers were spinning, and musicians were playing flutes and pipes."[36] Hardly any of the singers, dancers, and musicians mentioned in the emperor's description are found in the extant painting. The figures in the boats in the extant painting are not clear enough for viewers to tell what they are doing, and strictly speaking, the buildings in the extant painting are not "painted with the aid of a ruler." The painting Zhu Yuanzhang described more closely resembles another work formerly attributed to Li Song titled *Scenic Attractions of West Lake* in the Freer Gallery of Art (see fig. 1.1). It depicts the scenery around West Lake in clockwise order.

Art historians believe that this scroll was painted after the fall of the Southern Song and before the mid-fifteenth century. "The pure delight of West Lake" is written in four large characters at the beginning, contributed by Cheng Nanyun (d. 1458). Hui-shu Lee dates this hand scroll to the early Yuan, because the "use of the misty ink-wash technique for the distant mountain, minute description of figures, architecture, and other motifs" is similar to the style of the Yuan dynasty painter Qian Xuan (1239–1299). Lee also argues that despite the fact that it was most likely painted at a later time, the scroll reflected Southern Song scenery around the lake.[37] Historian Chen Hui, after a detailed study of this scroll, focusing on cross-referencing the content of the painting and historical documents, concludes that it was painted in the spring of 1267 based on the construction dates of the structures it depicts.[38] Either way, the painting could not have been painted by Li Song, but was likely to have been inspired by him or a copy of a painting similar to his.

This painting offers a different type of realistic representation; it is less topographic but more photographic. The inscription by Qing scholar Li E at the end of the scroll also illustrates the tendency to decipher paintings using knowledge of real place names. Li E compared this painting with the records in *Old Affairs of the Martial Grove* to explain different sites in his lengthy colophon. Li E's inscription again demonstrates that the painting and viewing of real scenery mainly focused on signposts. It also notes the important cross-references between images and textual records of geographical knowledge. The information about the Southern Song sites remained popular in later times.

As a eulogy to a harmonious political time, this painting attempts to showcase the prosperity of the lake, along with urban citizens' proclivity for excursions. In *Scenic Attractions of West Lake*, the painter meticulously depicted the details of wine houses, temples, bridges, causeways, city walls, water locks, and ponds along the city wall. The artist even included the advertisement banner of a wine house and the instrument players on small boats. The realistic touch is no longer limited to the natural landscape and physical locations, but now extends to people within the landscape, especially to depictions of the locations where they liked to gather and the food and drink they were fond of consuming. This painting is more detailed and informative than any other painting or map; it offered the most straightforward depiction of the physical appearance of the lake at the time, although it might well be romanticized.

In both Southern Song and later paintings, one outstanding feature was the interconnectedness between paintings and maps. The practice of reading paintings interwoven with geographical knowledge influenced the experience of traveling, viewing, and depicting. Viewers of these paintings were always fond of decoding these visualizations. In the process of encoding, painters incorporated the natural landscape into their cultural framework by reconciling artistic rendition with the realistic tradition of mapmaking. Their own sightseeing experiences and awareness of the expected audiences for their paintings motivated them to paint the landscape truthfully. In the process of decoding, the viewers tested their knowledge of the physical landscape, cross-checking the image with their own experience. Their readings of paintings and their traveling within the landscape were interdependent. In both cases, the visualization of landscape was influenced by the gazetteer maps of the lake, a tradition first established during the Southern Song.

The topographic tradition, on the one hand, reinforced the lake as a real place, a place that inspired and called for an actual visit and real personal experience. On the other hand, West Lake also became a topographic model that imbued the natural landscape with a state of order and a sense of mastery. The lake needed to be real, but images also needed to be artistic—both painterly and planimetric. Viewers and painters applied their knowledge of the visual culture when they interacted with the real landscape. Their experience was shaped by the visual models that they had already seen.

THE DEPICTION OF SIGHTSEEING EXPERIENCE AND EMOTION IN ALBUM PAINTINGS

While hand-scroll paintings were used to capture panoramic views of the lake's scenery, fan paintings depicted specific scenic sites. An account of a Jin embassy to Hangzhou records that "Suddenly, they [the Jin emissaries] turned their heads and looked back at the city's hilly slopes, where houses were stacked layer upon layer. Temples, towers, and terraces of varying heights looked like immortal palaces amidst falling flowers. [The Jin emissaries] got off the carriage and walked along, all enthusiastically praising the vista by saying that inside the city and along the lake were the scenes of a thousand fan paintings."[39] Album leaf painting became an established and well-represented artistic format during the Song dynasty, especially after the twelfth century. Unlike the long-established hand scroll or hanging scroll, which customarily covered a distance beyond what the human eye is capable of absorbing in a single glance, an album leaf painting is a more faithful representation of scenes that are visible within the field of a single observer's vision at a single moment. Moreover, albums and fan paintings were suitable for the imperial family to present to officials as awards.

In these paintings, the excursion itself rather than the landscape was the real theme.[40] The figures depicted are different from the tiny ones in Li Song's hand scroll, and they also contrast with the numberless crowds in the *Scenic Attractions of West Lake* scroll, who enjoy the material aspects of their visits to the lake. In album paintings, a few sightseers were portrayed gazing at the landscape. With no intention of depicting the entire landscape, these paintings usually crop one corner of the lake. The relationship between figures and landscape is characterized by an affective attachment.

SIGHTSEERS AMONG LANDSCAPE

The diagonal composition was useful in representing a corner of scenery and its interaction with sightseers. The anonymous fan painting *Spring Dawn at West Lake* (ca. thirteenth century, figure 4.2) focuses on the corner

FIGURE 4.2. *Spring Dawn at West Lake*, ca. thirteenth century. Anonymous. Ink on silk, 23.6 × 25.8 cm. Image of fan painting provided by the Palace Museum, Beijing.

of Solitary Mountain on the north bank of the lake, judging from the distant vista of the Protecting Chu Pagoda on a hill. On Solitary Mountain, several simply depicted buildings are hidden among the trees. The focus of the painting, however, is not these trees and buildings, but the small boat on the lake surface. In Southern Song paintings, a boat was usually interpreted as "the connection of the owners with the outside world" because it recalled the reality of traveling via waterways.[41] In the boat are two people, one holding an oar, the other sitting in the front with a zither-like object on his knees. The latter figure is gazing toward the left and thus leads the viewers to imagine the beautiful scenery on the other side of the lake. The painter applied light ink and green color to suggest a misty spring morning.

Spring dawns were popular subjects for artists in the Southern Song. Another extant example is *Painting of Spring Dawn at the Lake and Mountains* by Chen Qingbo (ca. mid-thirteenth century, figure 4.3). Chen was a court painter well known for his depictions of West Lake scenery; it is,

FIGURE 4.3. *Painting of Spring Dawn at the Lake and Mountains.* ca. mid-thirteenth century. Chen Qingbo. Ink and color on silk, 25 × 26.7 cm. Image provided by the Palace Museum, Beijing.

therefore, reasonable to assume that this fan painting was intended to represent West Lake as well.[42] This painting's composition is similar to that of *Spring Dawn at West Lake.* A causeway, on which a group of buildings hides among the trees, extends from the middle right to the upper left to connect with the distant mountains. On the lower left, a figure dressed like a scholar is riding a horse, followed by two servants, one carrying an umbrella and the other transporting luggage. They are heading to the left, but the scholar is looking back at the buildings on the causeway. This detail connects the two parts of the painting with a diagonal line. In both fan paintings, most of the paper is left blank, implying a lake surface and a misty environment, which again was a main feature of Southern Song art. The most famous artists who painted only a small portion of the paper were Ma Yuan (ca. 1190–1225) and Xia Gui (ca. 1190–1230), who were also known as "One Corner Ma" and "Half Side Xia," respectively.[43]

The emphasis in both paintings is on people wandering among scenery: in Chen's painting, it is the scholar riding on the horse, and in the other one, it is the scholar sitting in the boat. Both painters used the direction of a figure's gaze to lead viewers to notice the depiction of the natural scenery or to imagine the larger environment beyond the paintings' frames. Both paintings create a distance between the prominent scenery and the figures. The natural landscape is within reach but still untouchable. The light rendering of distant mountains (and the pagoda) further enhances the desire for quiet and pure nature. People who view these two paintings would naturally adopt the viewing angle of the figures in the paintings, extending their gaze and imagination from the lower left corner to the vast natural landscape. The depiction of the travelers invites the viewers to step into the painting to experience natural beauty at close hand and more personally.

Travelers in Southern Song paintings were handled differently from those in Northern Song landscape paintings. Under the brush of Northern Song painters, such as Fan Kuan, travelers were tiny and hardly noticeable. Fan wanted to depict a monumental mountain in order to inspire viewers' respect for nature. Another Northern Song painting, *Along the River during the Qingming Festival* by Zhang Zeduan (1085–1145), depicted figures traveling through a suburb to visit a graveyard. These figures, however, are not appreciating the aesthetics of the natural environment. In Southern Song paintings, the travelers are engaging with the landscape while simultaneously gazing at it. The size of the figure was also enlarged compared to the surroundings. They are enjoying the surrounding beautiful scenery with pleasure and ease. The relationship between people and the natural landscape is one of equality and thus is interactive.

The difference in the depiction of landscape conveyed the change in the perception of nature that occurred during the Southern Song. These Southern Song paintings include causeway paths leading into the distance, hermits and mountain dwellers, and small structures for enjoying the scenery at ease. These additions conveyed the idea that the landscape was not only a product of artistic representation but also a space for human habitation. These paintings made West Lake suitable for sightseeing and residence, an idealized place, as Guo Xi described in *The Lofty Message of Forest and Streams* (Linquan gaozhi):

> It is an accepted opinion that in landscapes there are those through which you may travel, those in which you may sightsee, those through which you may wander and those in which you may live. Any paintings attaining these effects is to be considered excellent, but those suitable for traveling and sightseeing are not as [great an] achievement as those ideal for wandering

> through and living in. Why is this? If you survey present-day scenery, in a hundred miles of land to be settled, only about one out of three places will be suitable for wandering and living, yet they will undoubtedly be selected as such.[44]

Guo's artistic theory, though formulated during the Northern Song, was not implemented until the Southern Song. What he articulated in this essay paved the way for a more affective rendering of the landscape. And the practical application of this artistic theory in real paintings was inseparable from the growth of sightseeing activities in real life. The emperor and the imperial family patronized the court painters and their art, and urban residents enjoyed similar or copied art. All of them wanted either a more humanized nature for leisure life or an escape from the hustle and bustle of the city. As art historian James Cahill argues, it was the noise of the city that drove the Southern Song painters to value quiet and straightforward scenery.[45] These paintings were motivated by the desire to escape from both physical and psychological pressures in the city.[46] In addition, painters' daily observations of sightseers around the lake and their constant gazing at the scenery allowed them to better follow Guo Xi's concept of depicting landscape as a livable space.

Painting informed by both the real scenery and the idealized living space connected with the philosophy of nature during the Song. Song dynasty thinkers believed that emotions could not only represent an individual's feeling but also give access to the reality of the world.[47] While painters demonstrated their attention to topography, they also wielded their brushes in the service of the emotions. Art historians have long noticed the phenomenon of depicting landscape by channeling emotion into the act of creation, otherwise known as the emotional brush. Art historian Wen Fong reads Song landscapes as "landscapes of emotion."[48] In Southern Song Hangzhou, sightseeing fostered the acquisition and recognition of inner coherence, which structured the capacity to guide the brush through emotional reflection.

POST-SONG PAINTINGS

After the Song, literati painters further developed the practice of depicting sightseers and the livable landscape. During the Ming dynasty, the practice of taking excursions to famous sites developed rapidly among the literati. Most of these excursions concentrated on suburban sites; they generated a number of album paintings by both literati and professional painters.[49] "Spring dawn at West Lake" continued to be a favorite post-Song painting theme, even when format and content changed along with broader artistic styles. For example, Xie Shichen's *Painting of Spring Dawn at West Lake* adopted a very different hanging scroll format, with lake water separating the foreground and distant mountains.[50] Despite the post-Song changes in format, composition, and brushwork reflected in this painting, Xie copied Chen Qingbo's depiction of travelers: once again, a scholar is riding on a donkey, followed by two servants, one carrying an umbrella, the other carrying the luggage.

After the Southern Song, painting West Lake was usually seen as an outlet for literati painters. Although literati began to connect the physical beauty of West Lake with visual representations during the Southern Song, they did not draw the scenery themselves. Court painters or professional painters created most paintings in the Southern Song. It was not until the Yuan dynasty that literati began to engage in painting and to contribute to the visual representation of West Lake. At that point, painting started to become a liberal art. Literati, with a certain amount of art training, began to acquire the ability to portray the beauty of West Lake through brushwork. Although they acknowledged that it was difficult to fully capture the essential beauty of the lake, they still painted it to record their trips and express their taste and emotions.

During the Yuan dynasty, many literati lamented the fall of the Song and refused to serve in the Mongol regime. Their lack of access to the government allowed and encouraged them to use their brushes to express dissent. Some of them, such as Qian Xuan, turned to painting for self-expression and as a way to pass the time. Qian's hand-scroll *Painting of Solitary Mountain* places Lin Bu on the left in a pavilion surrounded by plum blossoms and cranes.[51] In depicting Lin, Qian Xuan expressed his personal desire to live in reclusion. The use of green and blue, the flatness of the mountain rocks, and the lack of depth create a tranquil and unreal environment. There is almost no hint of the flow of time, which makes this hand scroll entirely different from Southern Song paintings. It is possible that Qian Xuan blamed the Southern Song government for losing China to the Mongols and therefore did not want to copy the Southern Song artistic tradition, but instead looked further back for aesthetic inspiration to the Tang, when China was more aggressive on the issue of northern and western nomads. The political instability of the Southern Song discouraged Yuan painters from following the artistic traditions of the previous dynasty in depicting West Lake, but after the establishment of the Ming, painters turned again to Southern Song art for inspiration in depicting the lake.

Ming literati painters especially emphasized the lake as a livable space. The Ming scholar and painter Li Liufang (1575–1629) once commented on the natural scenery of West Lake in an inscription on a painting: "Hangzhou is surrounded by [Zhe] River and [West] Lake. The mountains and water add radiance and beauty to each other, so the scenery is ever changing throughout the day and night. Stepping outside the city wall, your ears and eyes will be magnified. In small boats and straw sandals, you can find magnificent scenery everywhere. No other place under heaven surpasses West Lake: it is suitable for both living and wandering. Even if you eat, drink, and sleep here all day and night, you will never tire of it."[52] In this discussion of the lake's suitability for both wandering and living, Li emphasized its ever-changing scenery and how it fed the senses. These comments reflect his rich experience lingering at the lake, and they convey the advantages to painters who could observe the scenery closely while living nearby. He explained that time and light so greatly influenced the natural landscape that one painting could convey neither the actual beauty nor the artist's experience with nature.[53] He said, "You cannot paint the entire landscape, but still you should paint to record an impression."[54] Li, therefore, used his emotion-charged brush to depict mist and thus to convey his feelings about nature.[55] His depictions of West Lake are grounded more in the imagination than in a realistic view, even though he had sufficient personal exposure to the real landscape to paint it with geographic accuracy. Li's contemporary Song Maojin (ca. 1585–1620) also painted West Lake in a similar style, depicting a dreamlike landscape with very few brushstrokes.[56] Many of his album paintings of the lake emphasized the figures sitting and talking in small buildings within the landscape. The architecture and human life were highlighted rather than the mountains and waters. The attention to specific human constructions furthered the concept of a livable landscape.

At the same time, Ming literati also emphasized the feeling of nostalgia inherent in the lake's long cultural tradition. Dong Qichang's (1555–1636) hanging scroll *Painting of the Poetic Meaning of Lin Hejing* is an homage to two elements of tradition.[57] One is the Song dynasty scholar Lin Bu (also known as Lin Hejing), who is remembered for his enjoyment of nature and his avoidance of "vulgar" things. The other is the painting style of Ni Zan (1301–1374), one of the four famous literati painters of the Yuan dynasty. Dong's painting replicated Ni Zan's signature composition: the use of water to separate the foreground and distant mountains.[58] This painting resonates much more with artistic conventions than with the actual scenery. It was more a means to pay tribute to the cultural tradition and to emphasize the painter's cultural identity. Without the hint from the title, it would be hard to confirm that the painting depicted Solitary Mountain. The cultural memory embodied in the landscape outweighed the physical reality emphasized in the Southern Song paintings. The emphasis on the rich cultural past idealized the natural environment. The affective bond with West Lake was tightly woven together with and enhanced by awareness of the past.[59]

While it was not unusual for literati to imbue their landscape paintings with emotion during the late imperial periods, the Southern Song tradition of depicting West Lake lyrically established the theme of the lake as an embodiment of real experiences and a carrier for travelers' feelings. The misty brushwork favored in the Southern Song was especially suitable for adding sentiment to the natural landscape. From the earliest depictions of West Lake—which coincided with increased excursions to the lake—this particular landscape was closely associated with the mobility and mentality of sightseers.

CONCLUSION: THE PARADOX OF PHYSICAL REALITY AND VISUAL REPRESENTATION

Southern Song paintings of West Lake both depicted topography and conveyed sightseers' experiences and emotions. They were not only representations of excursions but also elegant artistic creations. The realistic and emotional visualization of West Lake attempted to record newly acquired knowledge about the natural landscape. Maps with place names embodied the emergence of new knowledge; topographic paintings represented the attempt to faithfully record nature; emotion-charged painting encompassed the desire to communicate with nature. Visual images functioned as a channel through which artists and viewers could make sense of the natural environment.

The fondness for depicting real places and the circulation of place names canonized the Song dynasty records. Famous sites in historical documents profoundly shaped the later choices of painters and mapmakers. After the Southern Song, West Lake changed physically as a result of war and later construction. Depictions of this landscape in paintings and prints, however, did not change along with these physical alterations. Instead, they adhered to quite persistent styles and conventions in capturing the lake. Some of the later paintings that topographically represented the lake even included particular Song sites regardless of the fact that they had by that time disappeared. The Leifeng Pagoda was badly damaged during the war at the end of the Southern Song, but later paintings still depicted it in its prime.[60] Also, as seen in the colophon of *Scenic Attractions of West Lake*, comparing paintings to the actual sites recorded in Song documents became an enjoyable game for literati like Li E. The Song dynasty left behind traditions of not only how to depict the lake but also how to train one's focus and how to visualize.

The convention of highlighting an idealized interaction between people and nature also prevented many painters from depicting the busy commercial activities that animated this landscape. A majority of paintings discussed in this chapter depict tranquil and misty scenery, emphasizing harmony between people and nature. Neither the excessive human-made floating paddies nor the flurry of commerce providing sensual enjoyment appeared in these paintings. The lake remained accessible yet untouchable, livable but not vulgar. Instead, these paintings paid more attention to artistic conventions, historical memories, and important sites. The focus on these sites made the lake immune to temporal changes in its physical shape.[61] To attract visitors and purchasers, later images also romanticized the experience of people in the natural landscape. They seemed to be based on an idealized version of Southern Song nature, making it hard to determine whether it was Southern Song West Lake or Southern Song visual depictions of West Lake that were memorized.

Therefore, visual images of West Lake gave rise to a discrepancy between the constantly changing appearance of nature and the persistent cultural memory of the lake. Nature as a physical entity and the aesthetic conventions were interdependent and mutually deconstructive. Each of the two fueled and promoted the other. While the persistent aesthetic rendering of the lake attracted so many visitors that their sheer numbers threatened to destroy the very beauty of the natural environment, the lake still depended on the continuation of these romanticized depictions to sustain its fame. In the service of aesthetic pursuits, people never stopped shaping the physical terrain, yet at the same time also praised it as a paradigm of idealized nature. The continuing changes in the physical landscape also created a simultaneous desire among artists and art patrons for paintings with certain aesthetic conventions and traditional motifs, as a way to preserve nostalgic memories of West Lake.

This paradox has become more evident since the introduction of modern technology. In today's China, the heavy daily traffic around the lake and the noisy crowds during holiday seasons create a jarring contrast with the purity and tranquility seen in so many photographs and videos of the lake.

The popular image of West Lake is still dominated by purity and tranquility. Famous sites of the Song dynasty still play an important role in painting, photography, and mapmaking, even though many of them no longer exist or have changed dramatically through the centuries. The contrasts remind us that the mutual dependence and tension between the landscape images and the reality of the physical environment have persisted over time, as has the idealized landscape rendered by the Southern Song brushes.

Cultural tropes established at West Lake during the Song dynasty not only have continued into later periods but also are being replicated in other parts of China. Part 3 (chapters 5 and 6) explores two of these tropes: the "middle landscape" model between pilgrimage and sightseeing, and the naming convention of "ten views." These tropes defined nature from a religious and an aesthetic perspective, respectively. Both contributed to the uniqueness of West Lake as a place and, at the same time, transformed this place into an appropriable cultural model that has played a unifying role in the formation of China's cultural geography.

PART III

The Cultural Trope of Nature

CHAPTER FIVE

PRAY AND PLAY

Pilgrimage and Sightseeing

WEST LAKE AND THE SURROUNDING MOUNTAINS WERE DOTTED with numerous religious sites. The Northern Song literatus Wang Sui (975–1033) noted in his description of the lake that "More than a hundred monasteries are scattered around the lake, echoing each other . . . this is indeed the finest scenery of the Zhe area, the place most worth visiting."[1] As this comment illustrates, the monasteries were regarded as the most notable feature of the lake and one factor that made it an outstanding regional destination. A large proportion of the sites labeled on the gazetteer map of West Lake were related to religion, including seventy Buddhist monasteries, twenty Daoist temples, fourteen shrines, eleven pagodas, and other places whose names suggest connections with religion (figure 5.1).

Noted along with other scenic spots and famous places, these temples were no longer treated merely as places of worship, but as sites of secular interest, worth visiting in their own right. Similarly, Zhou Mi also listed these religious sites together with other natural sites and cultural spots in a chapter in *Old Affairs of the Martial Grove* titled "Spectacular Scenery of the Lake and Its Mountains." This emerging phenomenon of incorporating religious sites into sightseeing images and discourses complicated both the nature of sightseeing activities themselves and the functions these sacred sites served.

Pilgrimage expeditions and sightseeing excursions to West Lake were interdependent, so that today it sometimes is difficult to distinguish between the two. Most of the accounts of trips to West Lake recorded during or soon after the event had elements of both. Pilgrims wanted others to know about their sightseeing expeditions; sightseers could rarely resist the temptation of going into a temple to offer incense and pray for good fortune.

FIGURE 5.1. Identification of religious sites around West Lake: rectangles = Buddhist monasteries, trapezoids = Daoist temples, triangles = shrines, ovals = pagodas and other sites linked to religion. Figure by the author, based on map of West Lake by engraver Wang Yao in *The Gazetteer of Hangzhou during the Xianchun Reign*, compiled by Qian Yueyou, ca. 1268–75. From Jiang Qingqing, *"Xianchun Lin'an zhi" Songban "jingcheng situ" fuyuan yanjiu*.

Although scholars have long discussed the development of religion during the Song, that development's relationship with leisure activities has received less attention. A fuller picture of West Lake as a cultural center for Hangzhou emerges along with investigation of how the natural landscape was experienced and conceptualized through the religious lens. This topic also offers insight into the discussion about the popularization of religion in the context of the expansion of urban lives and the reconceptualization of nature.

The blurred boundary between sacred and leisure travel was by no means unique to West Lake during the Southern Song. A similar phenomenon occurred in other places at other times and has attracted attention from both historians and religious-studies scholars. In China, pervasive confusion between pilgrims and sightseers occurred during the late Ming, as has been documented regarding pilgrimages to Mount Tai,[2] and the terms "pilgrim" and "tourist" are difficult to define in any mutually exclusive sense.[3] In medieval Japan, pilgrimages to sacred places such as the Kumano Shrine were valued; later, participation of ordinary people during the sixteenth century redefined the content and destinations of these pilgrimages,[4] affecting the intrinsic connection between play (*asobi*) and prayer, both conceptually and spatially.[5] The Middle Ages in Europe were marked by journeys and pilgrimages to holy places, and Geoffrey Chaucer's *Canterbury Tales* demonstrates that people began to take advantage of pilgrimages to explore the scenic beauty of the world along the way.[6]

While West Lake shared specific features with these cultural sites in other parts of the world, it is also unique in its proximity to both a city and a range of gentle surrounding mountains. These geographical conditions demanded less energy, time, and money from sightseers and pilgrims. While a pilgrimage usually meant long-distance travel, the religious sites around West Lake required only a day trip from the city. Furthermore, West Lake as a sightseeing destination and a public space for Hangzhou also hosted many religious festivals throughout the year, which further diversified the format of these short-distance temple visits. This context makes the English term "pilgrimage" less accurate. Two different terms in German distinguish between long-distance and short-distance pilgrimages: *Wallfahrt* refers to more frequent pilgrimages involving short distances, while *Pilgerfahrt* refers to less-frequent longer ones. In the Chinese context, *chaoshan jinxiang* (paying one's respect to mountains and offering incense) is a more accurate term for a short-distance pilgrimage.[7] Either *Wallfahrt* or *chaoshan jinxiang* would describe the religious activities discussed at West Lake in the Southern Song period.

The interdependence between pilgrimage and sightseeing redefined sightseers' appreciation of nature and provided temples with new strategies to attract visitors. During this process, religion and nature were interpreted paradoxically, and the complicated interaction between religious atmosphere and urban desire allowed West Lake to function as a "middle landscape" in which religious and urban space mingled.[8] The concept, which encompasses the popularization of religion through the less-noticed means of sightseeing, could prove useful in understanding the expansion of urban space.

THE POPULARIZATION OF RELIGION AROUND WEST LAKE

The Song dynasty witnessed the proliferation and popularization of different schools of religion, mainly through mingling of and exchanges between religious teachings.[9] The growing number of educated people and the increasing role of women expanded the body of lay believers, who absorbed diverse practices from different institutionalized religions without clearly differentiating among religious schools. Although many lay believers might profess to have a Confucian, Buddhist, or Daoist identity, they also participated in community rituals and subscribed to a broad range of socially prevalent values that blurred the divisions between different religions.

Scholars generally acknowledge the emergence of "popular religion" during Middle Period China, referring to the intense interaction among and blurred boundaries between religious teachings. Chinese popular religion derived from the ideal religious identity of "three religions being one" and should be understood as those religious practices of everyday life shared by all members of society.[10] Patricia Ebrey and Peter Gregory note the difficulty in contextualizing the concept of popular religion and use Eric Zurcher's model of "pyramid-shaped peaks" to explain the relations between popular religion and the three institutionalized religions: "As the peaks arise out of the same mass of undifferentiated 'popular' practice and belief, they begin to take form as discernible traditions."[11]

West Lake functioned as a stage for a variety of religions; while each type of religious site was staffed with its own clergy, its worshipers and donors might worship at and donate to sites connected to other religions as well. The state welcomed community-based religious ritual, as it constructed a sense of belonging to the newly established capital. Besides, the participation of a growing number of ordinary people expanded the income sources for the religious sites, so these temples were also willing to popularize their teachings in order to cater to lay believers.

The development of diverse religions benefited from state patronage. Although the Song state claimed Confucianism as its ruling ideology, it concurrently patronized Buddhism, Daoism, and local deities. By granting titles to local deities and patronizing religious ceremonies, the state and local governments played a vital role in constructing and promoting various temples.[12] State patronage was based on both the efficaciousness of temples and state inspection, so the wishes of the state played a significant role in whether or not a temple received official recognition. After the Jurchen invasion, the imperial court found religious support to be an effective force in its quest to claim and reinforce its political legitimacy.

Buddhism was the most prominent religion around West Lake, which served as a Buddhist pilgrimage center for China and even for East Asia. As early as the Southern Dynasties (420–589), the Jiangnan region was famous for its large number of Buddhist monasteries. More than three hundred monasteries were located in and around Hangzhou during the Tang dynasty. During the Five Dynasties, the local ruler Qian Liu, a devout Buddhist, built and refurbished many monasteries, some of which continued to be influential during the Song dynasty. Hangzhou was one of the few places during the Song where various Buddhist schools other than Chan were represented.[13] Moreover, many of these Hangzhou monasteries shouldered growing social responsibilities during the fall of the Northern Song by accepting refugees from the north and contributing extra economic income from their lands to the Song government.[14]

Daoism too enjoyed a prosperous history in the Song; a number of Northern Song emperors were well known for their faith in and patronage of Daoism.[15] Imperial support continued into the Southern Song, with the emergence of worship of the Daoist guardians dreamed of by the emperor or the empress dowager during their flight from the north to Hangzhou. Therefore, Hangzhou during the Southern Song acquired status as the site where imperial revival was evidenced through hosting the worship of these imperial guardians.

Later in the Southern Song, Hangzhou developed into an unparalleled location for the development of Buddhism and Daoism.[16] A total of 971 Buddhist monasteries were situated in Southern Song Hangzhou, centering on West Lake.[17] Although there were fewer Daoist temples, most of them enjoyed state patronage, and they occupied the best locations on the lake.[18] The diversity of other religions in Hangzhou was equally impressive, the result of the coexistence of deities transferred from Kaifeng, such as the god Pichang, with local deities such as Wutong. The warfare during the transition between the Northern and Southern Song resulted in an increase in the number of shrines to military patriots and newly acknowledged deities around the lake.

Visiting temples was built into the annual calendars of local residents. The primary reason for visiting a temple was to pray to the deities and to seek blessings such as favorable weather and cure of illness.[19] In the Southern Song, the uncertainty over the results of the civil service examinations and the unpredictability of business ventures also encouraged scholars and merchants to worship at local temples.[20] The need for donations and new believers encouraged temples to spread the word of their sacred powers. For example, the Upper Tianzhu Monastery (Shang Tianzhu) circulated quite a few miracle stories to prove that the Jurchen did not take away the monastery's authentic Guanyin statue.[21]

This religious flourishing profoundly influenced the geographical importance of West Lake. This area functioned mainly as a religious destination in the city life of Hangzhou.[22] It also helped to extend Hangzhou's outreach to the surrounding counties. While this might not have been as evident during the Song, the pilgrimages made by late Ming peasants helped enhance the center-periphery relationship between Hangzhou and the surrounding areas.[23]

APPRECIATION OF RELIGIOUS SITES AS PLACES OF INTEREST

Outings to temples were frequently mentioned in poems and described and shared orally. More than one-fifth of the poems in Dong Sigao's *One Hundred Poems of West Lake* are about visiting or staying in temples.[24] Local gazetteers and miscellaneous notes usually documented temples as points of local pride. The apparent efficaciousness of local temples could confirm in the popular imagination that deities had blessed a given spot. This might explain why the Tianzhu Monasteries and the Cold Spring Pavilion outside of the Soul's Retreat Monastery were included in the itinerary of the foreign emissaries from the Jin court when he visited the capital.[25] As the fame of these temples spread, it is not hard to imagine that local people would frequently be asked for directions to them, and these religious sites were thus noted on maps.

The religious sites were incorporated into the sightseeing routes. Nearly all the sites labeled on the map of West Lake were recorded in Zhou Mi's notes on various sightseeing routes. As table 5.1 shows, religious sites constituted a large percentage of the sites.

TABLE 5.1. Religious sites recorded in Zhou Mi's *Old Affairs of the Martial Grove*

Sightseeing route	Total sightseeing spots	Sites related to religion	Religious sites as percentage of sightseeing spots (%)
Fang Family Valley Route	50	38	76
Southern Mountain Route	67	47	70
Three Tianzhu Route	17	10	59
Northern Mountain Route	111	64	58
Big Wheat Hill (Damailing) Route	14	8	57
Ge Hill Route	122	52	43
Three Causeways Route	26	9	35
Small Wheat Hill (Xiaomailing) Route	38	13	34
Solitary Mountain Route	9	2	22

Among these sightseeing routes, two were especially popular: the Southern Mountain Route to the south end of the lake and the Three Tianzhu Route that offered a pilgrimage to the western mountain area. Most Hangzhou residents lived on the east side of the lake, and the main temples they visited were located on the west and south sides. The main destinations on the Southern Mountain Route, the Leifeng (lit., Thunder Peak) Pagoda and the Purity and Compassion Monastery (Jingcisi), were situated adjacent to one another on the south lakeshore and took about half an hour to reach from the city, an easy day trip. The Three Tianzhu Monasteries and the Soul's Retreat Monastery were farther away from the city but were more important religious sites. The Tianzhu Monasteries were already a pilgrimage destination for Guanyin worship before the emergence of Mount Putuo (Putuoshan), and the Soul's Retreat Monastery was known among literati from Su Shi's essay on the Cold Spring Pavilion and among commoners for a story of the famous eccentric monk Jidian (1148–1209).[26] Visitors had their choice of two approaches. One went past the Nanping (lit., Southern Screen) Hill and then headed into a hilly area. Lower Tianzhu Monastery (Xia Tianzhu) was about a two-hour walk from the city gate; both Middle Tianzhu Monastery (Zhong Tianzhu) and then Upper Tianzhu Monastery were reachable half an hour beyond that. The other approach involved a boat ride to Su Causeway, then passage through Small New Causeway to the mountain area. Either approach enabled city dwellers to complete the temple visit in one day. It is not hard to imagine that these city dwellers would take the opportunity to enjoy the lake scenery en route to the temples they set out to visit.

Moreover, nature and remoteness from earthly desire were much valued by religions, including Buddhism and Daoism, so a majority of temples were initially built in places with spectacular scenery. As Zhao Bian (1008–1084) noted in his couplet, "Lovely the lake and mountain scenery, which is the best under heaven. But all the scenery is concentrated where the Buddhist monasteries are."[27] Historical records often emphasized the natural beauty of religious sites as a principal reason they were considered as places of interest. For example, one local gazetteer glowingly describes the Three Worthies Hall: "Sitting in the middle of the Su Causeway, bowing toward the lake and mountains, the scenery is bright and vast. It is backed by continuing hills, with a thick and lush forest. Northern and Southern Hills, embracing misty green, all these are connected with the Su Causeway. Palace halls are unevenly laid out, pavilions sitting beside the dike, surrounded by flowers and bamboos."[28] This description emphasized two aspects of the scenic beauty: the surroundings or location of the shrine, and the vista from the shrine. While the first aspect has a panoramic-based perspective, focusing on how the site fits into the scenic context, the second has a narrower, site-centered perspective. The two aspects resemble the panoramic hand-scroll painting and the album leaf that captures a single view, respectively. These two perspectives were combined through the movement of sightseers. The sightseers' mobile perspective and emotional response were essential to the appreciation of the natural landscape-surrounded religious sites.

The interdependence of religious sites and scenic appreciation can be best illustrated with two examples. One is the Purity and Compassion Monastery, known for its evening bell that reminded sightseers of spatial and temporal change. The other is the Tianzhu Monasteries, which were colored by the desire for a tranquil and reclusive escape from the city. Located on the lake bank, the Purity and Compassion Monastery was backed by Nanping Hill, which was regarded as the most beautiful hill bordering the lake.[29] The top of the hill offered a view of the city and of the many boats that wove in and out of sight on the lake.[30] The temple itself was also famous for its extensive gardens where countless lotus flowers surrounded the splendid architecture and filled the beautiful ponds.[31] Moreover, this temple included the "Evening Bell from Nanping Hill," one of the iconic Ten Views of West Lake. The temple bell was known for two reasons. One was that the many hollows of Nanping Hill would echo the sound of the bell; the other was related to the location of the monastery and the timing of the Buddhist bell. The ringing of the bell announced the arrival of evening and the end of day trips. Contemporary poems about the bell referred to the sight of tourists going back home and monks returning to the temple from the city.[32] The changing of time, the symbolism of returning home, and the tension between city and suburb were combined and resonated in this evening bell. Its Buddhist meaning colored people's appreciation of Nanping Hill and emotionally annotated their leisure trips to the West Lake.

In addition to Buddhist symbols, abiding tranquility was a major element that attracted visitors. Natural scenery, rather than the efficaciousness of a temple visit, dominated the textual accounts of visits to the Tianzhu Monasteries and the Soul's Retreat Monastery. The Soul's Retreat Monastery, along with the Flying Hill (Feilaifeng) nearby, is within walking distance of the Tianzhu Monasteries, so documents, especially travel records, usually referred to these monasteries as a cluster. As Zhou Mi described, "The caves and cliffs are crystal clear and smooth, like the swirling dragon and auspicious phoenix, like layered plants with green sprouts, like ripple upon ripple, wave above wave."[33] The descriptions of natural beauty and quietness could be traced back to the Tang dynasty when Bai Juyi commented that in southeastern China, Hangzhou had the best landscape, and within Hangzhou, the Soul's Retreat Monastery commanded the best view. Later literati, especially Su Shi, made this spot a cultural pilgrimage destination.[34] The Tianzhu Monasteries, therefore, constituted another model for religious landscape: they offered an isolated natural setting for urban visitors, and their fame was sanctioned and preserved through literary works that depicted the surrounding landscape as an idealized nature. The monasteries themselves also regarded the scenic beauty as one of their attractions. One section in their temple gazetteer, devoted to "famous sites," details the nearby caves, hills, creeks, and forests.[35]

Although both the Purity and Compassion and the Tianzhu Monasteries were known as pilgrimage and sightseeing destinations, different people appreciated them in various ways. While it is difficult to neatly distinguish how diverse groups, as well as the state, conceptualized this religious landscape, their experiences were characterized by specific distinct features.

SEEKING LEGITIMACY: RELIGIOUS NATURE INTERPRETED BY THE STATE

Different schools of religion benefited from increasing state patronage during the Southern Song due to the dynasty's desire for legitimacy. In particular, Buddhism in Jiangnan was emphasized through the "Five Mountains and

Ten Monasteries" ranking system formulated by Emperor Ningzong.[36] This official ranking system encompassed the fifteen most important monasteries in the lower Yangzi area, three of which were located around West Lake. Incorporating these monasteries into the imperial discourse was both the foundation for imperial patronage provided to the monasteries and a symbolic way to claim the significance of the lower Yangzi provinces, the central region of the revived dynasty. Imperial patronage was given in exchange for religious support of the court's claims of legitimacy and peaceful rulership. For example, the Tianzhu Monasteries were built before the Song dynasty, and the Upper Tianzhu Monastery was known for worship of the white-robed Guanyin. After the Jurchen invasion, Emperor Gaozong ordered the damaged halls of these monasteries rebuilt in 1132 and made regular visits. Emperor Lizong's eulogy especially emphasized the power of the Guanyin bodhisattvas to protect commoners by granting a good harvest and pacifying military conflicts, both of which were primary concerns of the court.[37]

Furthermore, soon after the capital moved to Hangzhou, the state built many temples to worship guardians that were said to have protected members of the imperial family. When the Empress Dowager Wei (1080–1159), Emperor Gaozong's birth mother, traveled to Hangzhou after her release by the Jurchen, she dreamed of the four Daoist guardians (Tianpeng, Tianyou, Yisheng, and Zhenwu) and believed they had escorted her safely back home. Upon her arrival in Hangzhou, a grand temple was commissioned to worship these four sages. The Four Guardians Temple, located in the middle of the Su Causeway, was notable on maps and in literature alike. There, the imperial family prayed regularly and held grand ceremonies throughout the dynasty. The court wanted the four guardians to be worshiped and celebrated widely, as they conveyed to the common people the accessible and robust message that heaven still favored the Song dynasty. The Four Guardians Temple was not the only temple built concurrently with the commencement of the Southern Song; the shrine for Lord Cui was also constructed to worship the deity that was said to have protected Emperor Gaozong on his way to the south.[38]

State patronage was essential to the well-being of religious sites, and at the same time, it also endowed them with nonreligious attractions. For example, in 1175 Emperor Xiaozong bestowed upon the Purity and Compassion Monastery the title of "Great Being of Broad and Extensive Efficacious Responses Guanyin-Teaching Monastery," evidenced with a handwritten plaque. This type of honor was bestowed on temples along with the award of precious artifacts. Both the imperial plaques and the generous grants enriched the temple's collection of treasures, which were open to the public on special occasions, as a new way to attract visitors and, subsequently, potential donations. The Tianzhu Monasteries were famous for their exquisite lanterns and attracted curious city dwellers on the Lantern Festival.[39] Similarly, two wooden statues of deities housed in the Four Guardians Temple attracted the attention of contemporary literati. These sculptures were made with precious wood and large pearls on the day Empress Dowager Wei came back from the north.[40]

The desire to emphasize the blessing of heaven also encouraged the Song court to consider West Lake as a "life-releasing pond." This idea originated with the Buddhist practice of releasing fish and turtles into bodies of water to free them and thus to accumulate merit. Releasing life was a popular theme in Song anecdotes and poems.[41] As the number of lay believers participating in festivals grew, the life-releasing ritual was commercialized and moved beyond the space of the temple. During the Northern Song, as Cai Xiang recorded, "Boats on West Lake were filled with fish and shrimp, which were released in the clear waves."[42]

The official acknowledgment of the lake as a life-releasing pond, however, was more closely linked to political concerns. West Lake acquired the title of "life-releasing pond" during the Northern Song when Wang Qinruo proposed that it be used to accumulate merit for the state. Two reasons motivated Wang to make this request. One was his possible desire to win favor from the ruler; the other was associated with his relationships with local Buddhist monks. When Wang Qinruo was appointed as the governor of Hangzhou in 1019, leaders of the major Buddhist institutions assembled to greet him.[43] Wang maintained a good relationship with the local religious powers, and it was not unlikely that he felt an obligation or even was directly asked to promote the influence of Buddhism in Hangzhou.

West Lake's Buddhist-derived title was repeatedly confirmed during the Southern Song. During the Shaoxing reign, the local governor asked the court to reinstate the role of West Lake as a life-releasing pond in order to prohibit lake fishing. The local government then constructed the Virtue Growing Hall (Deshengtang) next to the lake containing a stele with carved inscriptions that dissuaded people from killing wildlife.[44] Scholars also performed laudatory declamations commemorating the lake as a life-releasing pond and stressing that heaven had blessed the Song dynasty from generation to generation.[45]

Building life-releasing ponds was a national phenomenon in Song China. More than twenty essays about these ponds were included in *Complete Song*

Dynasty Essays (Quan Song wen). As Zhao Xinggen concludes, this body of writing about releasing life centered on two concepts: loyalty toward the imperial family and emphasis on the Neo-Confucian teaching of respecting the emperor.[46] Few of these writings mentioned the influence of Buddhism or used any Buddhist discourse; one even stressed that building a pavilion had nothing to do with Buddhism.[47] The main concern for some scholars was an environmental issue.[48] With rapid agricultural development and the growing use of land by the large population, the potential problems of overexploitation caused by economic expansion began to attract attention. Assigning the title of life releasing to West Lake was likely to have been a strategy appropriated by local officials.

Religious belief in accumulating merit built the natural space of the lake into the political framework. The state used the life-releasing concept to symbolically strengthen the connection between blessing from heaven and the common people's ordinary ritual. The municipal government and local elites employed the life-releasing discourse to gain political capital. No matter how the life-releasing ritual was interpreted, the association with West Lake was real. Through the natural landscape, therefore, Buddhist teaching was interwoven with political concerns.

The belief that a specific landscape embodied the fate of the state was not only held by officials, but was also used by monks as a means to preserve the natural settings around their temples. During the Southern Song, the Nine-*li* Pine (Jiulisong) area was under the control of monks from the Gathering Celebration Monastery (Jiqingsi). When Prime Minister Shi Miyuan (1164–1233) wanted to chop down pine trees to build his house there, monks wrote poems and memorials criticizing this plan. They used references to Buddhist merit and the fortunes of the state to force Shi to give up. Han Tuozhou was also criticized and stopped by monks when he wanted to build his tomb at the Flying Hill. Monks from the Soul's Retreat Monastery insisted that this hill embodied the spirit of the Son of Heaven.[49] Although the monks utilized discourses similar to those used by the state, their reasoning was likely different. The monks appropriated the political discourses to achieve the goal of preserving their religious sites and especially the scenic beauty of their natural surroundings.

The state also constructed the religious landscape through its management of religious festivals. By imposing supervision and guidance on the operation of religious festivals at the lake, the government sought to enhance its administration of leisure life and thus to claim control over the annual calendar. Festivals frequently took place at West Lake, and many of them were associated with religion. These events drew the common people to the lake and were often the main reason for their presence there. Both *Old Affairs of the Martial Grove* and *Record of the Millet Dream* record a series of festivals month by month. The first lunar month started with the Spring Festival. The eighth day of the second month was the birthday of the True Lord of Mount Tai. After that came the birthday of the True Lord of Protecting Sages in the third month, followed by Buddha's Birthday in the fourth month. The fifth month was marked by the Double Fifth Festival, which was relatively secular. The sixth day of the sixth month was the birthday of Lord Cui. The fifteenth day of the seventh month was the Ghost Festival that commemorated the dead. Mid-autumn Day and the Chongyang Festival were next, and the rest of the year was filled with preparations for the New Year and imperial rituals.[50]

The Hangzhou government used religious festivals to promote excursions to West Lake. On the birthday of the True Lord of Mount Tai, the government organized a boat race and announced the opening of the commercial market on the lake. The government's announcement of the beginning of boating on a particular day each year embodied its control over urban life, and making the announcement on a religious festival day added the bonus of sacred legitimation. The simultaneity of these events gave urban residents a stronger reason to leave the city and thus increased revenue for the government.[51] More importantly, festival celebrations were both necessary and intentional outlets for common people.[52] Festivals fulfilled urbanites' shared desires to escape from their daily routines, while also providing the local government with an opportunity to reaffirm its administrative role and enhance its prestige. Moreover, festivals also marked seasonal change, another important area of government control, as the smooth transition of seasons could be interpreted as a blessing from heaven, a boon much sought after during the Southern Song. These festivals were especially important in the cities, where residents, no longer tied to farming, needed events to remind them of seasonal changes.

SEEKING TRANQUIL ESCAPE: RELIGIOUS LANDSCAPE INTERPRETED BY LITERATI

While many literati served as officials of the state or municipal governments, members of this group experienced the religious landscape differently in their spare time. In his official capacity, Su Shi wrote a memorial on the importance of protecting West Lake as a way to accumulate merit for the state and increase government revenue, but in his time off, he traveled with monks through the religious landscape as a transcending experience. Pure and tranquil joy, as opposed to the "noisy dirt" of the mundane world, was what attracted Su and many other literati.

During the Southern Song, Hangzhou hosted the civil service examinations every three years. The number of candidates for these examinations increased enormously, growing from 79,000 in the eleventh century to an estimated 400,000 in the thirteenth.[53] These literati usually took full advantage of religious nature by staying in temples and traveling with monks. Many literati visited the temples around West Lake to pray for good fortune in the civil service examinations. Several temples around the lake were especially famous for helping candidates to pass their exams. Upper Tianzhu Monastery was well known at that time for its one hundred fortune-telling drawings.[54] Many of these lots foretold success in the examinations, with illustrated figures dressed as literati, which suggested that scholars were the primary intended audience.[55] *Book of Hearsay* included several stories about supernatural phenomena and divination connected with the civil service examinations.[56]

"Upper Tianzhu Goddess of Mercy" (Shangzhu Guanyin) was a *Book of Hearsay* story about a scholar's two visits to the Upper Tianzhu Monastery. The protagonist and his friends, who have come to Hangzhou for the exams, pray for divination; he even dreams about drawing lots the day before his second visit, and his dream is very realistic and detailed. Not only does the dream resemble the real lot drawing, but the examination results also confirm the fortune foretold by the lot. The story presents a mixture of different types of divination, including drawing of lots in a temple, dreaming, and fortune-telling by a Daoist priest. All of these were ways literati could seek to learn about their fate before their exams. How accurately this reflected the reality at the time is hard to ascertain. Some literati, such as the scholar in this *Book of Hearsay* story, might not have believed in the lot drawn at the temple, but would have wanted to go there nonetheless as a social outing or responsibility. Visiting the temples, for literati, was more about belonging to a social circle than about adhering to a religious framework.

Moreover, these literati visitors also encouraged temples to assume new functions and offer new activities, including providing accommodation and serving vegetarian food and tea. The tradition of temples providing lodging for sightseers and examination takers started early in the Song dynasty. Buddhist monks practiced a tradition of traveling around to different temples, which originally provided accommodations for them. Later, literati also frequently stayed at temples. Su Shi, for example, stayed in the Water and Land Monastery (Shuilusi) near West Lake for a short period to enjoy the simple, quiet life there.[57] In the year of the examination, the inns in the city of Hangzhou could not accommodate the large number of exam takers, so temples offered additional lodging.

Temples were sometimes preferred to regular inns. In addition to the quiet environment and cheaper rent in temples, the possibility of taking baths there was another reason they were sought out first.[58] The surrounding mountains of West Lake offered ample sources of good spring water. The Pacifying State Monastery (Anguosi), for instance, was known for the bathing it provided, as was acknowledged by Su Shi.[59] The vegetarian food served at the temples was another lure for the literati. The monk Zanning (919–1001) was known for cooking bamboo shoots, and he compiled a catalog with details of the varieties of bamboo shoots grown around his temple.[60] In a poem about visiting the Soul's Retreat Monastery, Cao Xun (1098–1174) wrote, "I also like the vegetarian dishes, with fragrant vegetables and bamboo shoots."[61]

The most famous product associated with the temples was probably green tea. The temperate climate and rugged environment around West Lake are very suitable for tea cultivation. Local gazetteers documented the fragrant forest tea from the Lower Tianzhu Monastery and the white cloud tea from the Upper Tianzhu Monastery.[62] Many talented monks were good at making tea; since the Song dynasty, practicing Chan Buddhism was believed to share the same essential nature as making tea. The frequent references to tea in the literature of Song dynasty's Chan Buddhism shows that tea was a basic daily necessity in Chan monasteries. "Go Drink Tea!" (Chi cha qu), the famous expression attributed to the Chan master Zhaozhou Congshen (778–897), circulated widely in Song dynasty Chan literature.[63] A letter by the monk Jujian (1164–1246) inviting his friend for tea at the Soul's Retreat Monastery demonstrated extensive knowledge of tea making.[64] Literati such as Zhu Xi (1130–1200) wrote a significant number of poems about their pursuit of fragrant tea and tea parties in temples.[65] Making tea and inviting scholars to share it was a way for monks to build connections with the literati.

In addition to the cultivation of tea, the vegetation around the monasteries also became an attraction. The Tianzhu Monasteries, for instance, had been famous for their osmanthus trees since the Tang dynasty, when authors extolled the pure fragrance of the osmanthus flower in midautumn and depicted scenes in which the flowers scattered down like rain.[66] Similarly, azalea blossoms made the Bodhi Monastery (Putisi) famous.[67] For Hangzhou residents, crowded living conditions limited the planting of flowers and trees within the city, so raining osmanthus petals would easily capture visitors' attention.

During their temple visits, the literati's recurring themes were a longing for tranquility and the drawing of a contrast with the busy life of the city. In a poem, Tu Long (1543–1605) commented about these temples:

> Though not very far from the city,
> [Temples] presented a Buddhist environment.
> Birds sing among bamboos and hearing this,
> One can become enlightened.
> The lake scenery becomes misty during the evening,
> And the sounds of the sutra become even subtler.[68]

This Ming dynasty poem conveyed a Chan Buddhist sensibility, which had already been valued among Song dynasty literati and contrasted with rapid development and the city's hustle and bustle. The crowded urban life of Hangzhou exerted psychological pressures on its residents that enhanced the spiritual appeal of natural landscape. The appreciation of tranquil nature was already established in the idealized, reclusive lifestyle of the literati tradition, and Chan teaching during the Song made it even more appealing to literati who wanted an escape from earthly lives.

Literati's visits and writing contributed significantly to the establishment of sites and particular views by communicating multiple sensory impressions. Despite the literati's fondness for Chan teaching, their writing about religious sites was filled with descriptions of their sensory experiences in the landscape. This sophisticated combination of different sensory stimuli made the religious sites into places of interest. The location of monasteries was vital, as it determined the scenery visitors could embrace. The features of the landscape were evaluated aesthetically, with emphasis on the difference from urban life's crowds and clamor. In addition to visual aesthetics, visitors also looked for sounds such as the ringing bell that connected the inside and outside of a space, as well as continuity over time. The smell of flowers added elegance and natural atmosphere. More important, the making of a site, which mainly consisted of natural elements, involved human beings. It relied on the writing and rewriting of the "tranquil place," the subconscious combination of different senses, and even the mimicking of nature in the design of a garden.

Frequent literati sightseeing within the religious landscape enhanced scholars' contacts with monks. These contacts often were intentional, both because of the need to build local community and out of a shared fondness for Chan discourse. These interactions were already quite noticeable during the Northern Song. When Su Shi served as the local official in Hangzhou, he often visited the monks Cenliao and Biancai by boat and exchanged poems with them.[69] The growing number of monks in Southern Song Hangzhou further increased their local influence. The monastic population in the Southern Song reached around two hundred thousand in 1257. Major temples in Hangzhou, like the Purity and Compassion Monastery and the Soul's Retreat Monastery, each housed one to two thousand monks.[70]

Literary talent had been regarded as a valuable asset for the clergy. During the Northern Song, the monks Qingshun and Kejiu lived near the famous sites around West Lake and seldom went into Hangzhou. Records about these two concentrated on praise for their avoidance of the city and for their literary talents. Once, Su Shi traveled to the lake and found a well-written poem on a temple wall. He liked it so much that he inquired about the identity of the author, who turned out to be the monk Qingshun.[71] Thereafter, Qingshun's fame spread widely, and his virtues set the standard for later monks.

A shared fondness for tranquil lake scenery and writing reinforced the connections between monks and literati. They went sightseeing together and wrote poems as an elegant game. The names of some monks appear in the literary records not for their Buddhist erudition, but for their participation in literary sightseeing. It was recorded that the Northern Song monk Qisong (1007–1072) chose to stay at the temples in Hangzhou due to his love of natural beauty.[72] Once, when Yang Pan and another scholar visited him, they all toured the Soul's Retreat and Tianzhu Monasteries for several days, during which time they wrote a total of sixty-four poems. When they compiled these poems into an anthology, the two literati entrusted Qisong with the task of writing the preface for it. In it, he wrote, "Official Yang asked me to write the foreword; I dare not do it before officials in the court. Yang said, 'We are among the mountains and forest. We only talk about Dao, not power.' So I humbly wrote this. . . . We are different in our Confucianism and Buddhism, as well as serving in the court versus living reclusively. We meet here today, because our internal interests go along with each other." In explaining why he wrote the preface, Qisong was acutely aware of the difference between monk and literati, natural environment and court, religious rules and the mundane world. But he then emphasized their internal connections or interests—the love of poetry and natural landscape.

In the afterword, Qisong retained his humble position and emphasized his good relations with renowned literati: "I have been in the Central Wu area for more than twenty years. I have embarrassed the scholars who have traveled with me many times. In the past, Assistant Minister Lang Jian [968–1056] had the best relationship with me. He was known across the country for his poetic talents, and I was asked to respond to his poems. . . . How many people would be happy to travel with me, a monk who is dressed in Buddhist robes?"[73] Qisong's targeted audience was potential literati readers. He articulated his respect for scholar-officials and therefore placed himself in the middle of their elite networks.

The articulation of mutual support between literati and monks arose from the fact that West Lake was an appropriate contact zone for both groups.[74] Restricted by monastery rules and the standards set by Qingshun and Kejiu, monks would have left themselves open to criticism if they had met literati in the city. The lake, therefore, provided the two groups with a bridge between their respective worlds. This contact could also be very pragmatic, for the local elite sought to enhance their communities, and the monks hoped for recognition from the local government. Scholars' official duties usually encouraged them to be open and pragmatic in dealings with the religious people.[75] For the monks, the new system of appointing an abbot to major temples from a national pool of candidates encouraged their cultivation of good relationships with influential scholars. They needed scholars' recommendations to acquire a government appointment and thus advance in the monastic system.

COMMERCIAL ENJOYMENT: RELIGIOUS NATURE ENGAGED BY RESIDENTS OF THE CAPITAL

Ordinary residents of Hangzhou usually visited the temples on religious festivals. Of these festivals, some had been celebrated since the Tang dynasty, some were related to the Southern Song imperial family, and some were colored by local beliefs. Though they honored different deities that were celebrated in diverse ways, these festivals shared certain characteristics, as Gernet explains: "The primary purpose of these annual festivals was to get rid of breaths that had become vitiated, of pestilences and of demons, to recreate everything so that it should be new and pristine, to inaugurate a lucky period, and to open the way for beneficial influences. At the same time, they offered entertainments, which gave free rein to play-loving instincts, and times of merry-making during which constraints of daily life could be forgotten."[76]

This discussion highlights two aspects of festivals: their religious function and their function as entertainment. The entertainment component of the celebrations led ordinary urban residents to treat these festivals as excuses to travel outside the city. Their outings to temples and their engagement in religious rituals were quite different from the religious involvement of the state and the literati. While the state was more concerned about claiming political legitimacy through religious ritual, the common people took these events as occasions for leisure sightseeing. While the literati visited the lake for a tranquil escape from the city, the active engagement of ordinary urban residents motivated the emergence of worldly enjoyment within the religious landscape.

The mixing of religious outings and entertainment was common throughout the year. Hangzhou residents, who were criticized for too actively pursuing luxury and leisure, sought to discover and invent leisure sightseeing activities on any occasion. For example, the Qingming Festival, long emphasized by Confucianism as the major day to worship the ancestors, fell at a perfect time to enjoy splendid spring scenery. The east side of Hangzhou was bounded by the Zhe River, the south side was the site of the imperial palace, and the north side was the location of the garrison, leaving only the west side, the area around West Lake, suitable for burying the dead. On the day of the Qingming Festival, after worshiping at the graves of their ancestors, people would picnic beside the famous gardens or eat on boats, accompanied by music. In the evenings, people would return home with various local products from the lake.[77] The grief of mourning at the tombs would have dissipated gradually.[78]

The leisure activities of the common people during festivals were not always in tune with intent of the government. Honoring the birthday of Lord Cui was a tradition that went back at least to the Northern Song. On that day, hundreds of dramatic productions and other types of public entertainment that were staged in and around temples went on all night.[79] By the Southern Song, this festival was no longer merely the birthday celebration of a local deity, but had become a major occasion of political ritual, as Lord Cui was then regarded as a symbol of heaven's blessing of the Song imperial family.[80] The Northern Song's earthly enjoyment of Lord Cui's birthday gave way to a highly institutionalized imperial spectacle in the Southern Song.

The festival began with the inner court sending out royal messengers to offer incense, which was followed by visits of noblemen and imperial relatives, gentry, and commoners to the Lord Cui Temple (Cui Fujunmiao). Wu Zimu, after briefly recording these religious activities, moved on to document in detail the subsequent sightseeing activity on the lake: "On this day, all the decorated boats on West Lake gathered along the dikes. People enjoyed the cool breeze on the lake, escaping from the humid weather. They indulged themselves in sleeping in the shade of the willow trees, fully absorbing the fragrance of the lotus flowers. Untying their hair and clothes, they ate fruits that were kept cool in cold water. Drinking led some to sing wildly; others played [the game of] Go or fished in the water."[81]

The fact that urban residents were more engaged with leisure activities on this day was due to the deity's lack of local connections. Born in northern China, Lord Cui was never very influential in the Jiangnan region before the Southern Song. Although the court was eager to emphasize the festival of his birth in order to promote dynastic legitimacy, the birthday of Lord Cui did not resonate deeply with the local people. For the residents of Hangzhou, this was nevertheless an occasion to escape the heat and humidity in the crowded city.

Even when urban residents did participate in religious rituals as expected by the state, commercial elements crept into their religious practices. While literati records and official documents described the life-releasing ritual as an imperial spectacle, the mass activity component of this ritual was commercialized and leisured. Contemporary documents never discuss who sold the lay believers the fish and turtles they released into the lake—it could have been profit-seeking monks; it could also have been the proprietors of the small boats who usually sold cooked soup and seafood. Either way, the life-releasing ritual was transformed from a religious or political occasion into a commercial opportunity. Spiritual teaching was commoditized to meet sightseers' and lay believers' desires.

Religious practices and their meanings were further profaned with the increasing engagement of women believers. The Purity and Compassion Monastery had a Maitreya Buddha Hall that was popular with female visitors who always rubbed the big belly of the Buddha as a way to pray for children. This practice revealed an interesting misinterpretation of Buddhism in the mentality of the common people.[82] While the big belly of the Maitreya Buddha does have a religious meaning, female lay believers associated it with fecundity. The circulation of fertility anecdotes drew more visitors and potentially more donations, but it also clouded the true meaning of religious teaching. It is ironic to consider that while Buddhist teaching emphasized escaping from the mundane world and ignoring profane concerns, in reality religious sites such as this offered reassurance about and even promised fulfillment of a basic worldly desire.

Earthly desire also encouraged the members of the clergy to offer more commercialized services. One of the most important commercial attractions was the shops and booths in front of or near temple gates. Temple fairs developed rapidly throughout the Song, and the Prime Minister Monastery (Xiangguosi) in Northern Song Kaifeng was famous for its secular market.[83] This type of temple-based commerce further expanded during the Southern Song due to the relaxed regulation of markets at West Lake. The best-known markets included those outside the Three Worthies Hall, the Four Guardians Temple, and the Soul's Retreat Monastery. [84]

Businesses started by selling incense to pilgrims and later included secular souvenirs. In addition, members of the clergy also participated in the sightseeing market. As Lu You (1125–1210) wrote, "In the commercial area of West Lake, many mountain monks became businessmen."[85] In almost every temple, there were "reception monks" who were responsible for guiding visitors. In the beginning, they guided monks from other temples as well as pilgrims. But as excursions became increasingly popular, these "reception monks" became guides for sightseers. This was soon criticized by literati as a greedy practice aimed at fame or profit, especially when the involvement of temples in the commercial market brought undesirable results.[86] Ming scholar Li Ding (ca. 1593–1612) even compared these monasteries to pawnshops and banks, lamenting their loss of tranquility and purity.[87]

Festivals led to further commercialization of temples. On Buddha Shakyamuni's birthday (the eighth day of the fourth lunar month), for instance, the most popular ritual was called "Buddha bathing."[88] While the majority of rituals were held in the monasteries before the eleventh century, monks in the twelfth century began to extend their ceremonies beyond the monastery setting. Monks and nuns carried copper Buddha statues in small basins filled with sugar water and covered by flowered huts. They visited wealthy families and used small ladles to bathe the Buddha statues with the syrup as they asked for donations.[89] This ritual had broken through its previous spatial confines; reaching beyond the monasteries expanded the audiences for this ceremony, and practicing these rituals at people's doors secured more donations. The ceremony was transformed into a portable but more mundane ritual.

The increasingly popularized interpretation of religion also led to more profane themes in religious carvings. Catering to the demands of leisure sightseers, monasteries functioned as museums that preserved Buddhist-energized cultural relics, including sutra pillars, pagodas, bells, and stone carvings. Stone carvings were scattered all around the lake, on the Mist and Cloudy Cliff (Yanxialing) to the north, around the Phoenix Hill to the south, and on the Flying Hill to the west. Carvings were created during the Five Dynasties, flourished during the Song period, and continued into the Ming era. While a majority of these carvings took the traditional form of a sacred niche with a seated Buddha, some depicted religious stories. For instance, one Northern Song stone carving at the Flying Hill depicted the story of a pilgrimage with four monks and two horses in a line. Its targeted audience was likely the common people who preferred the adventurous story of a pilgrimage to serious religious teaching.

WHAT IS RELIGIOUS NATURE?

In Southern Song West Lake, religious pursuits and the experience of nature were inseparable and interdependent. Natural scenery functioned as a major component of the religious sites around the lake, and the religions offered new meanings to the natural setting of the lake. Religious sites and the natural landscape, in many people's viewpoints, resembled each other.

Different people sought to build spirituality into their own frameworks of political legitimacy, literary discourses, and commercial enjoyment. The state and the imperial family sought to employ religious sites to reinforce their legitimacy and to promote dynastic revival during the Southern Song. These goals added new religious sites to the natural environment and politicized the experience of nature. Literati phrased their appreciation of religious sites in the literary discourses with which they were familiar. Their complimentary descriptions of the natural beauty of these religious sites were closely associated with the literary ideal of reclusive life. Their visits to and impressions of religious sites were much colored by traces of famous historical scholars and historical writings. From the perspective of the common people, religion could also be considered an extension of their urban life, due to the leisured nature of their temple visits. Their mass involvement sustained many temples and resulted in human efforts to reshape nature. The municipal government built a causeway to serve the increasing number of pilgrims to the mountains west of the lake.

Therefore, two questions (which were also posed by contemporary literati) arise: Was the religious nature of the temples profaned because of people's visits and their interpretations of these religious experiences? Did these visits, as pilgrimages or sightseeing or both, detract from the natural quality of this religious nature? The answers to these questions reveal a paradox. Scholars during the Southern Song, and especially during later imperial times, seemed to believe that the common people's intrusive participation was a disturbance of tranquil nature. But profaned nature, if that was actually the result, was not caused solely by the actions of the common people.

The imperial family's experience with religious nature resulted in an attempt to reconstruct nature in miniature in the imperial garden. There, Emperor Xiaozong ordered the digging of a new pond and the construction of an artificial hill using rocks. He named the hill the "Flying Hill," and he also named a nearby pavilion in his garden "Cold Spring." These construction projects were motivated by the emperor's ambition to re-create nature through a human-made garden. The emperor even commented on his own garden after the new projects were finished: "Who said that human construction is not natural? The thousands of cliffs and tens of thousands of valleys conceal clouds and smoke."[90] Both Emperor Xiaozong and Emperor Gaozong wrote about how their experience in their newly reconstructed garden perfectly captured their experience in nature. They were aware of the difference between the miniature landscape in the imperial garden and real nature, but nonetheless strove to prove that they could perfectly copy nature. While religious sites offered inspiration on how to construct "nature," the fact that religious nature could be reproduced on a smaller scale implied the collapse of religiousness; nature and imperial enjoyment of it was under the control of imperial construction.

It might seem that the literati's experience of nature was primarily spiritual—a search for tranquility and a location for religious chanting. However, as an excessive number of literati visited cultural landmarks such as the Cold Spring Pavilion, some came not solely in pursuit of religious goals, but also to follow the literati tradition. They were touring nature as depicted in previous literary works and wrote new words about half-real and half-imagined nature. These writings were disseminated to popular markets and added to guidebooks, thus transforming certain cultural sites into "must-see" spots. Thereafter, regular literati visits, though driven by a longing for the previously documented tranquility and reclusiveness of the monasteries, potentially jeopardized the silence of these places.[91]

The increasing engagement of the common people further detracted from religious nature, as their leisured enjoyment during religious festivals rendered it less tranquil and more profane. Markets and businesses sprouted up near the temples; worldly desires for food and entertainment could be satisfied in shrines and on festivals. The profaneness of religious sightseeing encompassed not only the efforts of urban residents to enjoy the sensory commercialization, but also the efforts of the temples and the clergy themselves to cater to such secular desires.

In response to the burgeoning of sightseeing activities, the clergy strove to develop new functions to make temples desirable sightseeing destinations. Like Beijing temples in late imperial China, these religious spaces served tourist purposes by functioning as museums, libraries, and gardens.[92] Similarly, Song dynasty temples provided accommodation and guide services and also functioned as museums. Some of their attractions were gifts from nature, such as hills, creeks, and beautiful vegetation. Others reflected the efforts of temples and monasteries to promote their fame and attract more visitors. Their connections with commercial markets contributed to the fame and continuity of these temples. Comparison of local gazetteers of the thirteenth and the seventeenth centuries shows that temples that existed for more than four centuries were known for their secular markets.[93]

The question of whether people's increasing visits jeopardized the religious nature of these sites, therefore, revealed a paradox. While nature was much colored by religious meaning, it was also a belief in the efficacy of a religious blessing that brought increased visits along with profane elements from urban lives. On the one hand, this factor enhanced the influence of religious teaching, but on the other hand, it also disturbed the untouched nature and diluted the spirituality associated with these sites.

CONCLUSION: WEST LAKE AS A MIDDLE LANDSCAPE

As in most traditional societies, praying to the gods and seeking pleasure, which are both leisure activities, shared similarities. Both temple visits and excursions involved geographical movement, departing from the daily routine and getting out of the busy city, purchasing entertainment and trivial mementos, and interacting with different social groups. Praying and playing were transformable and interdependent.

This integration of religious and leisure activities helped transform West Lake into a middle landscape that diluted the boundary between religious and urban space. The term "middle landscape" was first applied by Peter G. Rowe to describe the intermediate and transitional suburban landscape between a big city and remote areas.[94] While Song dynasty West Lake was different from modern suburban landscapes, it acted as an intermediary between the city and the distant mountain areas. As a place that simultaneously embodied sacred power and hosted worldly entertainment, the lake can be viewed as a model of negotiation between praying and playing, as well as an analytical framework for discussing this negotiation.

As a middle landscape, West Lake was not only important in the expansion of urban space, it also facilitated people's social interactions. By visiting the lake's many temples and by participating in its religious festivals, urban residents acquired sacred experiences. They were able to escape temporarily from their established work, social status, and daily lives. Similarly, monks could also put aside their sutra chanting, temple cleaning, and other routine work. They actively sought to communicate with lay patrons, believers, and scholars.

This pattern continued after the Song and appeared in other places. As Zhang Dai (1597–1679) recorded, during the Ming dynasty Mount Tai functioned both as a pilgrimage center and as a destination where tourism developed to include various packages to appeal to all those who wished to ascend the mountain. These packages included inns, service, food en route to the mountaintop, and evening entertainment. While the food provided on the mountaintop was vegetarian, the food offered in the inns contained meat.[95] Compared to Song dynasty West Lake, religious tourism to pilgrimage destinations in the late Ming was more systematized and commercialized.

Moreover, in today's China, residents of the Shanghai metropolitan area visit West Lake regularly. They pray for blessings, donate money, and at the same time also take tourist pictures to post on social media. Historically famous temples, such as the Tianzhu and Soul's Retreat Monasteries, continue to offer sites for worship, and monks and local residents still engage in tourist-oriented commercial activities around the lake, such as selling entrance tickets, incense, souvenirs, and transportation services. The local government continues to regulate religious life by issuing pilgrimage certificates to believers and incorporating temples into cultural protection projects. The Song dynasty not only initiated this religious tourism but also contributed to today's tourist discourses by adding a historical dimension to these religious sites.

CHAPTER SIX

TEN VIEWS OF WEST LAKE

A Naming Convention

IN 1924 THE LEIFENG PAGODA, WHICH HAD STOOD FOR MORE than a thousand years beside West Lake, suddenly collapsed. This news, seemingly insignificant in such a politically unstable era, drew the attention of not only local people but also the elite from all over the country. Literati used the opportunity to lament historical change and to argue in favor of having the tower rebuilt in order to keep the set of the Ten Views of West Lake intact. The well-known writer Lu Xun (1881–1936), however, had criticized traditional Chinese culture, writing in his characteristically satirical tone, "Many of us in China . . . have a sort of 'ten views syndrome' or at least an 'eight views syndrome,' which reached epidemic proportions in the Qing dynasty, I should say. Look through any county annals, and you will find the district has ten sights, if not eight, such as 'Moonlight on a Distant Village,' 'Quiet Monastery and Clear Bell,' 'Ancient Pool and Crystal Water.'"[1] What bothered Lu Xun was the formulaic practice of assigning eight or ten four-character poetic phrases to epitomize the best local scenic sites. This widely influential naming convention derived from the Southern Song Ten Views of West Lake.

At the time Lu Xun wrote, the Ten Views of West Lake had served for centuries as a creative discourse that helped shape how people interacted with the natural landscape. The place names associated with West Lake defined the spots that drew visitors' eyes and influenced how these viewers interpreted what they saw. Drawing extensively from the actual local scenery, this place-energized visual culture was intricately interconnected with social activities and cultural norms. It was rooted in, and in turn enhanced, local pride. And more broadly, it allowed any visitor to feel more familiar with the landscape when they were in it.

The Ten Views of West Lake developed and circulated as a sightseeing discourse. While the tradition of sightseeing around West Lake dates back to the Tang dynasty, it was Song visitors who initiated the process of systematically selecting its iconic spots. When exposed to a new environment, sightseers use focal points to help them assimilate, and they tend to assign symbolic meanings to these focal locations. Their habits are embedded in the circulating cultural styles and images of this place.[2] This cultural way of viewing surrounding nature helped visitors to connect with the landscape. Humanist geographer Yi-fu Tuan labels this affective bond between people and place "topophilia."[3] Once the Ten Views of West Lake were enriched through art and literature, they became a checklist for sightseers who wished to take in what West Lake had to offer. Gazing at the sites, representing them in words or pictures, and circulating these artistic creations created a way of seeing and thinking about natural scenery that could be both personal and communal. Poems about and paintings of the lake also evoked a sense of being there for people who were physically unable to visit. Specific locations and seasonal changes are especially emphasized in this process.

This naming convention stemmed from and shaped the cultural trope of nature in China. The Ten Views, which appeared in poetry, paintings, and popular discourses, were constructed to evoke simultaneously a cultural landmark, an artistic motif, and a culturally laden naming convention.[4] The canonization of the Ten Views and the wide circulation of this naming convention served as a unifying force in the creation of Chinese cultural geography.

THE ORIGINS OF THE TEN VIEWS

The earliest extant reference to the Ten Views of West Lake is found in Zhu Mu's (d. 1255) record. He wrote, "People who were fond of things used to name [the scenery] using ten titles: Autumn Moon above the Placid Lake, Spring Dawn at Su Causeway, Remnant Snow on Broken Bridge, Sunset on Leifeng Pagoda, Evening Bell from Nanping Hill, Lotus Breeze at Qu Winery, Watching Fish at Flower Cove, Listening to the Orioles by the Willow Ripples, Three Stupas and the Reflecting Moon, and Twin Peaks Piercing the Clouds."[5] The earliest extant paintings of and poems on the Ten Views also date to the 1250s and 1260s, indicating that this set of views was invented during that period. Zhao Xigu (ca. 1237–1252) suggested that painters—not scholars—came up with the titles first.[6] This association of the

TABLE 6.1. The Ten Views of West Lake

Title*	Location/architecture	Construction date	Season for visiting	Time of day	Weather	Plants	Activity
1. Autumn Moon above the Placid Lake (Pinghu qiuyue)	Temple of the Dragon King (Longwangmiao)	Song dynasty (960–1279)	Autumn	Night	Clear		Viewing
2. Spring Dawn at Su Causeway (Sudi chunxiao)	Su Causeway	Northern Song (1089)	Spring	Dawn			Viewing and feeling
3. Remnant Snow on Broken Bridge (Duanqiao canxue)	White Causeway	Before the Tang dynasty (618–907)	Winter		After snow		Viewing from distance
4. Sunset on Leifeng Pagoda (Leifeng xizhao)	Leifeng Pagoda	Song Dynasty (975)		Dusk	Clear		Viewing
5. Evening Bell from Nanping Hill (Nanping wanzhong)	Purity and Compassion Monastery	Five Dynasties (954)		Dusk			Listening
6. Lotus Breeze at Qu Winery (Quyuan hefeng)	Qu Winery	Southern Song (1127–1279)	Summer		Breeze	Lotus	Viewing, smell-ing, and feeling
7. Watching Fish at Flower Cove (Huagang guanyu)	At the foot of Hua Family Mountain (Huajiashan)	Southern Song			Clear	Flower	Fish viewing
8. Listening to the Orioles by the Willow Ripples (Liulang wenying)	Assembled Scenery Garden	Xiaozong reign (1162–89)	Spring		Breeze	Willow	Listening and viewing
9. Three Stupas and the Reflecting Moon (Santan yingyue)	Three pagodas in the heart of the lake	Northern Song (ca. 1089)		Night	Clear		Viewing
10. Twin Peaks Piercing the Clouds (Liangfeng chayun)	Among the mountains west of the lake	Tang dynasty	Spring or autumn		Misty		Viewing

Source: Duan, "Ten Views of West Lake," 155.

* Numbers for the titles correspond to locations shown in figure 6.1.

Ten Views with painting was confirmed by Wu Zimu, who wrote, "In recent times the ten most spectacular scenes of the four seasons around West Lake and its mountains have been illustrated by painters."[7] The tradition of using four characters to name Song dynasty imperial paintings of landscapes further substantiates the claim that the Ten Views were first created by painters.[8]

The Ten Views were meant to convey the essence of the West Lake experience through a set of sights and associated activities correlated with specific times of day and seasons (table 6.1, figure 6.1). Views—even the words used in their names—encompassed not only a particular aspect of a scenic spot, along with the poetic or historical reference it should evoke, but also the appropriate circumstances for viewing, which could include season, time of day, weather, and the spectator's mood.[9] The Ten Views thus circulated as a symbol of the lake. In *Bamboo Lyric Songs of West Lake* by Yang Weizhen (1296–1370), mentioned in chapter 1, Leisure, the female narrator of the poem refers to West Lake, saying, "next to the Ten Views Pond is my home."[10]

Naming scenic places with poetic titles was an enduring literati tradition. The Ten Views of West Lake reflect the influence of site names used in Tang and Northern Song gardens. While the site names in Tang gardens were usually references to the site's location, function, and scenery, the Northern Song garden owners paid more emphasis on emotions and the cultural associations evoked by the site.[11] In the Tang period, Wang Wei (699–759) wrote poems for some of his beloved sites in the Wangchuan Villa, including Southern Hillock (Nancha), Willow Ripples (Liulang), and Northern Hillock (Beicha). These titles are reminiscent of the first two characters in the titles of the Ten Views, such as "Qu Winery," "Willow Ripples," and "Twin Peaks." Northern Song site names, such as Reading Hall (Dushutang), Fishing Hut (Diaoyu'an), Pavilion for Playing with Water (Nongshuixuan), and Pavilion for Watering Flowers (Jiaohuating) in the Garden of Solitary Enjoyment of Sima Guang (1019–86) bring to mind "Watching Fish" and "Listening to Orioles" in the Ten Views of West Lake. By the Southern Song dynasty, the two naming traditions, which emphasized natural scenery and human activity, respectively, had been fused.

The emphasis on place in the Ten Views also derived from the traditions of visual culture. The Tang painters Wang Wei and Lu Hong (ca. 740) painted pictures of their own gardens. Each of the album leaves in Lu Hong's *Ten Images of My Grass Hut* has a site name, such as "Writing Grass Hall" or "Expecting Immortal Steps," and includes a figure sitting or wandering in the landscape.[12] Each album by Lu also features a short description of the

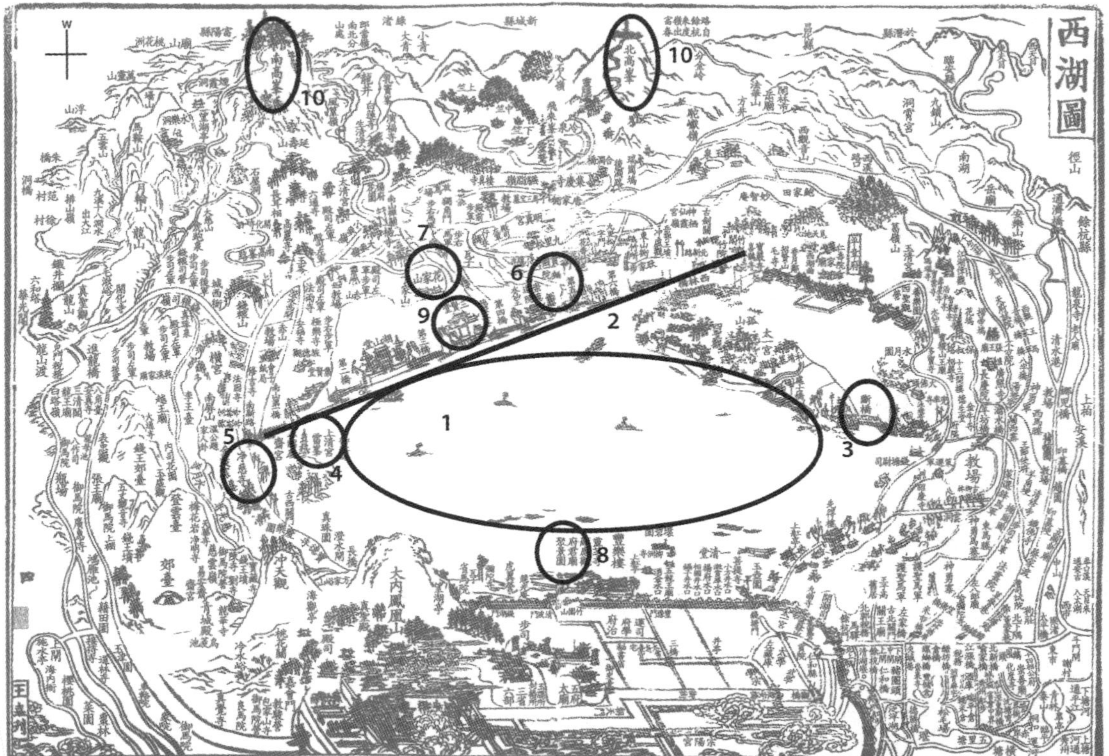

FIGURE 6.1. Locations of the Ten Views, based on the Southern Song map of West Lake by engraver Wang Yao in *The Gazetteer of Hangzhou during the Xianchun Reign*, compiled by Qian Yueyou, ca. 1268–75. Numbers correspond to the list in table 6.1. Figure by the author, based on Jiang Qingqing, *"Xianchun Lin'an zhi" Songban "jingcheng situ" fuyuan yanjiu*.

site's geography and history, followed by one or two poems related to the place. Both the format of ten associated album paintings and the emphasis on the representation of actual sites with figures suggest a possible inspiration for the Ten Views of West Lake.

The artistic tradition of album painting also fueled the practice of using four-character titles for views and putting a number of views into one collection. Earlier researchers have long drawn attention to the practice of naming eight or ten sites with four-character poetic titles and have pointed to connections between the Ten Views and the earlier convention of the Eight Views of the Xiao and Xiang Rivers. The earliest extant pictorial example of the Eight Views is by the Northern Song literatus Song Di (ca. 1023–1032). Their titles are "Wild Geese Descending to Sandbar," "Returning Sail off Distant Shore," "Mountain Market, Clear with Rising Mist," "River and Sky in Evening Snow," "Autumn Moon over Lake Dongting," "Night Rain on Xiao and Xiang," "Evening Bell from Mist-Shrouded Temple," and "Fishing Village in Evening Glow."[13] Past scholarship demonstrates that interconnections between textual and visual records contributed to the wide circulation of specific sets of views, or visualizations, of nature.[14] Indeed, the Ten Views are reminiscent of the verse-like structures of the Eight Views, in that putting any two titles together forms a couplet.[15] For instance, both "Twin Peaks Piercing the Clouds" and "Three Stupas and the Reflecting Moon" follow the same format of a number plus a structure or mountain plus a verb and end with a natural element in the sky. Three of the four sets of West Lake poems changed the original sequence of the ten titles, as Zhu Mu and Wu Zimu recorded them. The reason for rearranging the ten titles seems to have been to seek better pairing possibilities.[16]

While sharing similar connections between visual and textual records, the Ten Views differ from the Eight Views in several respects—above all, in the former's emphasis on specific locations and the inclusion of more human activities. While it was not until the Yuan dynasty that literati started to connect the Eight Views with actual locations in the Hunan area, eight of the Ten Views at West Lake included a specific place or structure from the very beginning.[17] What might seem a minor elaboration of adding specific locales to the Eight Views in actuality had major consequences as it changed how people saw nature.

In addition to being inspired by the visual culture, the Ten Views were also rooted in the tradition of poetry writing. Writing a set of ten poems describing different scenic spots and the seasons in one place was a literary convention dating at least to the Northern Song. Ouyang Xiu, for example, wrote ten lyric songs with the same title of "Picking Mulberries" (Cai sangzi) about the Slender West Lake (Shouxihu) in Yingzhou. Each song begins by describing an attraction of the lake, such as "After the late spring rain, West Lake is good" or "Carrying wine on the decorated boat, West Lake is good." The ten songs cover the scenery year-round.[18] The ambitious structure of presenting one place at different times, through different flowers and activities, is similar to the West Lake Ten Views. Another Northern Song poet, Pan Lang (d. 1009), also wrote ten lyric songs with the same rhyming scheme and format about Hangzhou based on his memories of the scenic beauty and his past excursions. Each lyric song describes one place in Hangzhou, such as West Lake, Solitary Mountain, and the Zhe River. This set of lyric songs circulated widely and was praised by Su Shi. The scholar Shi Manqing (994–1041) even commissioned paintings to represent Pan's poems.[19] This convention of writing a suite of poems to depict one spectacular site further inspired the creation of ten individual yet associated views for West Lake.

The Ten Views would not have become nearly as famous had it not been for the Jurchen conquest of north China and the Song relocation of the political center south to Hangzhou. Cahill suggests that a deep feeling of nostalgia arose due to both the loss of the north and the connection with China's idealized past.[20] The Ten Views were invented and received as an idealized model of human engagement with the natural scenery and the resulting artistic creations. This idealized model embodied the essence of Chinese culture and historical concepts of nature, thus generating ownership and power that could dilute the feelings of nostalgia. Place names, as archaeologist Jacquetta Hawkes points out, closely associated people with their territories.[21] Naming sites, recording names in literature, and inventing the ten titles evoking poetic and artistic allusions together reflected a conscious construction of local pride and a deep longing for the Chinese past.

THE TEN VIEWS DURING THE SOUTHERN SONG

The Ten Views manifest a particular method of describing a place and the unity of place, people, and act. Most of the views include diverse elements that are suitable for a painting or ready for a poem. The coupling of poems and paintings was a well-established practice in Song times, especially among court painters.[22] The ten titles evoke connections with specific places and seasonal moods. The Southern Song poems about and paintings of the Ten Views established them as a trope for later appropriation.

POEMS ABOUT THE TEN VIEWS

At least four collections of ten poems on the Ten Views of West Lake survive from the Southern Song dynasty, written by Zhang Ju (ca. 1253–1258), Wang Wei (ca. 1256), Zhou Mi, and Chen Yunping (ca. 1275).[23] The Ten Views likely served as topics for poetry competitions on many occasions. Zhou Mi had read Zhang Ju's poems and wanted to write his own versions to compete with them. Zhou also invited Chen to write, using this group of titles and the same rhymes for the poems.[24]

Many poems could be read as miniature trip diaries that indicated where and how the sightseers had spent their time. For example, all of the poems about "Three Stupas and the Reflecting Moon" indicate that the scene was viewed from a boat. Interestingly, all four poets depicted a similar scene for "Spring Dawn at Su Causeway." The sightseers enjoyed themselves around the lake all night; in the early morning, the courtesans, just awakened, had not yet put on their makeup, while those who were eager to meet the girls had already arrived on horseback.[25] It is unclear why all of the poems shared this theme; the later poets may have copied the earlier themes intentionally, perhaps to combine respect for past masters with a claim of their own knowledge of that specific place.

Comparisons between poems about the Eight Views and the Ten Views reveal a striking difference. While poems about the Eight Views conveyed the sentiments of someone in exile (such as "Night Rain on Xiao and Xiang"), poems about the Ten Views usually depicted flourishing sightseeing activities, even when the poems focused on the sunset, which was usually thought to arouse sorrowful feelings.[26] For example, in his poem about "Sunset on Leifeng Pagoda," Zhou Mi does not depict the end of an excursion in a sentimental way; rather, the poet adds to the joyful picture of sightseeing by emphasizing the continuing pleasure, the decorated carts, and the silver candles.[27] Southern Song scholar-officials often wrote about West Lake to sing the praises of the central government.[28] The formation of the Ten Views and the joyful emotion make a political point in emphasizing the happy sightseers who indulged themselves at West Lake.

PAINTINGS OF THE TEN VIEWS

The formation of the Ten Views as an invention of contemporary painters attests to the importance of framing and selecting scenic elements to form a particular view. The format of album painting worked well for capturing the Ten Views. The independent but still interconnected leaves of an album facilitated the presentation of a set number of scenes. The fact that each composition was painted as part of a set made it easier for viewers to identify each leaf. Specific landmark features function as indicators of which view each album leaf is depicting and can trigger viewers' mental images of the site, even though the rest of the compositional elements are not very realistic.

The Southern Song academy painters produced several sets of the Ten Views, and some artists created more than one.[29] Yet, despite this, the album by Ye Xiaoyan (ca. 1253–1258) is the only extant Song period depiction.[30] Little is known about Ye, and his Ten Views album is his only surviving work. Ye's debts to Ma Yuan and Xia Gui can be seen in this album in the frequent application of the axe-cut textual stroke and the distinctive rendering of misty scenery. Recurring themes and visual elements and the use of particular techniques were all essential in reproducing and reinforcing the characteristic visual culture of West Lake. It is quite possible that Ye's paintings of the Ten Views were closely based on or even copied from an earlier masterpiece. If Ye's painting was based on another lost masterpiece, this could explain the discrepancy between the thoughtful arrangement of the visual elements and his less impressive brushwork.

Depictions of the Ten Views of West Lake and the Eight Views of the Xiao and Xiang Rivers reveal clear influences from one another.[31] Some Southern Song painters, such as the monk Muqi (ca. 1200–after 1279), based their paintings of the Eight Views on their observations of West Lake scenery.[32] This practice in turn encouraged painters to borrow inspiration from Eight Views paintings when they depicted the Ten Views. For example, Ye Xiaoyan's album leaf *Listening to the Orioles by the Willow Ripples* echoes Monk Muqi's album leaf *Returning Sail off Distant Shore*, with the depiction of a nearby lakeshore and a misty rendering of distant waters.[33] Though influenced by depictions of the Eight Views, Ye's painting demonstrates very different intentions. Ye's utmost concern was to make sure that each of the ten leaves could be easily identified.[34] He made every effort to convey the information in each title by appropriating and arranging varying visual elements such as trees, mountains, buildings, and figures in the miniature format. Even images lacking specific identifying features contain clues that link the depicted scenery to a specific view. For instance, in *Autumn Moon above the Placid Lake*, while there is no specific landmark to identify the "placid lake," Ye depicted a sharply obtruding peak intended to contrast with and therefore attract viewers' attention to the calm lake.

Like the other West Lake paintings discussed in chapter 4, Ye's visual representations of the Ten Views are influenced by artistic traditions and at the same time also evoke and echo the actual sightseeing experience. What differentiates Ye Xiaoyan's painting from the Tang dynasty paintings about specific locations was his apparent assumption that the viewers already knew the sites he was depicting. While Lu Hong's paintings offer an illustrated introduction to these sites, Ye's depiction is less topographic. Due to the sightseeing activities and the circulation of poems about West Lake, it was natural for viewers to notice these signposts around the lake. Based on these experiences, viewers of the paintings could decode Ye's visual clues to discern the identity of each view, which offered them a sense of accomplishment. Just as those familiar with the skyline of New York can easily recognize the Empire State Building from its unique shape and its frequent appearance in photos, Southern Song visitors to West Lake must have had a similar experience: standing beside the lake, when they looked at the distant hills, two peaks stood out because of the two pagodas located there, and if they looked at the Southern Hill, the silhouette of the Leifeng Pagoda and the eaves of Buddhist monasteries revealed behind the trees would have caught their attention. Both the depiction and the identification of nature in the album paintings called viewers to come to the actual site in order to spiritually join others who had done the same and thus created a community based around a place.

THE REPRESENTATION OF PLACE AND TIME IN THE TEN VIEWS

The Ten Views of West Lake demonstrated a deliberate utilization of place and time. Depicting the natural landscape involves a complicated process of conceptualizing and abstracting the natural elements.[35] Specific places can serve as anchors for people to construct their personal identities and facilitate the joining of meaningful words and images.[36] These places became signposts in collective memory for inspiring writings and cultural topics.[37] Meanwhile, the Ten Views also evoke specific seasons or even times of day. Time functions as an important coordinate in one's memory. By connecting sites with more universal emotional attachments to nature, the Ten Views encourage spectators to recall and reflect upon their past experiences while contemplating the specific places around West Lake.

Many of the Ten Views are based on specific physical sites or structures, such as the Leifeng Pagoda, the Purity and Compassion Monastery, and the Su Causeway (see table 6.1). Poems about the Ten Views usually center on these places, and in Ye's painting, these locations were the foci. The emphasis on physical sites also enabled the artists to represent the scenery in a closer and more intimate way. Chen Yunping's poems, for example, often mention the relevant place names near each view, such as the Small New Causeway next to the view of "Lotus Breeze at Qu Winery" and the six bridges in the poem on "Spring Dawn at Su Causeway." He used these locations to construct his movement in the scenery, presenting multiple perspectives from which the site could be closely observed. In addition, a comparison of Ye's painting with Li Song's hand scroll, which also includes most of the Ten Views, reveals in Ye's work an alternative way to direct the perspective of viewers. Taking a bird's-eye view, Li Song ambitiously represented the entire lake from a high and distant standpoint. In Ye's painting of "Spring Dawn at Su Causeway," instead of trying to show the entire Su Causeway, he rendered only one of the six bridges that connected the causeway. These techniques helped to draw viewers close to the scenery to create an intimate atmosphere. The zooming-in writing strategy and painting technique enhanced the viewers' affective bond and personal identification with the place.

The emphasis on physical sites also shaped the representation of travelers, who were often deliberately included in both poems and paintings. Some views, such as "Watching Fish at Flower Cove," mention sightseeing activity in the title. Here, Ye depicted a figure boating on the lake in a leisurely manner and directed the viewers' attention to the open surface of the lake. Most of the poetry about this view also used the author's gaze to direct the readers' imaginations to the broader lake and also to the passage of time. The second half of Zhang Ju's ten poems, for example, all begin with the iconic Golden Flood Tower (Yongjinlou), which was on the east side of the lake, near the city gate. References to "gazing at the Golden Flood Tower" or "looking out from the Golden Flood Tower" placed readers in a broader space from which they could imagine looking back at the city or down the lake from a higher point. The experience of sightseeing was enhanced and broadened in these poems.

In addition to the attention given to specific places and the accompanying gazing perspective, the seasonal dimension of the Ten Views merits further discussion, as it offers clues about what to see at particular times. Among the Ten Views in table 6.1, two are about spring and one (each) is about summer, autumn, and winter. A theme commonly seen in Southern Song art is the articulation of seasonal moods.[38] Many Southern Song paintings were devoted to the depiction of seasonal scenery and activities, such as Liu Songnian's *Landscape Painting of the Four Seasons* and Ma Lin's *Clear Summer among the Lotus*. Wu Zimu, in his records of the Ten Views, rearranged the sequence of the ten titles so that they would better correspond with the natural order of seasons and time.[39]

The attention to seasonal features was also widely and consistently seen in other types of literati writings on West Lake. Wu Zimu listed some of these seasonal symbols in *Record of the Millet Dream*, indicating an acute awareness of seasonal change: "In spring, flowers and willows compete in beauty, while lotus and pomegranates bloom in summer. In autumn, the fragrance of cassia floats in the air, and in winter, jade-like plums bloom amidst the whirling flakes of auspicious snow. The scenes of the four seasons are ever changing, and these things that gratify the heart and give pleasure proceed endlessly apace."[40] Zhou Mi in his *Old Affairs of the Martial Grove* also included the scholar Zhang Yuezhai's documentation of favorite things to do in different seasons and on different festivals.[41] Zhang listed several dozen activities for each month, paying attention to seasonal weather, flowers, food, and festivals.

Furthermore, the use of the annual calendar as an organizing structure in Wu Zimu's capital journal also evidenced sensitivity to seasonal changes. This new organizational strategy demonstrated an attempt to categorize and systematize the newly expanding volume of knowledge. The effort to make sense of new experience with the natural landscape conveyed the desire to order the changing world of factual knowledge. The loss of the north created even a greater urgency for the Southern Song to prove its legitimacy, and the rapidly growing commercial sightseeing also created a need to establish order. Literary works and paintings reveal rhetorical and artistic strategies to imbue the state with order, and the sensitivity to changing time was both the motivation for and the product of these strategies.

In addition to sensitivity to seasonal changes, the Ten Views also suggest a fondness for capturing transient moments such as dawn and dusk. Southern Song writers loved to lament the loss of youth (traditionally symbolized by early morning and early spring) and the transient nature of the physical world. These moments were conveyed through events like dusk, sunset, and nightfall, as well as a breeze or gentle rain.[42] It was after the capital moved to Hangzhou that court painters developed a repertoire of artistic techniques that allowed them to archive the fleeting moment. The representation of vicissitudes of the moment was made possible by a sense of historical time: the possibility that things as they are known might change.

It was common for tourists to notice the change that beloved scenery underwent in the space of one season or one day. This tendency echoed

Northern Song artistic theory, as Guo Xi wrote: "Clouds and vapor in a real landscape differ through the four seasons. They are genial in spring, profuse in summer, sparse in autumn and somber in winter. . . . A mountain in the morning has a different appearance than in the evening. Bright and dull days give further mutations. This is called 'the changing aspects of different times do not stay the same,' thus can one mountain combine in itself the significant aspects of several thousand mountains."[43] From dawn to dusk, the passing of time enabled sightseers to perceive the concurrent changes in light, shadow, mist, and wind. The same pagoda appeared more vivid against a sunset, especially when sightseers were at the same time saying goodbye to the lake on their way back home. The ten titles advertised the greatest touring and gazing experiences by pointing out the best time for enjoying each site. For example, Qu Winery was always blessed with the smell of wine floating in the wind, but it was at its best when accompanied by the smell of lotus flowers in the summer. Moreover, time not only functioned as the most important coordinate in a person's memory, but also endowed the Ten Views with universal meanings. Viewers responded in similar ways to watching the sunset or seeing the reflection of the moon on water. These shared reactions made it easier for those who had never been to the lake to imagine themselves standing on its shore.

The emergence of sensitivity to the seasons and the conscious emphasis on geographical knowledge during the same period were not coincidental. Both were products of the growing proclivity to experience and interact with the natural environment. Time and place functioned as coordinates that were used to interpret nature and interaction with nature. Time and place also offered a naming convention and a ready-made framework for later tourists and scholars to use in inventing new views of West Lake and other places of interest after the Song dynasty.

THE TEN VIEWS AS A TROPE: DEVELOPMENT AFTER THE SONG

Sightseers after the Southern Song kept appropriating the Ten Views to serve their interests. Post-Song literature and art continually manipulated the conventions established during the Southern Song. This section looks into the later development of the Ten Views in response to commercialization, political desires, and modern techniques. The emergence of similar vista names for places at West Lake and for other scenic sites testified to the influence of the Southern Song naming convention. The evolution of the

Ten Views transformed them into a trope that could be adopted and at the same time also caused them to depart from the real landscape.

THE TEN VIEWS IN LITERATI CIRCLES

Despite a short period of disfavor immediately after the fall of the Southern Song, the Ten Views became a topic for literati painters as well as court painters. This came about as part of a significant development in literati painting during the Yuan dynasty. The sole set of extant album paintings of the Ten Views painted during the Yuan and recorded in the Qing dynasty catalog was the work of Wu Zhen (1280–1354), regarded as one of the four best literati painters of that era.[44] From then on, the Ten Views remained a favorite topic for literati artistic creations.

While the physical appearance of the sites associated with the Ten Views kept changing, the ten titles remained intact. Some sites mentioned in the original titles, such as the Qu Winery, disappeared with the Song court. Li Ding commented in his *A Short History of West Lake* (Xihu xiaoshi): "Of what were previously called the Ten Views, half are no longer identifiable."[45] Sun Cheng'en (1485–1565) also said, "The splendor of West Lake is well known all over the country, but if you are looking for the scenery on which the ten titles were based, you will not find it all."[46] However, these sites continued as subjects for new paintings. For example, the Ming dynasty painter Qi Min, a native of Hangzhou, still used the ten titles in his album paintings and still used poems directly linked to the ten titles to accompany them.[47] The Ten Views continued to direct the way the literati viewed the scenery of West Lake. Yi-Fu Tuan rightly observes that culture can influence how people perceive and see things that don't exist; he calls this "group hallucination."[48] This "hallucination," or more specifically the "nostalgic memory," shaped post-Song annotations of the Ten Views in miscellaneous notes, poems, and album paintings. These representations confirmed the geographical information, proper activities, and cultural values hidden in the ten titles.

Ming literati, trained in both writing and painting skills, were fond of referencing the Ten Views in elegant literary and artistic creations. Writing poems about the Ten Views became a popular literati activity. The protagonist in a late Ming popular story even wrote such a set of poems during his visit to the lake. Although tangential to the plot of the story, the ten poems were included to cater to literati readers and others who would appreciate the poems about famous sites. They contributed an additional element of entertainment and a sense of elegant culture to the story.[49] Another common scholarly practice was to contribute inscriptions for the album paintings of the Ten Views done by friends or to provide illustrations for the poems written by others. This usually led to social gatherings in which the ten unique but linked topics provided literati with an interesting and cultured game. Sun Cheng'en once recorded that his friend Tang Qingzhi showed him paintings of the Ten Views and asked for poems. After Sun wrote a short poem for each view, Tang Chaoyi, another friend, liked one of them so much that he asked someone to copy that painting and requested Sun to inscribe the poems on this copied painting.[50] Similarly, Qing dynasty scholars also wrote a number of poems on the Ten Views, and some continued the literary game of following Zhou Mi's rhymes in writing their ten poems.[51]

Eventually, modern literati visitors to West Lake started to reflect on and question the meaning of the Ten Views. In 1935 the author of *Notes on West Lake* (Xihu biji) commented that the Ten Views were only empty titles and poked fun at the imperial inscriptions on the Ten Views at the lakeshore by proposing his own version of these views, such as "Dancing in the Jinguo Hotel" or "Purchasing Antiques at the Yue Tomb."[52] The satirical tone and the creation of vulgar versions of the Ten Views echoed Lu Xun's criticism. Indeed, as commercial tourism developed, the articulation and representation of the Ten Views, first in commercial wood-block prints and later in modern pictures catering to mass tourism, gave rise to conflicting forces that drew visitors to the inherent cultural memory of West Lake as a place and framed their personal visual experience. Some scholars were more concerned that the Ten Views might restrict the depiction and appreciation of West Lake. At the end of the collection of Ten Views wood-block prints that he compiled, Li Yimeng (1903–1990) noted, "Talking about the Ten Views and imagining the scenery of the past is fine, but actual touring should not follow these Ten Views. It is meaningless for people to think they are still the essence of the lake scenery."[53] Although he valued the historical images of the Ten Views, Li proposed that West Lake images should extend beyond them and include other good sites.

THE TEN VIEWS IN A POLITICAL FRAMEWORK

The growing importance of the Ten Views in political discourse was associated with the fact that gradually they came to be considered by the literati as embodiments of the value of Chinese cultural geography. This continued the Southern Song literary trend of regarding places as carriers of dynastic nostalgia and collective memories. Furthermore, the fall of the Ming and its replacement by the Qing dynasty shocked Chinese literati and affected the way Chinese scholars wrote about the Ten Views. From the eyes of literati, the lake embodied the cultural values and political past. For instance, the poems of Zhang Dai about the Ten Views during the early Qing were a dream-like journey back to the late Ming.[54] These poems closely depicted time changing—not just the changes in a single day or season, but also the long-term historical development connecting the Southern Song and his time.[55] The value accorded by literati to West Lake brought it to the attention of the Manchu rulers.

Qing dynasty emperors, motivated by the desire to reinforce the legitimacy of their rule in China, were crucial patrons for the circulation and standardization of the Ten Views. During his inspection tours to the south, the Kangxi emperor (1654–1722, r. 1661–1722) wrote calligraphy for each of the ten titles, which was later inscribed on steles beside each scene, thus standardizing the Ten Views. *The Gazetteer of West Lake* (Xihu zhi), compiled under the supervision of the local minister Li Wei (1687–1738) during the Yongzheng reign (1722–35), included the Ten Views and other views named in the same fashion, along with detailed geographical and historical information.[56] The introduction to each vista usually began with one sentence on its history during the Song dynasty, then turned to Kangxi's visits to the site and the inscription he left. It confirmed the specific locations and times of the emperor's visits during his tours. For example, Kangxi changed the "Evening Bell" in the title "Evening Bell from Nanping Hill" into "Morning Bell," a change given particular emphasis in the gazetteer.[57] The last and most detailed part of the gazetteer entries focused on occurrences during the Yongzheng reign and primarily on local government accomplishments in repairing and enhancing the scenery. The political discourse of patronizing and ordering the cultural model of nature was as important as the description of the landscape. In addition, the Qianlong emperor (1711–1799, r. 1735–96) contributed at least five series of poems on the Ten Views and added poems to pair with Ye Xiaoyan's album paintings.[58] Such imperial appreciation of the Ten Views conveyed the political message of admiration for Chinese culture and the geography of the Jiangnan region, the cultural center of the Han literati.

The images of the Ten Views in Qing gazetteers provide an instructive contrast with Ming dynasty printed images. Adhering to the ordered landscape of wood-block and topographic representations, these Qing dynasty imperial images presented a controlled view of nature. These images had evident topographic characteristics: the realistic presentation of the natural scenery with sites included on imperial tours clearly labeled (figure 6.2).

FIGURE 6.2. *Spring Dawn at Su Causeway*, 1735. Wood-block print. Reproduced from Fu and Li, *The Gazetteer of West Lake* (Xihu zhi), 3.7–8.

Other imperial paintings followed the same fashion. Both Wang Yuanqi (1642–1715) and Dong Bangda (1699–1769) were asked by the emperor to paint hand scrolls titled *Panoramic Image of West Lake's Ten Views*. Both artists followed Li Song's precedent by starting from Phoenix Hill on the left and ending with Precious Stone Hill on the right. Yet both paintings not only include place names but also use techniques more often seen in wood-block prints. These paintings were created under the patronage of the emperor and clearly for the practical use of emperors. When Emperor Qianlong visited southern China in 1751, he brought Dong's paintings created in the previous year to compare to the real scenery.[59]

THE TEN VIEWS IN THE POPULAR MARKET

Starting in the late Ming, the Ten Views entered the popular market. The places associated with the Ten Views were located by the lakeside and thus were accessible for quick tours. When sightseeing activities around West Lake became popular among ordinary people, who did not have the money or the time to venture deep into the surrounding mountains, the ten scenic spots became top "must-see" attractions. Consequently, the potential audience for visual representations of the Ten Views grew, and publishers responded to this increased demand by creating printed images. The most

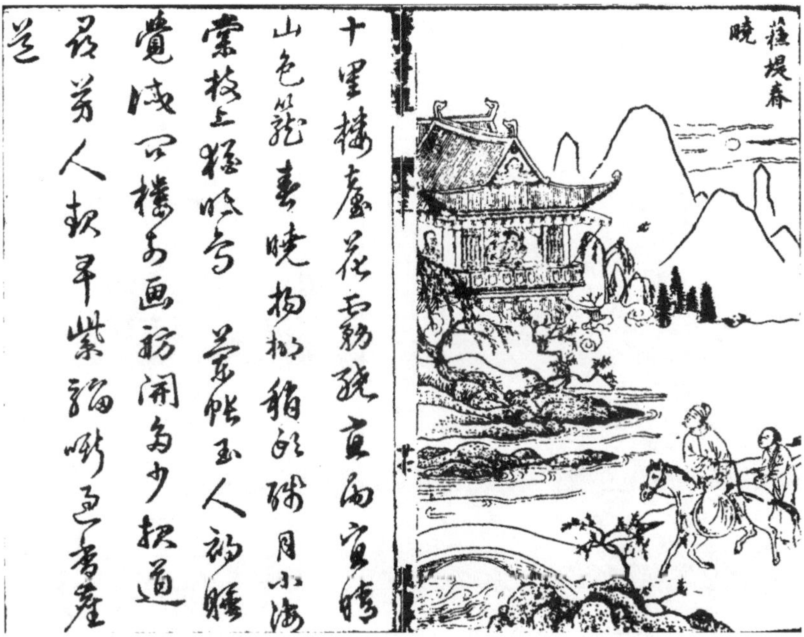

FIGURE 6.3. *Spring Dawn at Su Causeway* with accompanying poem, 1609. Wood-block print. From Yang Erzeng, *Newly Compiled Striking Views within the Seas* (Xinjuan hainei qiguan), 3.407.

famous set was the one included in *Newly Compiled Striking Views within the Seas* (Xinjuan hainei qiguan) by Yang Erzeng (ca. 1612), which became available in 1609 (figure 6.3). This collection was meant to serve as a travel guidebook, promoting the local identity and responding to the fashion of tourism. The tourist souvenir images collected in this book also functioned as post-travel memory and tools for armchair traveling.[60] This set of wood-block prints of West Lake copied and adapted the images from Yu Sichong's 1579 book *Categorized Notes of West Lake Gazetteer* (Xihu zhi leichao) by reducing full-page images to half-page (figure 6.4).[61] Yang's prints also juxtapose images with poems in different calligraphic styles.

Yang's images reflect the influences of both landscape-painting manuals, which offered basic iconic representations of the natural environment, and wood-block drama illustrations, which usually emphasized diagonal tension between figures. Figure 6.3, for instance, vividly depicts the scenery presented in Southern Song poems about "Spring Dawn at Su Causeway," offering a stage for the courtesan and the sightseer and their interaction. These images visualized the literary trope of the Ten Views as established in the Southern Song. In responding to the popular market, these

FIGURE 6.4. *Spring Dawn at Su Causeway*, 1579. Wood-block print. From Yu Sichong, *Categorized Notes of West Lake Gazetteer* (Xihu zhi leichao), 1.

wood-block images also added an element of enjoyable viewing, broadening their appeal to include both elegant and mass-market audiences. Shih Shou-Chien points out that these images especially emphasized the sightseer's viewpoint as a way to document and inspire sightseeing experiences.[62] The incorporation of a female image may also be an effort to appeal to an expanded female readership.[63] The multiple layers of narrative and the flexible imaginary representations drew the viewers' eyes. While following the aesthetic tradition of presenting to viewers both familiar natural scenery and engaging activities, these images also evoked local pride and fulfilled commercial purposes.[64]

Moreover, with a combination of poems, paintings, and calligraphy, this set of printed images catered to the literati taste for interchangeability of poems and paintings, as well as wealthy people's desire to consume high culture in one entity. The images were not as elegant as the Southern Song paintings or as informative as the Qing dynasty gazetteer maps, and infamous literati contributed to the poems, unlike the prestigious writers of the Song. Instead, this set of images popularized the literati trope of the Ten Views and packaged elite taste in a tourist brochure aimed at providing information for those who wanted to travel. During this commercialization,

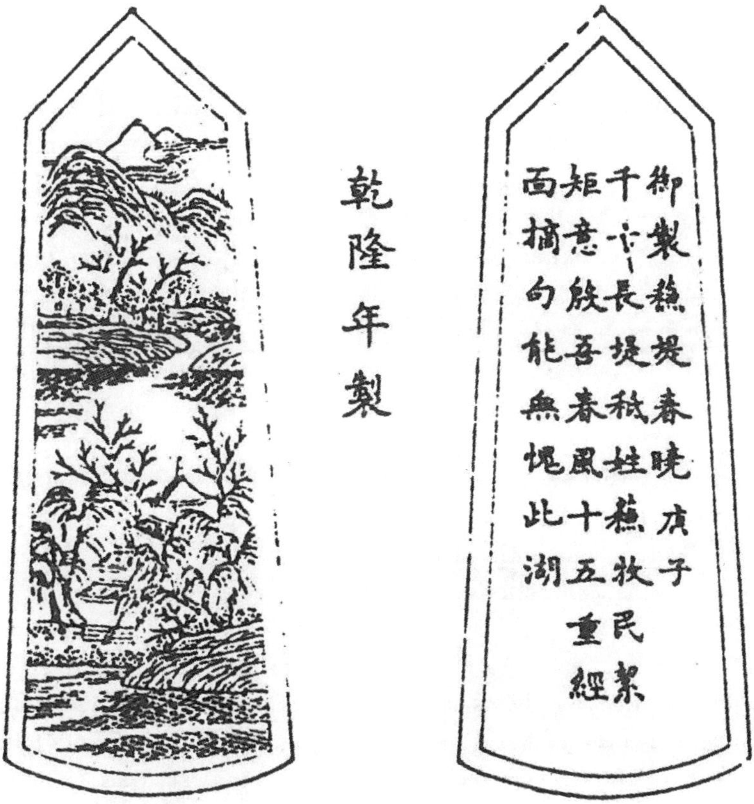

FIGURE 6.5. Drawing of an ink stick carved with an illustration of *Spring Dawn at Su Causeway*, with accompanying poem by Emperor Qianlong. Wood-block print. Artist unknown. From the collection "Ink-sticks of the Paintings of and Poems about Places of Interest at West Lake Made by the Emperor" (Yuzhi Xihu mingsheng tushi mo). From Wang Jinsheng, *Wangshi jianguzhai mosou*, 1a.

the Ten Views as a trope recommended a universal and sometimes formulaic experience. Consumers of these books and images saw them as embodiments of elite culture, as suggestions for sightseeing, and as a particular way of seeing and processing.

Further commercialization of the Ten Views occurred during the eighteenth century. The theme of West Lake expanded beyond the traditional mediums of art or poetry and entered material culture, appearing on articles such as ink sticks (figure 6.5) and embroidered works.[65] The adoption of the Ten Views as a theme for everyday objects revealed the wide circulation of this trope as a commercial profit-making method. The serialization of the Ten Views, which was evident in Southern Song album paintings, became a retail strategy to sell a collection of objects at once. Consumers bought this type of product as a way of accumulating cultural capital and participating in the literary traditions. The images of the Ten Views on these material objects became more formulaic. They either copied the graphics features in earlier paintings or were painted so as to directly translate the ten titles. For example, the scene in figures 6.5 is a simplistic image that makes extensive use of standardized components: willow trees, the landmarks mentioned in the relevant title (Su Causeway), and a stock landscape composition. It is not easy to identify the theme of the scene depicted without knowing that this is one of the Ten Views. Over time, the ten titles themselves became the foci, and sometimes even the only reference, for artistic creation. Drawing on well-circulated visual and textual materials, people could depict what was not available in real scenery but was epitomized in the culture. Ironically then, while these ten titles were invented in response to an affective bond with the natural environment, they also gradually placed personal connections with nature in jeopardy.

In modern times, the introduction of photography added new representations of the Ten Views. Photo albums from the early twentieth century used the ten titles for photos of specific locales and scenes. The adoption of photography facilitates armchair traveling and further contributes to the tourist gaze through photos circulated as commodities.[66] Thus, photography both spreads the popular gaze and provides a means for individuals to capture their own gazes, which empowers tourists. The Ten Views continue to provide a popular theme for photographers, even if more than half of the original landmarks in the titles are long gone.

As the Ten Views acquired a larger audience in the popular market, there have been attempts at reconstruction involving the rebuilding of relevant sites, the addition of signposts to explain each view, and, inevitably, the sale of a variety of souvenirs. This type of proposal appeared early in the twentieth century. Architectural historian Chen Congzhou (1918–2000), for instance, suggested adding lotus flowers to the lake so people could identify the "Lotus Breeze at Qu Winery" view.[67] Lu Xun very likely would have been disappointed to learn that the Leifeng Pagoda was rebuilt in 2002, complete with an elevator, as a way to re-create the Southern Song Ten Views and attract more tourists (figure 6.6). Modern visitors, arriving almost eight hundred years after the first appearance of the Ten Views, can still find these places and images of them on tourist maps, encounter them while walking around West Lake, capture the view of the Leifeng Pagoda against the sunset

FIGURE 6.6. Leifeng Pagoda, rebuilt in 2002. Photograph by Ricardo Mertsch, 2012. From Wikimedia Commons.

with their cameras, and purchase a group of ten postcards—each depicting one view like a modern ten-leaf album. The technology of producing mass images has preserved the Ten Views in a modern context and continues to shape the contemporary way of approaching the lake.

NEW VIEWS INSPIRED BY THE TEN VIEWS

The Ten Views also became a cultural allusion that inspired new titles and encouraged the active discovery of local scenery. During the Yuan dynasty, the Ten Views inspired the emergence of the so-called Ten Views of Qiantang partly as a response to geopolitical change involving Hangzhou.[68] No longer the national capital, Hangzhou (and West Lake) was included in the county of Qiantang, and local scholars started to pay more attention to Qiantang as an entity. The Ten Views of Qiantang clearly followed the model of the Ten Views of West Lake, evoking both place and time. Three of the ten new scenes, "West Lake Night Moon," "Misty Willows on Six Bridges," and "Double Peaks in White Clouds," stem from "Autumn Moon above the Placid Lake," "Spring Dawn at Su Causeway," and "Twin Peaks Piercing the Clouds," respectively. The other seven new scenes all include specific locations, such as Nine-*li* Pine, Cold Spring, Ge Hill, Solitary Mountain, and Zhe River. Most of the places in the Qiantang Ten Views were noted on the Southern Song map of West Lake. Meanwhile, the specific times (dawn and night) and the four seasons emphasized in the original Ten Views of West Lake remained in the Qiantang Ten Views. The formation of the new ten views demonstrates both the continuation of naming conventions and a conscious effort to create something different for the new political environment.

Ming scholars were fond of editing the titles of the Ten Views or coming up with new titles following the same naming convention. This adoption and playful use of the Ten Views paved the way for twisting and personalizing the ten titles. In *Eight Treatises on the Nurturing of Life* (Zunsheng bajian), Gao Lian (1573–1620) incorporated the Ten Views of West Lake into his suggestions for elegant seasonal activities. He also changed the title of "Remnant Snow on Broken Bridge" to "Treading on Snow on Broken Bridge," showing his fondness for actually walking in the snow rather than just viewing the snow scene.[69] Li Liufang, in his *Inscriptions on Armchair Travel Paintings of West Lake* (Xihu woyoutu tiba), included twenty colophons for album paintings. Each of them captures one scene, and some of them stemmed from yet were slightly different from the ten titles, such as "Watching Spring at Broken Bridge," "Dawn at Leifeng Pagoda," "Picking Water Grass at the Three Pagodas," and "Disappearing Fog at the Western Peaks."[70] This literary convention of combining specific locales with seasonal scenery and human activities was carried on from the original version of the Ten Views. Li strove to personalize his experience of the landscape, which came from his extended stay at and frequent travels around the lake. This practice of naming new sites in the same style as the Ten Views was also followed by Qing literati. For example, all of the one hundred titles in the Qing dynasty *One Hundred Poems of West Lake* (Xihu baiyong) by Zheng Yuejing take the form of four-character poems. The court-sponsored gazetteers also included more four-character scene-capturing titles.[71]

The practice of coming up with new views of West Lake has become a stimulus for promoting cultural life in contemporary Hangzhou. The local government has organized citizens to vote for several new versions of the Ten Views, as a strategy to promote local tourism and enrich mass culture. It is not very different from the creation of new titles by the Ming literati and the Qing court—all are strategies to order and claim ownership of nature. Most of the new Ten Views continue the Southern Song convention of combining place and time, such as "Osmanthus Rain at the Manlong Valley." Despite their origins in a mass popularity vote, the new version of the Ten Views cannot be compared to the original version in either its influence on tourist discourses or its artistic merit. Nevertheless, the continuing production of these numbered sets of views indicates that the Ten Views as a trope still endures as a particular manner of describing the landscape and registering new tourist attractions. It encourages corresponding acts of viewing and continues to enhance popular attachment to specific locations around West Lake.

Beginning in the Southern Song period, the convention of using ten views to present local scenery became a national practice that served both to reinforce local pride and to help any visitor to feel more familiar with the landscape. Meanwhile, the Ten Views also promoted competition among different places. Its applicability in different places and the potential for diverse artistic inventions allowed people to create new views. Eventually, local gazetteers for almost every county in China included a section devoted to places of interest. This practice even spread to Japan and Korea. For example, the Eight Views of the Xiao and Xiang Rivers and the Ten Views of West Lake together influenced the Eight Views of Ōmi in Japan.[72]

Many of the new views emerged and circulated as a result of local pride and imperial patronage. For example, the Ming court placed special emphasis on promoting views of Beijing to emphasize the cultural significance of the new capital. It started as the Eight Views of Yanjing (today's Beijing), and Wang Fu (1362–1416) did paintings about these views.[73] Later during the Xuande reign (1426–35), two other titles were added to raise the number of views to ten, and at the request of the emperor, Li Dongyang (1447–1516) wrote ten accompanying poems.[74] Wang's painting was later added to the Qing dynasty imperial collection, and in 1751 Emperor Qianlong standardized the eight titles. These views, including titles such as "Autumn Wind at Taiye Lake" and "Sunset at the Golden Terrace," encompass different seasons and all are associated with specific locations.

Poetry and paintings continued to give rise to and promote a set number of views, fueling the elaboration of local pride. For example, during the Ming and Qing dynasties, the Guanzhong plain had eight famous views, all following a similar naming convention. Some views clearly derived from the Ten Views of West Lake, such as "Morning Bell of the Goose Pagoda" and "Sunset at Mountain Li." In 1680 the local official Zhu Jiyi wrote poems and created paintings for each of these eight views. His paintings and poems were engraved on stone steles, which are now in the Stele Forest in Xi'an, a city on the Guanzhong plain. Almost all the eight images centered on the depiction of the signpost relevant to each title, such as the Ba Bridge (Baqiao) and the Grass Hall (Caotang).

As other local patrons indiscriminately adopted the Ten Views model, most of the post-Song views became more formulaic. They usually include images of sunsets, snow, morning scenes, and certain types of trees; different locations such as hills and rivers were also added to the titles for the purpose of localization. Although some of these were initially rooted in real scenery and might well have carried cultural allusions, people who were not locals would never have heard of these places and would also have found the depiction of seasonal scenery clichéd. The lack of both creative invention and circulation of poems and paintings about these views also made them unfamiliar and insignificant to outsiders. Therefore, the gap between real experiences and the stereotyped names grew. Consequently, the Qing dynasty literatus Zha Qichang (1713–1761) observed that local people routinely designated a requisite number of stereotyped titles, even in the gazetteers of remote areas. Commenting on the excessive use of eight or ten views, Zha complained, "This is really a bad habit."[75] His concern was later echoed in Lu Xun's withering criticism of the "ten views syndrome."

CONCLUSION: THE NAMING CONVENTION

The cultural trope of the Ten Views was produced, reproduced, and circulated in multiple mediums by numerous actors. In this culture-building process, the interplay and tension between text and image became pervasive, and neither texts nor pictures alone dominated people's interpretations of the lake. Rather, words and images merged in their influences on the viewers and upon each other to capture ephemeral moments and to associate them indelibly with this cultural landmark. Given the wide circulation of poems about and images of West Lake, even those who failed to pay a physical visit could enjoy a virtual experience of it. In this way, everyone could share a unifying set of memories with individual and even nostalgic resonance for anyone who contemplated this showplace of the new capital during the Southern Song.

The Ten Views of West Lake as a sightseeing discourse inspired people's enthusiasm for travel, and the development of this naming convention reveals the significant role of mobility in history. The invention and circulation of the Ten Views encompass the mobile perspective in imagined or real traveling; the representation of these views in various mediums and especially on the commercial market was a response to different types and growing numbers of tourists; the emergence of additional views centering on West Lake evidences expanding travel into the landscape; the appropriation of this naming convention by other locations represents the movement of information. This naming convention was and continues to be intricately associated with traveling, gazing, and the circulation of information.

The wide spread of the Ten Views as a trope represented a unifying force in Chinese culture: the integration of emotional aesthetic appreciation and real experiences with nature. The combination of these two ways of recognizing nature derived from sensitivity to changing time and the stable identity of place. Moreover, this trope served as a literary vehicle for artistic creations centering on cultural geography and also as a popular discourse open to all and available for appropriation by different people for different purposes. It also illustrated how people narrated their local histories and conversed with visitors. As a result, the Ten Views model that started at Southern Song West Lake gradually became an enduring feature of Chinese culture that was shared by different places and by people with diverse identities.

EPILOGUE

TODAY, WEST LAKE IS ONE OF THE MOST POPULAR DESTINATIONS in China, attracting both domestic and foreign visitors. The moment they arrive in Hangzhou, tourists are welcomed by posters, advertisements, and travel agents promoting the lake, whose scenery still somewhat resembles that in the traditional paintings. The lakefront and all the causeways are still adorned with peach trees and willows, as described in the Southern Song gazetteers. The lake is surrounded by inns, restaurants, shops, and museums. Food with local and seasonal features, or historical significance, is available nearly everywhere. Boats take tourists across the lake, stopping by the Lake Heart Island (Huxindao). Games, performers, and craftspeople with their creations are crowded around the lake and overflowing the small municipal parks and public squares. Walking around the lake, visitors are greeted by statues of historical figures and plaques detailing the histories of specific sites; they also find coin-making machines that allow them to create souvenir coins with depictions of the Ten Views. The rich scenery also extends to the surrounding mountains, where visitors can hike, visit temples, and purchase good tea.

In many respects, tourism around West Lake still echoes the features of sightseeing associated with the Southern Song. The lake remains a "leisure zone" for the people of Hangzhou. Temples that became famous during the Southern Song continue to be the most visited sites on today's tourist map. Nearly all the tourists—whether they are Buddhists or not—pay a visit to the Tianzhu and Soul's Retreat Monasteries. Just as in the Southern Song, the lake inspires artists and writers. The life of West Lake has been and continues to be closely related to the fate of Hangzhou. Since the Song dynasty, the expansion of the city has motivated urban residents to embrace the natural environment outside the city wall, and nowadays the development of the surrounding small towns has made West Lake a link between the city of Hangzhou and its hinterlands.[1] The city boundary, which loosened during the Song, continued to blur and even to disappear. As early as the Qing dynasty, the government kept the city gates entirely open during festivals, thus allowing merchants to triple their profits in one night.[2] The modern city limits have already expanded west beyond the lake.

Yet much has changed dramatically in the seven centuries that separate us from the Song. The imperial house that once dominated the sightseeing activities during the Southern Song no longer exists. The lake has shrunken considerably since the Song due to the lack of maintenance and no longer provides drinking water. Over the centuries, West Lake has been transformed from a natural landscape that inspired the production of knowledge into a human-made lake that embodies idealized nature and cultural memories—one could even call it a *bonsai*.[3] Physical change in the lake was one factor that contributed to this process, and the ongoing cultural construction and interpretation was another factor.

During the Southern Song, the lake was a stage for imperial rituals; it also provided a backdrop for a collection of shops and mazes of crooked alleys; it was a platform for great officials and rich merchants, as well as an ideal place for lay believers and illicit lovers; it was deeply influenced by the urban economy and culture of Hangzhou, and yet it was also a natural landscape. It witnessed the emergence of a new understanding in the system of producing knowledge and a new cultural trope of naming nature. However, West Lake in the Southern Song was far from the idealized perfection portrayed in some documents. The lake began to arouse criticism, with literati blaming its beautiful scenery for bewitching the imperial court and officials, sapping their willingness to retake the north by force. A famous poem by Lin Sheng (ca. 1174–1189) on the walls inside an inn at the lake implies as much:

> Mountains after green mountains and towers beyond towers,
> When is the singing and dancing on West Lake to end?
> The warm breeze intoxicates sightseers,
> They easily mistake Hangzhou for Bianzhou [the Northern Song
> capital Kaifeng].[4]

The amusements offered at West Lake and the scenery around its shores were thus deemed responsible for distracting sightseers.

The sharp contrast between the pleasures of West Lake and the sad memory of losing north China led many literati to project blame onto the lake during the Yuan dynasty. Southern Song writers who lived into the Yuan dynasty, such as Liu Yiqing, the author of *Anecdotes of Qiantang*

(Qiantang yishi), seemed to believe that the Southern Song had been in a process of deterioration from the outset.[5] Liu Yiqing attributed the loss of the dynasty mainly to the ineptitude of officials such as Jia Sidao and emperors like Lizong, who wasted time at West Lake. "How could the world not go wrong?" Liu asked.[6] Additionally, things that were praised during the Southern Song, such as Emperor Gaozong's literary efforts while on an excursion to the lake, became targets of criticism during the Yuan dynasty. The story of Emperor Gaozong commenting on a scholar's poem on the wall of a lakeside inn, discussed in chapter 1, was reinterpreted in a totally different way by Fang Hui, who used it to lament the loss of the country to the Mongols:

> "Wind through the Pines" was chanted by tens of thousands of people,
> But now it has turned out to be remnant regrets that were deposited on
> the misty lake . . .
> After war ends, an old horse sleeps on the vacant causeway;
> With banquets now rare, empty boats are moored in the lonely harbor.[7]

This poem, which points out ironic aspects of the poem "Wind through the Pines" and laments the demise of the dynasty, suggests a connection between the emperor's indulgence in sightseeing and dynastic decline. Although their own experiences with leisurely excursions encouraged the literati to remember the lake with fondness, they were also irritated by the extravagant sightseeing trips of the imperial family and important officials, especially those who had given up trying to recover lost territory.

The lack of government support, in addition to the critical attitude toward West Lake, contributed to the lake's decline under the Yuan dynasty. The Mongol rulers placed their political and economic emphasis on northern China, and Hangzhou was decimated and no longer received the attention it did in the Southern Song. West Lake was ignored by the government, and its surface gradually became clogged with weed-like water chestnuts.

Despite the lack of attention from literati during this period, the lake's reputation began to spread across the Eurasian continent. This was partly due to the expanded territory of the Mongol Empire. Marco Polo was among the first to introduce Hangzhou and West Lake to Europeans, who were very impressed by the well-developed urban culture and sightseeing facilities.[8] Abraham Cresques, probably the best mapmaker of the fourteenth century, patronized by Peter of Aragon, created the *Catalan Atlas* in 1375.[9] This detailed Eurasian map incorporated information from Marco Polo's records. Hangzhou was depicted on the map as a castle and identified as

FIGURE E.1. Detail of Hangzhou and West Lake in *Catalan Atlas*, 1375. Abraham Cresques. Hand-colored engraving on paper, 20.5 × 26 in. Bibliothèque Nationale de France, Paris.

"Quinsay," the term used in Marco Polo's account and probably a Latinized transliteration of the term *xingzai* (exile location). Cresques also drew a pond of water on the edge of the castle, indicating the inclusion of West Lake in the Western imagination (figure E.1).

It was not until the middle of the Ming dynasty that officials attempted to restore the lake, by which point it had already dried up several times.[10] A dredging project that took place in 1508, overseen by the determined local governor Yang Mengying, was the most significant. The chief obstacle he faced was again the diked paddies planted by the local gentry.[11] The conflict between the economic aspirations of powerful local families and the ecological concerns of the municipal government persisted after the Southern Song. Eventually, his project enhanced the charm of the scenery by adding another dike and a human-made island in the middle of the lake. Yang later compiled *The Record of Dredging and Restoring West Lake* (Junfu Xihu lu), which included all relevant memorials and eight illustrations that indicated the geographic relationship between the lake and urban construction. In the preface, Yang claimed that the purpose of this particular dredging project was to "restore the previous scenery."[12] He also built the Four Worthies Hall (Sixiantang) to memorialize Li Bi, Su Shi, Bai Juyi, and Lin Bu. Consequently, Tian Rucheng listed Yang, along with Bai Juyi and Su Shi, as the three figures who made the biggest contributions to the lake.[13]

As the lake scenery was restored in the Ming, the literati began to regain an interest in recording the history of West Lake. The late Ming witnessed the burgeoning of tourism involving literati and ordinary people alike. Travel writings and guidebooks circulated on an unprecedented scale. Scholars consider this boom in sightseeing a new stage of leisure life and a fashion rooted in urban culture.[14] Unlike the imperial-centered, capital city–driven sightseeing during the Southern Song, the expansion of excursions during the late Ming was fueled by Hangzhou's development as a cultural center for the Jiangnan region and a national silk production center. At that time, scholars who lived or sojourned there were usually from local gentry families and seldom served in the government. The development of transportation and the growing wealth accumulated by gentry families allowed these literati to go sightseeing more frequently. They also needed these sightseeing gatherings to maintain their cultural circles. Writing and publishing what they saw and experienced was an important form of self-expression and social communication. The increasing number of readers also motivated the recording of sightseeing activities at famous destinations.

During the Ming dynasty, a more coherent approach to documenting the lake emerged. Tian Rucheng contributed two encyclopedic works about the lake and devoted special attention to the history of excursions. In addition to these two large volumes, other literati also produced numerous historical and literary works, such as Li Ding's *A Short History of West Lake* and Zhang Dai's *Searching for West Lake in Dreams* (Xihu mengxun). These texts recorded details of physical geography, cultural traditions related to the lake, and the authors' own sightseeing experiences. These records usually emphasized the sites and sightseeing routes formed during the Song dynasty. Zhang Dai, for example, organized his book by different famous sites and used the names of different sightseeing routes as titles for all the chapters. In documenting these sites, historical figures and especially anecdotes from the Southern Song were always the foci. These Ming literati also emphasized their personal sightseeing experiences. Zhang Dai described in detail the lake scenery after snow and his visit to the Lake Heart Pavilion.[15] His conversation with another sightseer in the pavilion added a personal touch to the scenery. Unlike the Song authors of the capital journals, these Ming literati were not only observers of but also participants in the sightseeing activities they described. Their connection with the landscape was more interactive.

During the late Ming, the rapid development of popularized excursions by ordinary people aroused new concern among the literati. Already in the Southern Song, scholars had promoted their cultural superiority through their appreciation of quiet lake scenery. For example, Song dynasty literatus Wang Shen (1155–1227) compared his own sightseeing with that of others in his poems. Wang usually chose to visit the lake at night to avoid noisy tourists. He wrote,

> Why do the bells hurry the dawn?
> I am afraid visitors will come one after another.
> After the worldly people go back,
> I will go boating alone and play on the jade flute. . . .
> People in the capital are all dreaming,
> So, I can have this bright moon sky of West Lake for myself.[16]

His poem conveys a subtle devaluation of others' sightseeing and indicates his tendency to distinguish himself by claiming the superiority of his taste. Among literati in the Ming dynasty, this tradition continued, became more widespread, and developed further, with increasing emphasis on sightseeing at specific times.

Ming literati attempted to set up aesthetic standards to distinguish themselves from other tourists. These attempts were motivated by status anxiety, a notion brought up by art historian Craig Clunas in his discussion of the late Ming art market.[17] Many of the Ming scholars were frustrated with the difficulty of passing the civil service examination and the rising status of merchants. As a result, the culture of taste emerged. Literati proclaimed that true appreciation of West Lake's natural beauty demanded a visit at the right time, usually evening, dusk, or snowy days, when the scenery was not disrupted by a noisy crowd. Zhang Dai, for instance, emphasized this in his account of sightseeing at West Lake on the fifteenth day of the seventh lunar month. Zhang divided travelers into the five categories of wealthy families, officials, famous monks, ordinary people, and literati.[18] He criticized those in the first four categories for not really watching the moon. Zhang placed himself and his friends outside the five categories. He said that only after ordinary travelers had left, when West Lake became quiet again, would he and his friends come out to enjoy the quiet moonlight. His criticism of vulgar tourists was linked to his desire to highlight the superiority of his own sightseeing style.

West Lake acquired political functions in imperial discourse during the Qing dynasty, especially in the early and high Qing. The visual images of West Lake experienced a revival as a result of active imperial patronage.[19] With a banner army stationed to guard the coastline, Hangzhou had military and political significance for the Qing court. The Jiangnan region, as the cultural center for the Han elite, also played an important role in the Qing court's efforts to legitimize itself. Both Kangxi and Qianlong conducted several inspection tours to the lower Yangzi region and stopped by West Lake nearly every time.[20] They both showed special interest in the West Lake scenery and even replicated the Su Causeway in Beijing's Summer Palace with the well-known six bridges. As a result of imperial interest, the Qing government compiled and published several informative gazetteers concerning West Lake, such as *The Gazetteer of West Lake* in 1731 and *West Lake Gazetteer Compilation* (Xihu zhizuan) in 1751. The compilation of the gazetteers reflected the intentional efforts of the imperial house and the local government to demonstrate their appreciation of Han culture. Through publicly demonstrated and documented patronage, the Manchu government claimed its ownership of the landscape and incorporated the Han culture into the new regime. The motivation was not much different from the emperors' learning of the Chinese language and the opening of a special civil service examination for the Han literati.[21]

Local elites also left numerous records about West Lake during the late Qing. A large number of miscellanies that focused on Hangzhou were included in the twelve-volume *General Compilation of Historical Sources on Hangzhou* (Wulin zhanggu congbian) at the end of the nineteenth century. This source is an example of the Qing dynasty intellectual trend of organizing historical sources and compiling collections of historical notes, and it also testifies to the growing local pride.[22]

During the Republican period (1912–49), Hangzhou was reconstructed to promote the development of a modern tourist industry. This was partly due to the emergence of Shanghai as the new economic center of the lower Yangzi delta; Hangzhou was reshaped as a cultural and tourist center to attract visitors from that city.[23] More guidebooks were published geared toward the needs of those who came only or mainly for tourist purposes. Among these books were *Revised and Enlarged Guide for Touring West Lake* (Zengding Xihu youlan zhinan) by Xu Ke (1869–1928) and *Firsthand Tourist Guide to Hangzhou* (Shidi buxing Hangzhou Xihu youlan zhinan) by Lu Feizhi (b. 1892), published in 1929.

Lu Feizhi's book, a good example of these publications, was driven by a demand similar to the one that gave birth to the "guide" during the Southern Song; it also provided a ready-to-use travel plan that was widely available to a much larger number of visitors. It begins with information on famous sites, organized into sections and sightseeing routes. Many of these sites were historical, and the information he presented followed the gazetteer style. Lu then devoted special attention to places of interest, followed by different seasonal scenery and festivals. The last part of Lu's book introduced a new feature: travel itineraries he had designed. These varied in length, ranging from half a day to fifteen days. He organized the itineraries into four categories according to the means of transportation used: walking, and then touring by boat, bus, or car. This design catered to the differing needs of visitors and the choices offered by a modernizing transportation infrastructure. The book was the result of Lu's twofold motivation. His first motivation was to provide a handy guide for the growing numbers of Chinese and foreign visitors, especially "old, young, and female" sightseers, taking advantage of the convenient transportation from Shanghai. In presenting this first motivation, Lu compared West Lake, which he called "China's big park," to Europe's Sweden.[24] Lu's second motivation was to correct what he found to be the inaccuracies of most other guidebooks. He mentioned his own accumulation of extensive records derived from frequent touring around the lake. This motivation was a continuation of Dong Sigao's pursuit of authenticity and emphasis on knowledge of local geography.

After the establishment of the People's Republic of China in 1949, the government provided further funding to develop local tourism and more tourist books were published. A 1950 dredging project at West Lake, the first major dredging effort since the high Qing period, was inspired by Mao's "man can conquer nature" concept. This project failed to achieve its original goal of adding the capacity of the lake and was also unsuccessful in terms of environmental protection.[25] Since then, however, West Lake has been incorporated into the administrative agenda of the local government and has continued to play a significant role in the urban life of Hangzhou. Today's Zhejiang provincial and Hangzhou municipal governments strive to maintain the natural scenery and enhance the cultural memories of West

Lake, in order to stimulate the tourist industry. Numerous historical sites have been excavated, repaired, and noted on tourist brochures.

With the rapid development of modern tourism, contemporary discussion also includes the damage that tourism does to nature. West Lake during the Song dynasty presents both the origin of today's conflicts between tourism and environmental protection and the hope for a possible balance between tourist-oriented development and ecological preservation. The lake's sustainability, however, can be the focal point of a prosperous sightseeing industry, involving the power of religious beliefs and landscape aesthetics in preserving the environment. History can inform the contemporary discussion about the environmental impact of sightseeing and tourism more generally.

Meanwhile, the constant emphasis on cultural conventions and historical memories made and continues to make West Lake a unique "place" that is also potentially "placeless"—a locale characterized by the homogenization of experience and the loss of uniqueness in identity.[26] Through the site-making process, sightseeing evoked identity and ownership, created cultural conventions, and repainted the relations between city and nature. These results generated a sense of place that fashioned the uniqueness of West Lake in Chinese culture. On the other hand, as sightseeing has become more commercialized since the late Ming, popular products with West Lake motifs, such as ink sticks, guidebooks, and postcards, have become more formulaic. Tourists could come to West Lake clouded by previous excursions that were encapsulated in historical documents or dazzled by universal commercial experiences. This process jeopardized the lake's uniqueness and the personal experience related to it.

Moreover, the writings about and paintings of West Lake that made it a unique cultural landmark marginalized the population that was essential to the lake's development. This included the laborers who dredged the lake and the merchants, artisans, and peasant families who lived and made a living outside the city. Therefore, through history West Lake as a place was simultaneously constructed and diluted. The relationship between place and placelessness was not dichotomized, but had already been hybridized as early as the premodern period. Place and placelessness are often created at the same time, through the same process, and even contribute to each other. It is this interdependence, not the perfect vision of West Lake, that makes it a place eminently worthy of discussion.

In the twenty-first century, West Lake was discovered as a global tourist destination, and the lake was reinvented and redefined as both an international and a national symbol of "Chineseness," as seen from the successful campaign to have the lake named a UNESCO World Heritage Site. The West Lake Museum was established in 2005 on the lakeshore and later became a cultural component in the UNESCO application.[27] It now has a library open to the public, which specializes in resources related to West Lake, with a research institute next to it. In 2016 the museum published a virtual-reality tour of West Lake on its WeChat account (a popular form of social media in China based on smartphones), showing and explaining the history of significant places around the lake—yet another incarnation of the kind of tourist paraphernalia produced in the Southern Song.[28] West Lake and its history have been incorporated into the building of Chinese culture and the Chinese nation-state. This place-making process is one ongoing theme that ties together eight hundred years of multifaceted attention to the lake.

APPENDIX

The two stories translated here are discussed in chapter 3.

1. THE WEST LAKE ADMINISTRATIVE ASSISTANT

Commandant Di, the third general in the Right Army of the Metropolitan Infantry Command, arranged for soldiers from all stockades to enter the city to receive their salaries on the sixth day of the second lunar month in 1192. Once they arrived at the Qianhu Gate, Di sat on a chair to wait for the city gate to open. When he felt something hard touching his feet, [he] took a candle to look down and saw a huge crab over three feet long, ugly and strange looking.

Di asked the attendant soldiers to catch it, tie it up, and take it to his home. He then sat down again and dozed off. He dreamed about an odd, ugly-looking person with a long beard who wore the green robe of an official, a soft turban, black boots, and a leather belt. Holding his tablet of authority, the person bowed and said, "I am the Administrative Assistant of West Lake, who was caught and tortured by you for coming out to play on the green field. I am worried that I will suffer in a boiling pot. Please, send a messenger back to your home, and ask them to spare my life. I will repay you generously. If I cannot escape from this disaster, although my petty life itself is worth nothing, I am afraid this could bring bad luck to your family—and that won't be a small thing."

When Di awoke, the city gate was open, and the army entered the city in ranks. Di had no time to ask anyone [to act as a messenger]. After completing his duties, he rode home, but his children had already cooked and eaten the crab, and all were surprised by the delicious taste. Only Di's wife had not touched the food. Di told her the dream and stopped her from eating. Not long after, all five children died from disease, one by one, and only Di and his wife survived.

2. SPIRITUAL TRAVEL AROUND WEST LAKE

Chen Wu, a peasant from Xinjin County in Leping, was hired to work on the Zhai family's farmlands. During his free time, he was also employed by others to carry luggage when they traveled to distant places. In the spring of the fourth year of Shaoxing [1134], he died at home from disease, but his body remained warm, so the family was not willing to bury him.

After three days, Chen suddenly woke up and said, "As I began to die, I felt my spirit leaving from my forehead. I saw my body lying on the bed, and my wife and children were crying. I called to them, but no one responded. There came a deity, referring to himself as 'general,' and he took me to other sick peoples' homes, and we enjoyed the food and wine those families offered. After he became drunk, he called me forward, saying, 'I hear that the scenery in West Lake is magnificent, but I regret that I have never been there. Now, since I have the chance to travel and inspect things, I want to go sightseeing around the lake. I would like you to be my guide. Once I have seen the lake, I will send you back.'

"He then asked his guards to put me in a cloth bag and carry me on the road. Along the way to Lin'an, every time he encountered families with offerings, he would hang the bag in which I was concealed under the eaves and warn me not to breathe. He gathered all the food and took it away hurriedly, without stopping for too long; he would then go on to the next household. We stopped at over ten places in a day. In the evening, the deity entered a temple and distributed wine and food among his followers, and they all returned to their altar positions and ate.

"After five days like this, we arrived in Lin'an and went sightseeing on the lake. The Tianzhu and Soul's Retreat Monasteries, the market, and the gardens—we visited them all one by one, except that the deity dared not enter the Daoist temples.

"Traveling along the coastline, we arrived in Fujian and then returned to Jianchang and Fuzhou in Jiangxi, resting at Zha's family home in Baigan. We hadn't sat for too long before a messenger came to say, 'Leave quickly, leave quickly.' Soon, a sharp crash of thunder shocked heaven and earth. A Daoist master appeared, wearing a star hat, carrying a sword, and holding water to recite an incantation. He kept reciting until fire consumed the house. All the guards grabbed the general and hurried him away, stepping on each other the whole way. I was still in the cloth bag and suddenly fell to the ground. After I woke up, I found myself here." Chen Wu then returned to life.

On this day, Kang Yizhong from Luoyang visited Zhai's family and witnessed this occurrence. Around late fall, Kang and Zhai went to Mount Song, and, as they passed Baigan, they paid a visit to Zha's family. The family told them, "The entire family fell ill during the epidemic this spring and recovered after the Daoist master performed the Five Thunders exorcism." This was in accordance with what Chen Wu said.

NOTES

Introduction

1 Lin'an was only a de facto capital for the Southern Song dynasty. It was never officially established as the capital, although in 1138 it was designated as the *xingzai*, or "exile location."

2 The term "Middle Period China" was first used by Patricia Ebrey and Peter Bol in 2014 at the first Middle Period Humanities Conference. It covers the years 800–1400 CE and includes the second half of the Tang dynasty (618–907) and the Liao (907–1123), Jin (1115–1234), Xi Xia (1038–1227), Song (960–1279), and Yuan (1215–1368) periods. The advantage of this label is that "it is broader than a dynasty or century, is less Eurocentric than 'medieval,' and does not carry associations of decline from a classical era." See Ebrey and Huang, *Visual and Material Cultures in Middle Period China*, 1.

3 Jin Wenjing, "Xihu zai Zhong Ri Han"; Idemitsu, *Ike Taiga no "Seikozu" nitsuite*; Miyazaki "Saiko wo meguru kaiga"; Yang and Fang, "Riben zaoyuan kongjian zhong de Xihu jingguan yixiang"; Chen Xiaofa, "Xuezhou Dengyang yu Hangzhou Xihu." For example of the lake's fame in Japan, see Tian Rucheng, *Xihu youlan zhiyu*, 3.551.

4 Polo and Manuel, *Travels of Marco Polo.*

5 The term "leisure zone" comes from art historian Jonathan Hay, who uses it to refer to an area that depicted the suburban landscape and was "devoted at least in part to a leisure culture featuring temples, pleasure boats, restaurants, tea houses, wine shops, and courtesans." Meyer-Fong, *Building Culture in Early Qing Yangzhou*, 133nn20, 26.

6 Fang et al., *Jin shu*, 15.15b.

7 Cronon, *Nature's Metropolis*, 17; Hargett, *Jade Mountains and Cinnabar Pools*, 6.

8 See Li Zehou, *Mei de lichen, Huaxia meixue, Meixue sijiang*, 283–84.

9 Tuan, *Topophilia*, 71.

10 For the Chinese concept of natural landscape, see Kubin, *Zhongguo wenren de ziranguan.*

11 Cronon, *Nature's Metropolis*, 18.

12 Moule, *Quinsai*, 13; Gernet, *Daily Life in China*, 26. For the scale of the city wall during the Qing dynasty, see Liping Wang, "Tourism and Spatial Change in Hangzhou, 1911–1927," 108.

13 Mote, "A Millennium of Chinese Urban History," 38.
14 Hartwell, "A Revolution in the Chinese Iron and Coal Industries in the Northern Sung, 960–1126 A.D."; Bol, *This Culture of Ours*; John Lee, "Recent Studies in English on the Tang-Song transition"; Osawa, "Tōdai henkakuki no rekishiteki igi"; Luo, "A Study of the Changes in the Tang-Song Transition Model."
15 For a discussion of the shift of transportation from northern China to the south, see Cao, *Songdai de jiaotong yu zhengzhi*, 61–88.
16 *Baishi changqing ji*, 20.13a–b.
17 *Su Shi quanji jiaozhu*, *shiji* 2, 9.848.
18 *Ouyang Xiu quanji*, 40.585.
19 Zhu Mu, *Fangyu shenglan*, 1.6b.
20 For discussion on terms used in traditional documents regarding traveling, see Hargett, *Jade Mountains and Cinnabar Pools*, 5–6, and Wu Ya-ting, "Movement Matters," 23–25, 49–71.
21 Urry and Jonas, *The Tourist Gaze 3.0*, 19.
22 For examples, see Wu Renshu, *Youyou fangxiang*, and Brook, *Confusions of Pleasure*.
23 Li Hsiao-ti, *Zhongguo de chengshi shenghuo*.
24 Cohen, "A Phenomenology of Tourist Experiences."
25 Nyíri, *Scenic Spots*, 95.
26 Nenzi, *Excursions in Identity*; Lomine, "Tourism in Augustan Society 44BC–AD69."
27 Urry and Jonas, *The Tourist Gaze 3.0*; Shaw and Williams, *Tourism and Tourism Spaces*.
28 Wu Ya-ting, "Movement Matters"; Ellen Cong Zhang, *Transformative Journeys*. Also see Ihara, *Sōdai Chūgoku o tabisuru*.
29 Hargett, *Jade Mountains and Cinnabar Pools*, 90.
30 Lin and Jin, *NanSong gudu Hangzhou*; Xu, *NanSong ducheng Lin'an*; He, *NanSong shi ji NanSong ducheng Lin'an yanjiu*; Umehara, *Chūgoku kinsei no toshi to bunka*; Song, "Songdai de xihu yu Hangzhou"; Dai, "Xihu de meili yu aichou"; Zhuansun, "Lin'an de fosi yu lüyou wenhua yanjiu"; Cheng Meng, "NanSong Lin'an Xihu jingqu jieri youle chutan"; Cheng and Wang, "Guanfang gonggong fuwu yu NanSong Xihu lüyou."
31 See Wu Renshu, *Pinwei shehua*, 177–214, and Brook, *Confusions of Pleasure*, 153–66.
32 Nyíri, *Scenic Spots*, 7. See also Brook, *Confusions of Pleasure*, 180.
33 Lam, et al., eds., *Senses of the City*, xiii.
34 See Dott, *Identity Reflections*, and Yu, "Pu-to Shan."
35 For discussions of geographical perspectives on historical study, see Genovese, Hochberg, and Fox, *Geographic Perspectives in History*, and Baker, *Geography and History*.
36 For examples, see Meyer-Fong, *Building Culture in Early Qing Yangzhou*, and Naquin, *Peking*.
37 Robson, *Power of Place*.
38 For the distinction between place and space, see Cresswell, *Place*, 7, 15–17; and Tuan, *Space and Place*, 6.
39 Cresswell, *Place*, 14; Relph, "Spirit of Place and Sense of Place in Virtual Realities," 19.
40 Mitchell, *Landscape and Power*, 1.

41 Gernet, *Daily Life in China*, 19–20.
42 De Pee, "Urban Acupuncture," 5. Also see de Pee, "Notebooks (*biji*) and Shifting Boundaries of Knowledge in Eleventh-Century China."
43 Hargett, *On the Road in Twelfth-Century China*, 1.
44 The term *biji* has been translated variously into English as "random jottings," "note-form literature," "occasional notes," "desultory notes," "miscellanies," and so on.
45 Ellen Cong Zhang, "To Be 'Erudite in Miscellaneous Knowledge'," 44.
46 Hargett, "Sketches," 560.
47 Ellen Cong Zhang, "To Be 'Erudite in Miscellaneous Knowledge'."
48 Gang Liu, "The Poetics of Miscellaneousness," 13.
49 Stephen West mentions the possibility that Wu Zimu's book dates to 1334, but more scholars tend to believe that the earlier date is more plausible. West, "The Interpretation of a Dream," 100–101.
50 De Pee, "Nature's Capital," 181.
51 West, "The Interpretation of a Dream."
52 Gang Liu, "The Poetics of Miscellaneousness," 76.
53 De Pee, "Nature's Capital," 183.
54 Hargett, *On the Road in Twelfth-Century China*, 4–5.
55 Hargett, *On the Road in Twelfth-Century China*, 45.
56 McDowall, *Qian Qianyi's Reflections on Yellow Mountain*, 144.
57 Lin and Jin, *NanSong gudu Hangzhou*, 359.
58 Hu, *Huaben xiaoshuo gailun*, 260–355.
59 The Five Mountains and Ten Monasteries were the fifteen most important monasteries in the Jiangnan area, three of which were located around West Lake. Chapter 5 discusses this in more detail. See also Zhang Shiqing, *Wushan Shicha Tu yu Nan-Song Jiangnan chansi.*
60 The Chinese title of this painting is *Xihu qingqu tu*, literally translated as *The Pure Delight of West Lake*. The English title used in this book follows the one used by the Freer Gallery of Art.
61 Lefebvre, *Production of Space*, 38–39.

Chapter One: Leisure

1 Zhou Mi, *Wulin jiushi*, 3.352.
2 Quan, "BeiSong Bianliang de shuchuru maoyi," 92–94; Ma, *Commercial Development and Urban Change in Sung China (960–1279)*; West, "Playing with Food."
3 See Ihara, *Chūgoku Kaifū no seikatsu to saiji.*
4 Shiba, *Commerce and Society in Sung China*, 202.
5 Chen Xiang, *Guling ji*, 19.1b.
6 Chen Guocan, "NanSong shimin jieceng tanxi," 1.161.
7 Chen Qiqing, *Jiading Chicheng zhi*, 37.
8 Shi, *Chunyou Lin'an zhi*, 10.9b.
9 *Xihu youlan zhiyu*, 6.107.
10 Gernet, *Daily Life in China*, 48.

11 For the fashion among Song elites of collecting books, calligraphies, antiquities, and paintings, see Ebrey, *Accumulating Culture*, 5.

12 De Pee, "Purchase on Power," 154.

13 Zhou Mi, *Wulin jiushi*, 3.353.

14 Shen, *Mengxi bitan*, 11.7a.

15 *Wulin jiushi*, 6.405, 6.414–21, 10.454–56.

16 *Wulin jiushi*, 3.351.

17 *Wulin jiushi*, 3.351.

18 Zhao Yanheng, *Yunlu manchao*, 5.9b–10a; Wu Zimu, *Mengliang lu*, 1.123.

19 This causeway's original name was the White Sand Causeway (Baishadi). People usually thought of it as the one built by Bai Juyi, but that causeway was in fact built to the north of this dike and no longer existed during the Southern Song.

20 Zhou Mi, *Wulin jiushi*, 3.352.

21 For more discussion of the government's use of sightseeing activities to reinforce political authority, see chapter 3.

22 *Wulin jiushi*, 3.353.

23 *Wulin jiushi*, 3.353.

24 *Wulin jiushi*, 3.351.

25 *Wulin jiushi*, 3.351.

26 For more discussion on purchasing souvenirs in Edo Japan, see Nenzi, *Excursions in Identity*, 152.

27 Collins-Kreiner and Zins, "Tourists and Souvenirs," 1, 18.

28 Wu Zimu, *Mengliang lu*, 2.133.

29 Zhou Mi, *Wulin jiushi*, 3.356.

30 *Qiandao gao, Chunxi gao*, 6.5b.

31 Liu and Ren, "Songdai nüxing shishang xiaofei."

32 Zhou Mi, *Wulin jiushi*, 3.305.

33 Wu Zimu, *Mengliang lu*, 19.291.

34 *Wulin jiushi*, 3.351–52.

35 See Li Song's painting *Itinerant Peddler*, preserved in the Palace Museum, Beijing.

36 Li and Zhu, eds., *Baibao zongzhen ji*, 62.

37 Naideweng, *Ducheng jisheng*, 90.

38 The length of the Song dynasty ship discovered in the South China Sea is 35.7 meters. Liu Zhiyuan, *Nanhai yihao de kaogu shijue*.

39 Shiba, *Commerce and Society in Sung China*, 6.

40 Gernet, *Daily Life in China*, 82.

41 Wu Zimu, *Mengliang lu*, 12.226.

42 For a detailed discussion of the water networks in Hangzhou, see chapter 2.

43 Yang Weizhen, *Xihu zhuzhi ci sanzhong*.

44 For more discussion on the depiction of boats in Song paintings, see chapter 4.

45 Xihu Laoren, *Fansheng lu*, 101.

46 *Fansheng lu*, 103–4.

47 Wu Zimu, *Mengliang lu*, 12.224.

48 Jiang Kui, *Baishi Daoren gequ*, 3.6b; Li E, *Songshi jishi*, 60.11b.

49 Li E, *Huchuan lu*, 132.

50 Wu Zimu, *Mengliang lu*, 12.224.
51 Zhou Hui, *Qingbo zazhi*, 12.9b.
52 Li E, *Huchuan lu*, 312.
53 *Xizihu shicui yutan*, 1187–88.
54 Zhou Mi, *Wulin jiushi*, 3.353.
55 *Wulin jiushi*, 3.353; Wu Zimu, *Mengliang lu*, 12.224.
56 Shiba, *Commerce and Society in Sung China*, 200, 212.
57 *Mengliang lu*, 12.224.
58 Zhou Mi, *Guixin zashi*, *xuji xia*.33a.
59 Wu Zimu, *Mengliang lu*, 12.224.
60 Zheng, *Anwantang ji*, 10.2a.
61 Yao, *Xuepo ji*, 44.13b.
62 Chen Qi, *Jianghu xiaoji*, 16.22a.
63 As Zhang Ju's poem says, "It is reported that the phoenix city [Hangzhou] hurried the [locking] key"; Wang, Shen, and Xuanye, *Yuxuan lidai shiyu*, 64.23a–b. Zhou Mi's poem also says, "Already urged the key of the phoenix city"; see Zha and Li, *Juemiao haoci jian*, 7.10b.
64 Tian Rucheng, *Xihu youlan zhiyu*, 16.319–20.
65 Wu Zimu, *Mengliang lu*, 12.224.
66 Xihu Laoren, *Fansheng lu*, 101.
67 Tuotuo, et al., *Song shi*, 134.4409.
68 *Song shi*, 134.4343.
69 "Songren shenghuo shuiping ji bizhi kaocha."
70 Tian Rucheng, *Xihu youlan zhiyu*, 6.107.
71 Simmel, "Fashion."
72 *Wulin jiushi*, 6.407; Zhou Qingyuan, *Xihu erji*, 11.195.
73 Tao, *Shuo fu*, 67 *xia*.22b–23a; Liu Xun, *Lingbiao luyi*, *shang*.5a.
74 West, "Playing with Food."
75 Wu Zimu, *Mengliang lu*, 13.229.
76 The Golden Flood Gate was also given the name of the Harvest and Comfort Gate during the Southern Song (ca. 1158–1279). See Ding Bing, *Wulin fangxiang zhi*, 1.374–75.
77 *Mengliang lu*, 12.219.
78 *Yijian zhi*, *zhi bu* 6.3152.
79 Zhou Qingyuan, *Xihu erji*, 11.195.
80 *Mengliang lu*,16.255.
81 Wu Zimu, *Mengliang lu*, 10.203.
82 Lü Zuqian, *Lidai zhidu xiangshuo*, 6.4a–b.
83 Zhou Qingyuan, *Xihu erji*, 11.195.
84 West, "Playing with Food," 74.
85 For example, see Zhou Mi, *Qidong yeyu*, 196–97.
86 Ellen Cong Zhang, "The Culture of Travel in Song China (960–1276)," 112–13, and "Communication, Collaboration, and Community, Inn-wall Writing during the Song (960–1279)."
87 For later literati's comments on this anecdote, see the epilogue.

88 Zhou Mi, *Wulin jiushi*, 3.353.
89 *Wulin jiushi*, 7.427.
90 Tian Rucheng, *Xihu youlan zhiyu*, 3.44; Liang Shaoren, *Liangban Qiuyu'an suibi*, 350.
91 Naideweng, *Ducheng jisheng*, 93.
92 Yuan, *Fengchuang xiaodu*, *xia*.17.
93 Li Xinchuan, *Jianyan yilai xi'nian yaolu*,173.2858; Lu You, *Laoxue'an biji*, 8.104.
94 Tian Rucheng, *Xihu youlan zhiyu*, 20.319; Zhou Mi, *Wulin jushi*, 3.305.
95 Zhuang, *Jilei bian*, *zhong*.15b.
96 *Mengliang lu*, 6.259.
97 Zhou Bida, *Erlaotang zazhi*, 3512–13.
98 Zhu Tinghuan, *Zengbu Wulin jiushi*, 8.16a–17b; Wu Zimu, *Mengliang lu*, 18.284.
99 *Zengbu Wulin jiushi*, 8.16a–17b.
100 Polo and Manuel, *Travels of Marco Polo*, 232.
101 Wu Zimu, *Mengliang lu*, 12.224.
102 *Xie lüe*, 2.7a.
103 Zhu Tinghuan, *Zengbu Wulin jiushi*, 8.16a–17b.
104 *Wulin jiushi*, 356–7.
105 Zhou Mi, *Wulin jiushi*, 409–10.
106 *Yijian zhi*, *zhi ji* 3, 2.902.
107 *Wulin jiushi*, 3.351.
108 Xihu Laoren, *Fansheng lu*, 99.
109 *Wulin jiushi*, 3.351.
110 De Pee, "Purchase on Power," 179.
111 Jianfei Zhu, *Chinese Spatial Strategies*, 90.

Chapter Two: Urbanization

1 Zhang Huiru, "NanSong Hangzhou shuihuanjing yu chengshi fazhan hudong guanxi yanjiu," 38.
2 Lin Zhengqiu, "Xihu gudai shujun zhili shi tanshu," 56–67.
3 Honda, "Sō Dai Kōshū oyobi kōhai chi no suiri to suiri soshiki"; Shiba, "Sō to Kōshū no shōgyō kaku"; Fujiwa, "Saiko hirakiei shōshi Minami Sō Linan kenkyū ni yose te."
4 Wu Songdi, "NanSong yimin yu Lin'an wenhua," 36.
5 Zhu Kezhen, "Zhongguo lishi shang de hanzai."
6 Tian Rucheng, *Xihu youlan zhiyu*, 24.436.
7 Ding, *Wulin zhanggu congbian*, 23.1a–b.
8 See Lin Zhengqiu, "Xihu gudai shujun zhili shi tanshu," 58.
9 Bai, *Baishi changqing ji*, 68.8a–10a.
10 *Baishi changqing ji*, 68.8b.
11 Wu Renchen, *Shiguo chunqiu*, 84.3b.
12 *Su Shi quanji jiaozhu, wenji* 5, 30.3288.
13 *Su Shi quanji jiaozhu, wenji* 5, 30.3297.
14 *Su Shi quanji jiaozhu, wenji* 5, 30.3289.
15 Zhou Bida, *Erlaotang zazhi*, 3512–13.

16 Scholarly opinions differ on the exact size of one *zhang* during the Song. It was probably around 3.07–3.22 meters. For more discussion, see Liu Chunying, "Cong BeiSong Dongjing waicheng de kaogu faxian tan BeiSong shiqi de yingzaochi."
17 One *guan* is about 1,000 *wen*.
18 Chen Menglei, *Gujin tushu jicheng*, 797–98.
19 The monks' names were Zhongwen, Zigui, Ruzheng, and Sitan. *Su Shi quanji jiaozhu, wenji* 5, 31.3354.
20 *Su Shi quanji jiaozhu, wenji* 5, 31.3353–54.
21 *Su Shi quanji jiaozhu, wenji* 5, 30.3290.
22 See de Pee, "Urban Acupuncture," 174, and de Pee, "Circulation and Flow."
23 For more discussion on the life-releasing ritual, see chapter 5.
24 *Su Shi quanji jiaozhu, wenji* 5, 30.3288–89.
25 Chen Menglei, *Gujin tushu jicheng*, 798.
26 *Su Shi quanji jiaozhu, wenji* 5, 30.3289.
27 For a detailed discussion of the Ten Views, See chapter 6.
28 See Wang Xiangzhi, *Yudi jisheng*, 2.39, and Zhu Mu, *Fangyu shenglan*, 1.5. Also see Jiang Qingqing, *"Xianchun Lin'an zhi" Songban "jingcheng situ" fuyuan yanjiu*, 285–89.
29 Xu Song, *Song huiyao jigao*, 17.22.
30 Tian Rucheng, *Xihu youlan zhiyu*, 21.389–90.
31 Qian Yueyou, *Xianchun Lin'an zhi*, 32.5a–b.
32 *Xianchun Lin'an zhi*, 33.4a–b.
33 Tuotuo, *Song shi*, 283.9562.
34 *Song shi*, 390.11958; *Song shi*, 361.11312.
35 Bai, *Baishi changqing ji*, 23.12b.
36 Tuotuo, *Song shi*, 361.11312.
37 *Jingkou qijiu zhuan*, 8.3b.
38 *Xihu youlan zhiyu*, 24.435.
39 Hofmann, "The Biographer's View of Craftsmanship."
40 Tian Rucheng, *Xihu youlan zhiyu*, 24.435.
41 Qian Yueyou, *Xianchun Lin'an zhi, juan* 22–39.
42 Ding, *Wulin zhanggu congbian*, 23.8a–b. One *zhong* is equal to 64 *hu*, about 6,400 *sheng*.
43 Zhu Tinghuan, *Zengbu Wulin jiushi*, 8.16a–17b.
44 For example, see Yang Wanli, *Chengzhai ji*, 23.2a.
45 Ye Sheng, *Shuidong riji*, 271.
46 Xu Song, *Song huiyao jigao*, 17.23–24.
47 Shi, *Chunyou Lin'an zhi*, 10.14a.
48 Naideweng, *Ducheng jisheng*, 90.
49 Qian Yueyou, *Xianchun Lin'an zhi*, 33.4b.
50 Zhou Zizhi, *Taicang timi ji*, 59.7a–b.
51 Li Huarui, *Songdai jiu de shengchan he zhengque*.
52 Lü Zuqian, *Lidai zhidu xiangshuo*, 6.4a–b.
53 *Taicang timi ji*, 59.7a–b.
54 Wu Zimu, *Mengliang lu*, 10.203–4.

55 Zhou Mi, *Wulin jiushi*, 6.412–13.
56 *Wulin jiushi*, 6.406–7.
57 For more discussion of the accommodations provided by temples, see chapter 5.
58 For example, see Jiang Teli, *Meishan xugao*, 12.3b.
59 Xihu Laoren, *Fansheng lu*, 101.
60 Naideweng, *Ducheng jisheng*, 83.
61 Wu Zimu, *Mengliang lu*, 16.256.
62 *Mengliang lu*, 1.128.

Chapter Three: Seeking Identity in Place

1 *Wulin jiushi*, 3.352; translation from de Pee, "Nature's Capital," 179.
2 Chen Zao, *Jianghu changweng ji*, 5.24a–b.
3 For example, see Li E, *Songshi jishi*, 50.26a–b.
4 De Pee, "Nature's Capital," 182.
5 Bol, "Reconceptualizing the Order of Things in Northern and Southern Song."
6 Egan, *The Problem of Beauty*, 109–61.
7 Hargett, *On the Road in Twelfth-Century China*, 280.
8 Ellen Cong Zhang, *Transformative Journeys*, 154–206.
9 West, "The Pains of Pleasure," 136.
10 Qian Yueyou, *Xianchun Lin'an zhi*, 33.23a.
11 *Baishi changqing ji*, 20.11a.
12 For more discussion of Su Shi and West Lake, see Ridgway, "Imagined Travel."
13 Fei Gun, *Liangxi manzhi*, 4.1b.
14 Shen Gua, *Mengxi bitan*,10.85.
15 Chen Si, *Liang Song mingxian xiaoji*, 162.12a–b.
16 Owen, *Remembrances*, 1.
17 *You Longjing ji*, 64.
18 *Transformative Journeys*, 178.
19 Liu Gang, "The 'Loss' of Purity."
20 For example, Chen Qi, a well-known publisher, published an anthology for the River and Lake Poetry Club. See Liu Fang, *Shengshi fanhua*, 168.
21 *Mengliang lu*, 19.292. See also Ouyang Guang, *SongYuan shishe yanjiu conggao*, and Xiao, "Xihu yinshe kao," 7.88–99.
22 *Pinzhou yudi pu*, 1.16a.
23 Deng, *Boya qin*, 1.28b–29b.
24 Wooldridge, *City of Virtues*, 7.
25 *Su Shi quanji jiaozhu, wenji* 5, 30.3289.
26 *Taicang timi ji*, 52.3b–4b.
27 Lian, "How Does an Objective Correlative Objectify?" 220.
28 For more discussion of the design and building of Southern Song Hangzhou, see Moule, *Quinsai*, 11–52; Gernet, *Daily Life in China*, 22–27; Wright, "The Cosmology of the Chinese City"; Xie, "Disembodied Historicity"; and Kracke, "Sung K'ai-feng."
29 Zhu Guozhen, *Yongchuang xiaopin*, 9.24a.

30 Qian Yueyou, *Xianchun Lin'an zhi*, 33.22a.
31 Tang Guizhang, ed., *Quan Song ci*, 2.839.
32 Naideweng, *Ducheng jisheng*, 75.
33 *Wulin jiushi*, 3.352.
34 See chapter 5.
35 Ebrey, "Taking Out the Grand Carriage."
36 Lin Fan, "The Local in the Imperial Vision," 10.
37 Qian Yueyou, *Xianchun Lin'an zhi*, 33.23b.
38 *Mingshui ji*, 7.37–38.
39 Aoyama, *Tō Sō jidai no kōtsū to chishi chizu no kenkyū*, 465–72; Bol, "The Rise of Local History"; Hymes, "Marriage, Descent Groups, and the Localist Strategy in Sung and Yuan Fu-chou"; Hargett, "Song Dynasty Local Gazetteers and Their Place in the History of Difangzhi Writing."
40 Wu Ya-ting, "Movement Matters," 220–23.
41 Bol, "The Rise of Local History," 46.
42 Lin Fan, "The Local in the Imperial Vision," 25.
43 Milburn, *Urbanization in Early and Medieval China*, 6–7.
44 Hargett, "Song Dynasty Local Gazetteers and Their Place in the History of Difangzhi Writing," 427.
45 Qian Yueyou, *Xianchun Lin'an zhi*, 32.7a–b.
46 Milburn, *Urbanization in Early and Medieval China*, 7.
47 For more information on the four capital journals, see the introduction.
48 *Mengliang lu*, 117.
49 West, "The Interpretation of a Dream."
50 *Wulin jiushi*, 3.311.
51 The Three Causeways referred to the Su Causeway, the White Causeway, and the Small New Causeway.
52 Xihu Laoren, *Fansheng lu*, 99. Six One Spring was named after Ouyang Xiu.
53 Ridgway,"Touring the City in Southern Song China," 2.
54 *Xihu baiyong*, 1–2.
55 *Transformative Journeys*, 175–80.
56 Davis, *Wind against the Mountain*, 24.
57 Lian, "How Does an Objective Correlative Objectify?" 222–26.
58 Tang Guizhang, ed., *Quan Song ci*, 5.3083.
59 *Quan Song ci*, 5.3138. The translation is by Shuen-fu Lin. See Chang and Owen, *Cambridge History of Chinese Literature*, vol. 1 (to 1375), 550–51.
60 Shuen-fu Lin, "Wen Jiweng of the Late Southern Song."
61 Hongsheng Zhang, "Consciousness of Adversity and the Spirit of Innovation," 87.
62 West, "The Pains of Pleasure," 142.
63 Ling Yuzhi, *Hong Mai nianpu*, 32. *Yijian zhi*, 4.1833.
64 Egan, "Crime, Violence, and Ghosts in the Lin'an Stories in *Yijian zhi*," 149.
65 For examples, see Inglis, *Hong Mai's Record of the Listener and Its Song Dynasty Context;* Hsiao-wen Cheng, "Traveling Stories and Untold Desires"; and Ellen Cong Zhang, Introduction to *Record of the Listener.*
66 Gerritsen, "Visions of Local Culture," 74–75.

67 Hong Mai, *Yijian zhi, zhi ji* 3, 2.902. For a full translation of this story, see Egan, "Crime, Violence, and Ghosts in the Lin'an Stories in *Yijian zhi*," 153–55. For the other two stories, see the appendix.
68 Ebrey, "Women, Money, and Class."
69 Hong Mai, *Yijian zhi, ding zhi* 4, 1.571.
70 Campany, *Strange Writing*, 266.
71 *Fengchuang xiaodu*, 219. The translation comes from West, "The Pains of Pleasure," 141.
72 Wang Mingqing, *Yuzhao xinzhi*, 13.138.
73 Hong Mai, *Yijian zhi, zhi ding* 8, 3.1032.
74 Ouyang Xiu, *Guitian lu*, 2.31.
75 Zhu Peng, *NanSong guji kao, shang*.4a.
76 Hong Mai, *Yijian zhi, zhi gui* 5, 3.1258.
77 For more discussion on this book, see Altenburger, "Layered Landscape," 118–26.

Chapter Four: A Topographic and Affective Place

1 *Guixin zashi, xu bian*, 203–4.
2 *Baishi changqing ji*, 23.7b.
3 Hu Zi, *Yuyin conghua, hou ji* 37.8a–b.
4 Zhang Chou, *Qinghe shuhua fang*, 3.383a; Gao Shiqi, *Jiangcun xiaoxia lu*, 7.1031; Wen Jia, *Qianshantang shuhua ji*, 8.51; Li E, *NanSong yuanhua lu*, 635; Wang Yuxian, *Huishi beikao*, 6.20b–21a. Though written records of paintings of West Lake date back to the Northern Song, the earliest extant art is from the Southern Song. See *Qinghe shuhua fang*, 4.143a, and Tian Yiheng, *Liuqing rizha*, 35.669.
5 Li Ding, *Xihu xiaoshi*, 1194.
6 For example, see Miyazaki, "Saiko wo meguru kaiga."
7 Hui-shu Lee, *Exquisite Moments*, 19–59.
8 For example, see Lihong Liu, "Collecting the Here and Now."
9 *Xihu youlan zhiyu*, 17.297.
10 Zhang Yanyuan, *Lidai minghua ji*, 130–31. For a translation of this text, see Bush and Shih, *Early Chinese Texts on Paintings*, 37. For more discussion of the development of depicting landscape in both visual and textual form, see Virag, "The Ethics of Visualization."
11 Wu Ya-ting, "Dushan."
12 Wu Ya-ting, "Movement Matters," 242–43; Hargett, *Jade Mountains and Cinnabar Pools*, 16.
13 Chen Ye, *NanSong huihua shi*, 53–56.
14 Shih, *Shanming guying*, 87.
15 Li and Zhu, eds., *Baibao zongzhen ji*, 62; Li You, *Guhang zaji*, 1.1b.
16 Wang not only contributed to the wood-block maps in local gazetteers but also left his name on *Changli xiansheng ji* (Anthology of Mr. Changli) and *Hedong xiansheng ji* (Anthology of Mr. Hedong). The compilers of both *Changli xiansheng ji* and *Xianchun lin'an zhi* were friends of Jia Sidao. See Jiang Qingqing, *"Xianchun Lin'an zhi" Songban "jingcheng situ" fuyuan yanjiu*, 21.

17 Jiang Qingqing, "*Xianchun Lin'an zhi*" *Songban* "*jingcheng situ*" *fuyuan yanjiu*, 38.
18 "*Xianchun Lin'an zhi*" *Songban* "*jingcheng situ*" *fuyuan yanjiu*, 206–93.
19 Powers, "Picturing Time in Song Painting and Poetry," 68.
20 De Weerdt, *Information, Territory, and Networks*, 35–75.
21 Tuan, *Space and Place*, 76–77.
22 De Weerdt, "The Cultural Logics of Map Reading," 239, 255–56, 260.
23 Li You, *Guhang zaji*, 1.1b.
24 Fan Lin, "The Local in the Imperial Vision," 31.
25 For annotated detailed images and more discussion, see Lee, *Exquisite Moments*, 24–25, and Xiaolin Duan, "Ten Views of West Lake," 174, figure 4.11.
26 On the historical map, I.2, the literary translation Imperial Phoenix Hill is used; on the modern map, I.1, it is labeled Phoenix Hill for readability.
27 "*Wulin jiushi.*"
28 Cahill, "The Imperial Painting Academy," 169.
29 Hui-shu Lee, *Exquisite Moments*, 22.
30 *Xuzhai minghua lu*, 12.632a.
31 *Lu Yanshan wenji*, 84.22a–b.
32 For a Japanese example, see *View of West Lake* by Kusumi Morikage (ca. 1620–1690) in the Metropolitan Museum of Art in New York City.
33 For an image of Xie's painting, see Xihu Bowuguan, *Lidai Xihu shuhua ji*, 78–79.
34 For an image of Dai's painting, see *Lidai Xihu shuhua ji*, 62–63.
35 Li E, *NanSong yuanhua lu*, 2.586.
36 *NanSong yuanhua lu*, 2.585.
37 "Picturing West Lake."
38 "*Xihu fansheng quanjing tu* wei NanSong yuanhua kao." Chen's conclusion is based on several facts. The first is that the Small New Causeway, built in 1242, was included in the painting, but the Lake and Mountain Hall (Hushantang), built in 1267, was not. The second is that the Memorial Garden for Yue Fei (1103–1142) in the painting shows both the Awarding Loyalty and Extending Blessing Monastery (Baozhongyanfusi), rebuilt between 1263 and 1267, and the Memorial Hall, so this painting could not have been painted earlier than 1267. The third is that the family temple of Jia Sidao, built in the second lunar month of 1267, is depicted in the painting. Chen points out that 1267 was a remarkable year. Possibly the court commissioned certain construction projects that year and then supported the painting of this scroll through patronage.
39 Xihu Laoren, *Fansheng lu*, 122–23. The translation is from Hui-shu Lee, *Exquisite Moments*, 19.
40 Shih, *Shanming guying*, 76.
41 Cahill, "The Imperial Painting Academy," 181.
42 Li E, *NanSong yuanhua lu*, 2.635.
43 City University of Hong Kong Chinese Civilisation Centre, *China: Five Thousand Years of History and Civilization*, 747.
44 Translation from Bush and Shih, *Early Chinese Texts on Painting*, 152–53.
45 *The Lyric Journey*, 54–55.
46 Thorp and Vinograd, *Chinese Art and Culture*, 242.

47 Virag, "The Ethics of Visualization."
48 *Beyond Representation*, 95.
49 Shih, *Shanming guying*, 186.
50 For an image of Xie's painting, see Xihu Bowuguan, *Lidai Xihu shuhua ji*, 77.
51 For an image of Qian's painting, see *Lidai Xihu shuhua ji*, 46–47.
52 *Tanyuan ji*, 12.15.
53 For further discussion of the representation of time and seasons in West Lake paintings, see chapter 6.
54 *Xihu woyou tu tiba*, 1094.
55 For an image of Li's painting, see Xihu Bowuguan, *Lidai Xihu shuhua ji*, 118–19.
56 For an image of Song's painting, see *Lidai Xihu shuhua ji*, 111.
57 For an image of Dong's painting, see *Lidai Xihu shuhua ji*, 117.
58 For examples of Ni Zan's painting, see Guoli, *Gugong shuhua tulu*, 4.301–2.
59 Tuan, *Topophilia*, 99.
60 Lu Ciyun, *Huruan zaji*, 27–28.
61 Ming and Qing painters generally confined themselves to the sites depicted by Song painters, adding only newly renovated structures such as Lake Heart Pavilion (Huxinting). Chen Menglei, *Gujin tushu jicheng*, 807–8.

Chapter Five: Pray and Play

1 Qian Yueyou, *Xianchun Lin'an zhi*, 33.16b.
2 Dott, *Identity Reflections.*
3 McDowall, *Qian Qianyi's Reflections on Yellow Mountain*, 85.
4 Moerman, *Localizing Paradise*, 235.
5 Hur, *Prayer and Play in Late Tokugawa Japan*, 24, 197–98.
6 Raj and Morpeth, *Religious Tourism and Pilgrimage Festivals Management*, 62–63. Also see Nolan and Nolan. "Religious Sites as Tourism Attractions in Europe."
7 Naquin and Yu, *Pilgrims and Sacred Sites in China*, 3, 11–12.
8 Rowe, *Making a Middle Landscape.*
9 Ebrey and Gregory, *Religion and Society in T'ang and Sung China*; Hansen, *Changing Gods in Medieval China, 1127–1276*; von Glahn, *The Sinister Way.*
10 Naquin and Yu, *Pilgrims and Sacred Sites in China*, 10.
11 *Religion and Society in T'ang and Sung China*, 28–29.
12 Hansen, *Changing Gods in Medieval China*, 162.
13 Mou, "NanSong Lin'an cheng simiao fenbu yanjiu"; Sun Xun, "Songdai Hangzhou simiao yanjiu"; Wang Zhongyao, "NanSong Lin'an ji MingQing Hangzhou daojiao gongguan kao"; Yuming Duan, "Kaifeng Daoist Temples in the Southern Song Dynasty Hangzhou."
14 Sun Liang, "NanSong shiqi Hangzhou fojiao wenhua chutan."
15 See Ebrey, *Emperor Huizong*, 324–60.
16 Qian Yueyou, *Xianchun Lin'an zhi*, 75.1a.
17 Zhuansun, "Lin'an fosi yu lüyou wenhua yanjiu"; Chi-Chiang Huang, "Elite and Clergy in Northern Sung Hangchou," 298.
18 Mou, "NanSong Lin'an cheng simiao fenbu yanjiu," 98.

19 Hansen, *Changing Gods in Medieval China*, 3.
20 Shi-shan Susan Huang, "Tianzhu Lingqian."
21 Yu, "Pu-to Shan."
22 Shiba, *Songdai Jiangnan jingjishi yanjiu*, 83–126.
23 Liping Wang, "Paradise for Sale," 89–137.
24 For detailed discussion on *Xihu baiyong*, see chapter 3.
25 Tuotuo, et al., *Song shi*, 119.2812.
26 Jidian and Sun Zhi, *Lingyinsi zhi*, 3.11b.
27 *Qingxian ji*, 5–12b.
28 Wu Zimu, *Mengliang lu*, 12.218.
29 Xia Ji, *Xihu lansheng shixu*, 214.
30 Monk Jixiang, *Jingcisi zhi*, 800.
31 Xu Fengji, *Qingbo xiaozhi*, 78; *Jingcisi zhi*, 23.815.
32 Zha Weiren, *Juemiao haoci jian*, 7.11b.
33 *Wulin jiushi*, 5.402–3.
34 Tian Rucheng, *Xihu youlan zhi*, 10.115–16.
35 Monk Guangbin, *Hangzhou Shang Tianzhu jiangsi zhi*, 10.240–59.
36 See Zhang Shiqing, *Wushan shisha tu yu NanSong Jiangnan chansi*.
37 Monk Guangbin, *Hangzhou Shang Tianzhu jiangsi zhi*, 11.14a, 1.10b.
38 Wu Zimu, *Mengliang lu*, 8.186.
39 Tian Rucheng, *Xihu youlan zhiyu* 3.50.
40 Zhou Mi, *Guixin zashi, xuji juan xia*.39b.
41 Monk Dahe, *Nanping Jingcisi zhi*, 23.304; Zhou Qingyuan, *Xihu erji*, 8.12.
42 *Duanming ji*, 3.16a–b.
43 Chi-Chiang Huang, "Elite and Clergy in Northern Sung Hangchou," 325.
44 Qian Yueyou, *Xianchun Lin'an zhi*, 32.12a.
45 Ye Shaoweng, *Sichao wenjian lu*, 13.169.
46 "Songdai fangsheng yu fangshengwen yanjiu."
47 Zeng and Liu, *Quan Song wen*, 5084.325.
48 *Quan Song wen*, 2201.81.
49 Zhuansun, "Lin'an fosi yu lüyou wenhua yanjiu."
50 Dai, "Xihu de meili yu aichou."
51 Wu Zimu, *Mengliang lu*, 1.128–9.
52 See Zhao Shiyu, *Kuanghuan yu richang*.
53 Hansen, *Changing Gods in Medieval China*, 7.
54 Shi-shan Susan Huang, "Tianzhu Lingqian."
55 Zheng Zhenduo, *Zhongguo gudai banhua congkan*, lot numbers 13, 18, 27, 35, 51, 54, 57, 83.
56 See "Shangzhu Guanyin," "Lin'an leisheng," "Yi Guanren jidi," from Hong Mai, *Yijian zhi, bing zhi* 9, 2.437; *san zhi xin* 8, 3.1447; *san zhi xin* 8, 3.1448.
57 *Su Shi quanji jiaozhu, shiji* 2, 8.769.
58 Fang Hao, "Songdai fojiao dui lüyou zhi gongxian," 33.
59 *Su Shi quanji jiaozhu, shiji* 4, 20.2158.
60 Li E, *Zengxiu Yunlinsi zhi*, 824.
61 *Zengxiu Yunlinsi zhi*, 22.731.

62 Tian Rucheng, *Xihu youlan zhiyu*, 24.385–86.
63 Puji, *Wudeng huiyuan*, 1565.93b19–21; Benn, *Tea in China*, 128.
64 Li E, *Zengxiu Yunlinsi zhi*, 22.692.
65 Tian Rucheng, *Xihu youlan zhi*, 4.55; Monk Guangbin, *Hangzhou Shang Tianzhu jiangsi zhi*, 366.
66 *Xihu youlan zhiyu*, 24.378–79.
67 *Xihu youlan zhiyu*, 2.382.
68 Monk Dahe, *Nanping Jicisi zhi*, 23.51.
69 Wu Zhijing, *Wulin fanzhi*, 185.
70 Zhuansun, "Lin'an fosi yu lüyou wenhua yanjiu," 16.
71 Tian Rucheng, *Xihu youlan zhiyu*, 14.243.
72 Yuanjing, *Wulin Xihu gaoseng shilüe deng bazhong*, 18.
73 Qisong, *Tanjin wenji*, 11.11b–13b.
74 Hui-shu Lee, *Exquisite Moment*, 40–43.
75 Chi-Chiang Huang, "Elite and Clergy in Northern Sung Hangzhou," 300.
76 *Daily Life in China*, 185.
77 For more discussion of these local products, see chapter 1.
78 Wu Zimu, *Mengliang lu*, 2.132–33.
79 Meng, *Dongjing meng hua lu*, 8.53.
80 *Mengliang lu*, 8.186.
81 *Mengliang lu*, 8.186.
82 Tian Rucheng, *Xihu youlan zhiyu*, 23.204.
83 Yang Junbo, "BeiSong Dongjing siyuan lüyou xiyinwu ji lüyou huodong yanjiu."
84 *Xihu youlan zhiyu*, 25.405; Zhou Mi, *Wulin jiushi*, 4.351.
85 *Wannan shigao*, 17.26b.
86 *Xihu youlan zhiyu*, 25.405.
87 *Xihu xiaoshi*, 1197.
88 Meng, *Dongjing meng hua lu*, 8.52.
89 Zhou Mi, *Wulin jiushi*, 3.354–55.
90 Tian Rucheng, *Xihu youlan zhiyu*, 3.36–37.
91 Gang Liu, "The 'Loss' of Purity."
92 Naquin, *Peking*, 249.
93 Liping Wang, "Paradise for Sale," 122.
94 *Making a Middle Landscape*, 1–2.
95 Zhang Dai, *Tao'an mengyi, Xihu mengxun*, 4.73. Also see Pei-yi Wu, "An Ambivalent Pilgrim to T'ai Shan in the Seventeenth Century."

Chapter Six: Ten Views of West Lake

This chapter is based in part on my previously published article "The Ten Views of West Lake." In addition to new research, it also includes a discussion of post-Song developments.

1 Lu, *Selected Works of Lu Hsun*, 96.
2 Urry and Jonas, *The Tourist Gaze 3.0*, 17.
3 *Topophilia*, 4.

4 Mitchell, *Iconology*, 13.
5 *Fangyu shenglan*, 1.6b–7a. The translation is from Hui-shu Lee, *Exquisite Moments*, 32.
6 *Dongtian qinglu ji*, 1.566.
7 *Mengliang lu*, 12.220.
8 Shih, *Shanming guying*, 82–83.
9 Nyíri, *Scenic Spots*, 9.
10 Liang Shaoren, *Liangban Qiuyu'an suibi*, 13.465.
11 Harrist, "Site Names and Their Meaning," 207.
12 For studies of Lu Hong's *Ten Images of My Grass Hut*, see Zhuang Shen, *Tang Lu Hong caotang shizhi tujuan kao*, and Wu Gangyi, "Lu Hong jiqi huaji wei'e yuanliu kaojian."
13 Shen, *Mengxi bitan*, 9.549. The translations of the eight titles are from Murck, "Eight Views of the Hsiao and Hsiang Rivers by Wang Hong," 216.
14 See Barnhart, "Shining Rivers"; I, "'Landscape Like a Picture' and 'Landscape in the Picture'"; Hui-shu Lee, *Empresses, Art, and Agency in Song Dynasty China*, 171–79; Miyazaki, "Saiko wo meguru kaiga," 203; Shih, *Yidong de Taohuayuan*, 23–25; and Murck, "Eight Views of the Hsiao and Hsiang Rivers."
15 "Eight Views of the Hsiao and Hsiang Rivers," 219–20.
16 For more discussion, see Duan, "Ten Views of West Lake," 159.
17 Murck, *Poetry and Painting in Song China*, 260.
18 Ouyang, *Ouyang Xiu quanji*, 131.1991–93.
19 Tang and Zhou, *TangSong ci jianshang cidian*, 2467.
20 Cahill, "The Imperial Painting Academy," 186.
21 *A Land*, 151.
22 Cahill, "The Imperial Painting Academy," 160–61, 165.
23 Tian Rucheng, *Xihu youlan zhiyu*, 10.153; Wang, Shen, and Xuanye, *Yuxuan lidai shiyu*, 64.23–26; Zha Weiren, *Juemiao haoci jian*, 7.11–12; Chen Yunping, *Rihu yuchang*, 80.663.
24 *Juemiao haoci jian*, 7.11; *Rihu yuchang*, 80.663.
25 For a translation of Zhou Mi's poem as an example, see Duan, "Ten Views of West Lake," 158.
26 Murck, *Poetry and Painting in Song China*.
27 Zha Weiren, *Juemiao haoci jian*, 7.10b. For translations, see Duan, "Ten Views of West Lake,"159.
28 See chapter 3.
29 Gao Shiqi, *Jiangcun xiaoxia lu*, 7.1031; Li E, *NanSong yuanhua lu*, 8.635. Art historians suggest that there are untitled Southern Song album leaves that are reminiscent of the titles of the Ten Views. Examples include *Travelers at Dusk* and Ma Yuan's *Bare Willows and Distant Mountains* in the Museum of Fine Arts, Boston; *Boating by a Willow Bank* in the Metropolitan Museum of Art; and Ma Yuan's *Walking on a Mountain Path in Spring* in the National Palace Museum. See Hui-shu Lee, *Exquisite Moments*, 68–69, 108–9, and Shih, *Shanming guying*, 76.
30 For plate illustrations, see Guoli, *Gugong shuhua tulu*, 22.74–79. Also see Li Yumin, "Xihu shijing tezhan."
31 Barnhart, "Shining Rivers," 55.

32 Hui-shu Lee, *Exquisite Moments*, 12.
33 For detailed images of Ye Xiaoyan's album, see Duan, "Ten Views of West Lake," 151–92. Also see Li Lincan, "Ye Xiaoyan de Xihu tu ji qita" and Barnhart, "Shining Rivers," 51 (fig. 26).
34 Lee, "The Domain of Empress Yang," 305.
35 Egan, "Nature and Higher Ideals in Texts on Calligraphy, Music, and Painting," 303.
36 Clunas, *Elegant Debts*, 93; Liu, "Collecting the Here and Now."
37 Y. Eugene Wang, "Tope and Topos," 489.
38 Hui-shu Lee, in *Exquisite Moments*, 41–42, attributes this feature to imperial interest in Daoism and Chan Buddhism, both of which emphasized an awareness of the transience of the human world.
39 *Mengliang lu*, 12.219.
40 *Mengliang lu*, 12.216–17, Translation from Hui-shu Lee, *Exquisite Moments*, 32.
41 For more discussion of festivals, see Duan, "Scenic Beauty outside the City," 145–55.
42 Loehr, *Great Painters of China*, 191; Powers, "Picturing Time in Song Painting and Poetry."
43 *Linquan gaozhi*. Translation from Bush and Shih, *Early Chinese Texts on Painting*, 152–53.
44 Bian, *Shigutang shuhua huikao*, 25.20a–b.
45 *Xihu xiaoshi*, 3.1194.
46 *Wenjian ji*, 34.3b–4a.
47 See Xihu Bowuguan, *Lidai Xihu shuhuaji*, 120–29.
48 *Topophilia*, 247.
49 Zhou Qingyuan, *Xihu erji*, 14.262–79.
50 *Wenjian ji*, 34.3a–b. For a discussion of Ming literati painting, see Cahill, *The Restless Landscape*.
51 For example, see Chen Yunping, *Rihu yuchang*, 26.540; Zhang Yun'ao, *Jinniuhu yuchang*, 105; and Yang Fengbao, *Xihu qiuliu ci*, 43–44.
52 Pin, *Xihu biji*, 511.
53 *Xihu shijing houji*, 961.
54 *Tao'an mengyi, Xihu mengxun*, 153–54.
55 Campbell, "The Ten Scenes of West Lake."
56 For more discussion on this gazetteer, see Altenburger, "Layered Landscape," 126–143.
57 Fu and Li, *Xihu zhi*, 3.26b.
58 See Guoli, *Gugong shuhua tulu*, 22.74–79.
59 Shih, *Shanming guying*, 299–300.
60 *Shanming guying*, 250. Also see Clunas, *Pictures and Visuality in Early Modern China*, 84.
61 Similar prints can also be found in *Hushan shenggai* (Conspectus of sights of the lakes and hills), published in color during the early seventeenth century. See Cohen and Monnet, *Impressions de Chine*, 152–53.
62 *Shanming guying*, 250–54.
63 See Clunas, *Pictures and Visuality in Early Modern China*, 160–64.

64 For further discussion of this set of Ming printed images, see Li-Chiang Lin, "A Study of the *Xinjuan hainei qiguan*, a Ming Dynasty Book of Famous Sites,"and Duan, "A Comparative Study of Two Series of Printed West Lake Ten Views."
65 For ink sticks, see Wang Jinsheng, *Wangshi jianguzhai mosou*, 1a. For embroidered works, see Li E, *Dongcheng zaji, juan xia*.18b–19a.
66 Urry and Jonas, *Tourist Gaze 3.0*, 166–67.
67 Chen Congzhou, *Zishi yumo*, 985.
68 The Qiantang Ten Views were "Misty Willows on Six Bridges," "Nine-*li* Cloudy Pine," "Singing Woodman around Mount Efficacious Rocks," "Roaring Monkey near Cold Spring," "Sunrise at Ge Hill," "Clear Snow at Solitary Mountain," "Night Market at the North Gate," "Autumn Wave of Zhe River," "West Lake Night Moon," and "Double Peaks in White Clouds." See Tian Rucheng, *Xihu youlan zhiyu*, 12.196–97.
69 *Zunsheng bajian*, 3.45b–46a.
70 Li Luifang, *Xihu woyoutu tiba*, 3.1094–1101.
71 For example, see Fu and Li, *Xihu zhi*, and Liang Shizheng, et al., *Xihu zhizuan*.
72 For more discussion of the influence of West Lake on Japanese and Korean culture, see Jin Wenjing, "Xihu zai Zhong Ri Han."
73 I, "A New Exploration on Qing Palace's Collection of Ming Dynasty Artist Wang Fu's Painting—'The Eight Views of Beijing.'"
74 *Huailutang ji*, 16.1–3.
75 Jin Ao, *Haining xianzhi*, 3.422.

Epilogue

1 Liping Wang, "Paradise for Sale," 89–137.
2 Fan, *Hangsu yifeng*, 19.33.
3 Yi-Fu Tuan, "A View of Geography," 101.
4 Tian Rucheng, *Xihu youlan zhi*, 1.2.
5 Gang Liu, "The Poetics of Miscellaneousness," 44, 59–60.
6 *Qiantang yishi*, 5.10b.
7 Ding, *Wulin fangxiang zhi*, 383.
8 Polo, Cordier, and Yule, *Book of Ser Marco Polo*, 77.238.
9 For more information, see Cresques and Grosjean, *Mapamundi, the Catalan Atlas of the Year 1375*.
10 Liping Wang, "Emperor Kangxi's Southern Tours and the Qing Restoration of West Lake."
11 Chen Menglei, *Gujin tushu jicheng*, 798–99.
12 *Junfu Xihu lu*, 806.
13 See *Xihu youlan zhiyu*, 11.187, 24.375.
14 Wu Renshu, *Pinwei shehua*, 177–213.
15 *Tao'an mengyi, Xihu mengxun*, 3.56.
16 *Fanghu cungao*, 3.6a.
17 Clunas, *Superfluous Things*.
18 *Tao'an mengyi, Xihu mengxun*, 7.111.

19 Hui-shu Lee, "Picturing West Lake."

20 Liping Wang, "Emperor Kangxi's Southern Tours and the Qing Restoration of West Lake"; Michael G. Chang, *A Court on Horseback*.

21 Chang and Owen, *Cambridge History of Chinese Literature*, vol. 2 (from 1375), 25.

22 For more discussion of Qing scholarship, see Elman, *Philosophy to Philology*.

23 Liping Wang, "Paradise for Sale," 208–63.

24 *Shidi buxing Hangzhou Xihu youlan zhinan*, 819–20.

25 He, "The Project of Dredging the West Lake in the 1950s and Its Ecological Consequences."

26 Relph, *Place and Placelessness*, 141.

27 State Administration of Cultural Heritage of People's Republic of China, "West Lake Cultural Landscape of Hangzhou," 15.

28 These modern developments might well provide a fruitful area for future scholarship, especially the issue of how the history of West Lake was appropriated in the discourse of national pride and developed through the use of new technology. Lam, et al., eds., *Senses of the City*, xvi.

BIBLIOGRAPHY

Primary Sources

Bai Juyi 白居易 (772–846). *Baishi changqing ji* 白氏長慶集. In *Siku quanshu*, Wenyuan ge edition.

Bian Yongyu 卞永譽 (1645–1712). *Shigutang shuhua huikao* 式古堂書畫匯考. In *Siku quanshu*, Wenyuan ge edition.

Cai Xiang 蔡襄 (1012–1067). *Duanming ji* 端明集. In *Siku quanshu*, Wenyuan ge edition.

Chen Congzhou 陳從周 (1918–2000). *Zishi yumo* 梓室余墨. In Wang Guoping, ed., *Xihu wenxian jicheng*, vol. 13.

Chen Menglei 陳夢雷 (1650–1741), et al., eds. *Gujin tushu jicheng* 古今圖書集成. In Wang Guoping, ed., *Xihu wenxian jicheng*, vol. 1.

Chen Qi 陳起 (ca. 13th century). *Jianghu xiaoji* 江湖小集. In *Siku quanshu*, Wenyuan ge edition.

Chen Qiqing 陳耆卿 (1180–1236). *Jiading Chicheng zhi* 嘉定赤城志. In *Siku quanshu*, Wenyuan ge edition.

Chen Si 陳思 (ca. 1225–1264) and Chen Shilong 陳世隆. *Liang Song mingxian xiaoji* 兩宋名賢小集. In *Siku quanshu*, Wenyuan ge edition.

Chen Xiang 陈襄 (1017–1080). *Guling ji* 古靈集. In *Siku quanshu*, Wenyuan ge edition.

Chen Yunping 陳允平 (ca. 1275–1278). *Rihu yuchang* 日湖漁唱. In *Congshu jicheng chubian* 叢書集成初編. Taipei: Xinwenfeng Chuban Gongsi, 1986.

Chen Zao 陳造 (1133–1203). *Jianghu changweng ji* 江湖長翁集. In *Siku quanshu*, Wenyuan ge edition.

Cheng Mi 程珌 (1164–1242). *Mingshui ji* 洺水集. In *Siku quanshu*, Wenyuan ge edition.

———. *You Longjing ji*. In Wang Guoping, ed., *Xihu wenxian jicheng*, vol. 14.

Deng Mu 鄧牧 (1247–1306). *Boya qin* 伯牙琴. In *Siku quanshu*, Wenyuan ge edition.

Ding Bing 丁丙 (1832–1899). *Wulin fangxiang zhi* 武林坊巷志. Hangzhou: Zhejiang Renmin Chubanshe, 1988.

———. *Wulin zhanggu congbian* 武林掌故叢編. Taipei: Tailian Guofeng Chubanshe, 1967.

Dong Sigao 董嗣杲 (ca. 13th century). *Xihu baiyong* 西湖百詠. In *Siku quanshu*, Wenyuan ge edition.

Fan Zushu 范祖述. *Hangsu yifeng* 杭俗遺風. In Wang Guoping, ed., *Xihu wenxian jicheng*, vol. 19.

Fang Xuanling 房玄齡 (578–648), et al. *Jin shu* 晉書. Beijing: Zhonghua Shuju, 1977.

Fei Gun 費袞 (ca. 12th–13th century). *Liangxi manzhi* 梁溪漫志. In *Siku quanshu,* Wenyuan ge edition.

Fu Wanglu 傅王露 (ca. 1715) and Li Wei 李衛 (1687–1738). *Xihu zhi* 西湖志. Hangzhou: Zhejiang Shuju, 1878.

Gao Lian 高濂 (ca. 16th century). *Zunsheng bajian* 遵生八牋. In *Siku quanshu,* Wenyuan ge edition.

Gao Shiqi 高士奇 (1645–1704). *Jiangcun xiaoxia lu* 江村消夏錄. In Lu Fusheng, et al., eds., *Zhongguo shuhua quanshu*, vol. 7.

Gao Sisun 高似孫 (ca. 1184). *Xie lüe* 蟹略. In *Siku quanshu,* Wenyuan ge edition.

Guo Xi 郭熙 (ca. 11th century). *Linquan gaozhi* 林泉高致. In *Siku quanshu,* Wenyuan ge edition.

Guoli Gugong Bowuyuan 國立故宮博物院. *Gugong shuhua tulu* 故宮書畫圖錄. Taipei: Guoli Gugong Bowuyuan, 1989.

———. *Songdai shuhua ceye mingpin tezhan* 宋代書畫冊頁名品特展. Taipei: Guoli Gugong Bowuyuan, 1995.

Hong Mai 洪邁 (1123–1202). *Yijian zhi* 夷堅志. Edited and annotated by He Zhuo 何卓. Beijing: Zhonghua Shuju, 1981.

Hu Zi 胡仔 (ca. 1147–1167). *Yuyin conghua* 漁隱叢話. In *Siku quanshu,* Wenyuan ge edition.

Hushan shenggai 湖山勝概. Preface by Chen Changxi 陳昌錫. In Bibliothèque Nationale de France, Paris.

Jiang Kui 姜夔 (1155–1221). *Baishi Daoren gequ* 白石道人歌曲. In *Siku quanshu,* Wenyuan ge edition.

Jiang Teli 姜特立 (b. 1125). *Meishan xugao* 梅山續藁. In *Siku quanshu,* Wenyuan ge edition.

Jidian 濟顛 (1148–1209) and Sun Zhi 孫治 (ca. 17th century). *Lingyinsi zhi* 靈隱寺志. In *Siku quanshu,* Wenyuan ge edition.

Jin Ao 金鰲, et al., eds. *Haining xianzhi* 海寧縣誌. Taipei: Chengwen Chubanshe, 1983.

Jingkou qijiu zhuan 京口耆舊傳. In *Siku quanshu*, Wenyuan ge edition.

Li Ding 李鼎 (ca. 1593). *Xihu xiaoshi* 西湖小史. In Wang Guoping, ed., *Xihu wenxian jicheng,* vol. 3.

Li Dongyang 李東陽 (1447–1516). *Huailutang ji* 懷麓堂集. In *Siku quanshu,* Wenyuan ge edition.

Li E 厲鶚 (1692–1752). *Dongcheng zaji* 東城雜記. In *Siku quanshu,* Wenyuan ge edition.

———. *Huchuan lu* 湖船錄. In Wang Guoping, ed., *Xihu wenxian jicheng*, vol. 8.

———. *NanSong yuanhua lu* 南宋院畫錄. In Wang Guoping, ed., *Xihu wenxian jicheng,* vol. 2.

———. *Songshi jishi* 宋詩紀事. In *Siku quanshu,* Wenyuan ge edition.

———. *Zengxiu Yunlinsi zhi* 增修雲林寺志. In Wang Guoping, ed., *Xihu wenxian jicheng,* vol. 22.

Li Liufang 李流芳 (1575–1629). *Tanyuan ji* 檀園集. In *Siku quanshu,* Wenyuan ge edition.

———. *Xihu woyoutu tiba* 西湖臥遊圖題跋. In Wang Guoping, ed., *Xihu wenxian jicheng,* vol. 3.

Li Xinchuan 李心傳 (1167–1244). *Jianyan yilai xi'nian yaolu* 建炎以來系年要錄. Beijing: Zhonghua Shuju, 1988.

Li Yimeng 李一氓 (1903–1990). *Xihu shijing houji* 西湖十景後記. In Wang Guoping, ed., *Xihu wenxian jicheng,* vol. 14.

Li Yinhan 李音翰 and Zhu Xuebo 朱學博, eds. *Baibao zongzhen ji* 百寶總珍集. Shanghai: Shanghai Shudian Chubanshe, 2015.

Li You 李有. *Guhang zaji* 古杭雜記. In Ding Bing, *Wulin zhanggu congbian*, vol. 1.

Liang Shaoren 梁紹壬 (b. 1792). *Liangban Qiuyu'an suibi* 兩般秋雨盦隨筆. Shanghai: Shanghai Guji Chubanshe, 1982.

Liang Shizheng 梁詩正 (1697–1763), et al. *Xihu zhizuan* 西湖志纂. Taipei: Taiwan Shangwu Yinshuguan, 1978.

Liu Xun 劉恂 (ca. 10th century). *Lingbiao luyi* 嶺表錄異. In *Siku quanshu,* Wenyuan ge edition.

Liu Yiqing 劉一清 (ca. 13th–14th century). *Qiantang yishi* 錢塘遺事. In *Siku quanshu,* Wenyuan ge edition.

Lu Ciyun 陸次云 (ca. 1662). *Huruan zaji* 湖儒雜記. In Wang Guoping, ed., *Xihu wenxian jicheng,* vol. 8.

Lu Feizhi 陸費執 (b. 1892). *Shidi buxing Hangzhou Xihu youlan zhinan* 實地步行杭州西湖遊覽指南. In Wang Guoping, ed., *Xihu wenxian jicheng*, vol. 19.

Lu Fusheng 盧輔圣, Cui Erping 崔爾平, and Jiang Hong 江宏, eds. *Zhongguo shuhua quanshu* 中國書畫全書. Shanghai: Shanghai Shuhua Chubanshe, 2000.

Lu Shen 陸深 (1477–1544). *Lu Yanshan wenji* 陸儼山文集. In *Siku quanshu,* Wenyuan ge edition.

Lu You 陸遊 (1125–1210). *Laoxue'an biji* 老學庵筆記. Beijing: Zhonghua Shuju, 1979.

———. *Wannan shigao* 宛南詩稿.

Lü Zuqian 呂祖謙 (1137–1181). *Lidai zhidu xiangshuo* 歷代制度詳說. In *Siku quanshu,* Wenyuan ge edition.

Meng Yuanlao 孟元老. *Dongjing meng hua lu* 東京夢華錄. In Meng Yuanlao, et al., *Dongjing meng hua lu (wai si zhong).*

Meng Yuanlao 孟元老, et al., *Dongjing meng hua lu (wai si zhong)* 東京夢華錄外四種. Annotated by Zhou Feng 周峰. Beijing: Wenhua Yishu Chubanshe, 1988.

Monk Dahe 釋大壑 (1525–1576). *Nanping Jingcisi zhi* 南屏淨慈寺志. In Wang Guoping, ed., *Xihu wenxian jicheng*, vol. 23.

Monk Guangbin 釋廣賓. *Hangzhou Shang Tianzhu jiangsi zhi* 杭州上天竺講寺志. Taipei: Mingwen Shuju, 1994.

Monk Jixiang 釋際祥. *Jingcisi zhi* 淨慈寺志. In Wang Guoping, ed., *Xihu wenxian jicheng,* vol. 23.

Naideweng 耐得翁. *Ducheng jisheng* 都城紀勝. In Meng Yuanlao, et al., *Dongjing meng hua lu (wai si zhong).*

Ouyang Xiu 歐陽修 (1007–1072). *Guitian lu* 歸田錄. In *Siku quanshu,* Wenyuan ge edition.

———. *Ouyang Xiu quanji* 歐陽修全集. Annotated by Li Yi'an 李逸安. Beijing: Zhonghua Shuju, 2001.

Pang Yuanji 龐元濟 (1864–1949). *Xuzhai minghua lu* 虛齋名畫錄. In Lu Fusheng, et al., eds., *Zhongguo shuhua quanshu,* vol. 12.

Pin Pin 品品. *Xihu biji* 西湖筆記. In Wang Guoping, ed., *Xihu wenxian jicheng,* vol. 14.

Puji 普濟. *Wudeng huiyuan* 五燈會元. In *Xu zang jing* 續臧經, Xiwenfeng Chuban Gongsi 新文豐出版公司. Taipei: Xiwenfeng Chuban Gongsi, 1993.

Qisong 契嵩 (1007–1071). *Tanjin wenji* 鐔津文集. In *Siku quanshu,* Wenyuan ge edition.

Qian Yueyou 潛說友. *Xianchun Lin'an zhi* 咸淳臨安志. In Zhonghua Shuju Bianjibu, *Song Yuan fangzhi congkan.*

Shen Gua 沈括 (1031–1095). *Mengxi bitan* 夢溪筆談. In *Siku quanshu,* Wenyuan ge edition.

Shi E 施諤. *Chunyou Lin'an zhi* 淳佑臨安志. In Zhonghua Shuju Bianjibu, *Song Yuan fangzhi congkan.*

Siku quanshu 四庫全書. Wenyuan ge 文淵閣 edition. Shanghai: Renmin Chubanshe, n.d. Online version; last accessed September 18, 2019. https://ctext.org/zhs.

Su Shi 蘇軾 (1037–1101). *Su Shi quanji jiaozhu* 蘇軾全集校注. Edited by Zhang Zhilie 張志烈, Ma Defu 馬德富, and Zhou Yukai 周裕鍇. Shijiazhuang: Hebei Renmin Chubanshe, 2010.

Sun Cheng'en 孫承恩 (1485–1565). *Wenjian ji* 文簡集. In *Siku quanshu,* Wenyuan ge edition.

Tang Guizhang 唐圭璋, ed. *Quan Song ci* 全宋詞. Beijing: Zhonghua Shuju, 1965.

Tao Zongyi 陶宗儀 (ca. 1360–1368). *Shuo fu* 說郛. In *Siku quanshu*, Wenyuan ge edition.

Tian Rucheng 田汝成 (ca. 1526). *Xihu youlan zhi* 西湖遊覽志. Hangzhou: Zhejiang Renmin Chubanshe, 1980.

———. *Xihu youlan zhiyu* 西湖遊覽志餘. Hangzhou: Zhejiang Renmin Chubanshe, 1980.

Tian Yiheng 田藝蘅 (ca. 1570). *Liuqing rizha* 留青日札. In Wang Guoping, ed., *Xihu wenxian jicheng,* vol. 13.

Tuotuo 脫脫, et al. *Song shi* 宋史. Beijing: Zhonghua Shuju, 1977.

Wang Guoping 王國平, ed. *Xihu wenxian jicheng* 西湖文獻集成. Hangzhou: Hangzhou Chubanshe, 2004.

Wang Jinsheng 汪近聖 (ca. 18th century). *Wangshi jianguzhai mosou* 汪氏鑑古齋墨藪. In Shanghai Guji Chubanshe 上海古籍出版社, *Xuxiu siku quanshu* 續修四庫全書. Shanghai: Shanghai Guji Chubanshe, 1995–2002.

Wang Keyu 汪砢玉 (b. 1587). *Xizihu shicui yutan* 西子湖拾翠餘談. In Wang Guoping, ed., *Xihu wenxian jicheng,* vol. 6.

Wang Mingqing 王明清 (ca. 1163–1224). *Yuzhao xinzhi* 玉照新志. In Wang Guoping, ed., *Xihu wenxian jicheng,* vol. 13.

Wang Shen 汪莘 (1155–1227). *Fanghu cungao* 方壺存稿. In *Siku quanshu,* Wenyuan ge edition.

Wang Xiangzhi 王象之 (ca. 1196). *Yudi jisheng* 輿地紀勝. Chengdu: Sichuan Daxue Chubanshe, 2005.

Wang Yiqing 王奕清 (1664–1737), Shen Chenyuan 沈辰垣 (ca. 1684), and Xuanye 玄燁 (1654–1722). *Yuxuan lidai shiyu* 御選歷代詩餘. In *Siku quanshu*, Wenyuan ge edition.

Wang Yuxian 王毓賢 (ca. 1691). *Huishi beikao* 繪事備考. In *Siku quanshu,* Wenyuan ge edition.

Wen Jia 文嘉 (1501–1583). *Qianshantang shuhuaji* 鈐山堂書畫記. In Lu Fusheng, et al., eds., *Zhongguo shuhua quanshu,* vol. 3.

Wu Renchen 吳任臣. *Shiguo chunqiu* 十國春秋. In *Siku quanshu,* Wenyuan ge edition.

Wu Zhijing 吳之鯨 (ca. 1609). *Wulin fanzhi* 武林梵志. In Wang Guoping, ed., *Xihu wenxian jicheng*, vol. 22.

Wu Zimu 吳自牧. *Mengliang lu* 夢粱錄. In Meng Yuanlao, et al., *Dongjing meng hua lu (wai si zhong).*

Xia Ji 夏基 (1623–ca. 1672). *Xihu lansheng shixu* 西湖覽勝詩序. In Wang Guoping, ed., *Xihu wenxian jicheng*, vol. 9.

Xihu Bowuguan 西湖博物館. *Lidai Xihu shuhuaji* 歷代西湖書畫集. Hangzhou: Hangzhou Chubanshe, 2010.

Xihu Laoren 西湖老人. *Fansheng lu* 繁盛錄. In Meng Yuanlao, et al., *Dongjing meng hua lu (wai si zhong).*

Xu Fengji 徐逢吉 (ca. 17th–18th century). *Qingbo xiaozhi* 清波小志. In Wang Guoping, ed., *Xihu wenxian jicheng*, vol. 8.

Xu Ke 徐珂 (1869–1928). *Zengding Xihu youlan zhinan* 增訂西湖遊覽指南. In Wang Guoping, ed., *Xihu wenxian jicheng*, vol. 10.

Xu Song 徐松 (1781–1848). *Song huiyao jigao* 宋會要輯稿. In *Siku quanshu,* Wenyuan ge edition.

Yang Erzeng 楊爾曾. *Xinjuan hainei qiguan* 新鐫海內奇觀. In Shanghai Guji Chubanshe, *Xuxiu siku quanshu*. Shanghai: Shanghai Guji Chubanshe, 2002.

Yang Fengbao 楊鳳苞. *Xihu qiuliu ci* 西湖秋柳詞. In Wang Guoping, ed., *Xihu wenxian jicheng,* vol. 27.

Yang Mengying 楊孟瑛 (1459–1518). *Junfu Xihu lu* 浚复西湖錄. In Wang Guoping, ed., *Xihu wenxian jicheng,* vol. 3.

Yang Wanli 楊萬里 (1127–1206). *Chengzhai ji* 誠齋集. In *Siku quanshu,* Wenyuan ge edition.

Yang Weizhen 楊維禎 (1296–1370). *Xihu zhuzhi ci* 西湖竹枝詞. In Yang Weizhen, et al., *Xihu zhuzhi ci sanzhong* 西湖竹枝詞三種. Hangzhou: Liuyi Shuju, 1928.

Yao Mian 姚勉 (b. 1216). *Xuepo ji* 雪坡集. In *Siku quanshu,* Wenyuan ge edition.

Ye Shaoweng 葉紹翁. *Sichao wenjian lu* 四朝聞見錄. In Wang Guoping, ed., *Xihu wenxian jicheng*, vol. 13.

Ye Sheng 葉盛. *Shuidong riji* 水東日記. In Wang Guoping, ed., *Xihu wenxian jicheng,* vol. 13.

Yu Sichong 俞思冲 (ca. 1595). *Xihu zhi leichao* 西湖志類鈔. Taipei: Chengwen Chubanshe, 1983.

Yuan Jiong 袁褧. *Fengchuang xiaodu* 楓窗小牘. In Zhu Yian 朱易安, et al., *Quan Song biji* 全宋筆記, vol. 4. Zhengzhou: Daxiang Chubanshe, 2008.

Yuanjing 元敬 (1011–1091), et al. *Wulin Xihu gaoseng shilüe deng bazhong* 武林西湖高僧事略等八種. Hangzhou: Hangzhou Chubanshe, 2006.

Zeng Zaozhuang 曾棗莊 and Liu Lin 劉琳, eds. *Quan Song wen* 全宋文. Chengdu: Bashu Shushe, 1988–1994.

Zha Weiren 查為仁 (1694–1749) and Li E 厲鶚. *Juemiao haoci jian* 絕妙好詞箋. In *Siku quanshu*, Wenyuan ge edition.

Zhang Chou 張丑 (1577–1643). *Qinghe shuhua fang* 清河書畫舫. In Lu Fusheng, et al., eds., *Zhongguo shuhua quanshu*, vol. 4.

Zhang Dai 張岱 (1597–1680). *Tao'an mengyi, Xihu mengxun* 陶庵夢憶.西湖夢尋. Shanghai: Shanghai Guji Chubanshe. 2009.

Zhang Yanyuan 張彥遠 (ca. 9th century). *Lidai minghua ji* 歷代名畫記. Beijing: Renmin Meishu Chubanshe. 1963.

Zhang Yun'ao 張雲璈 (1747–1829). *Jinniuhu yuchang* 金牛湖漁唱. In Wang Guoping, ed., *Xihu wenxian jicheng,* vol. 27.

Zhao Bian 趙抃 (1008–1084). *Qingxian ji* 清獻集. In *Siku quanshu,* Wenyuan ge edition.

Zhao Fan 赵蕃 (1143–1229). *Qiandao gao, Chunxi gao* 乾道稿 淳熙稿. In *Siku quanshu,* Wenyuan ge edition.

Zhao Xigu 趙希鵠 (ca. 1180–1240). *Dongtian qinglu ji* 洞天清錄集. In Huang Binhong 黃賓虹 and Deng Shi 鄧實, eds., *Meishu congshu* 美術叢書. Taipei: Yiwen Yinshuguan, 1960.

Zhao Yanheng 趙彥衛 (ca. 1195). *Yunlu manchao* 云麓漫钞. In *Siku quanshu,* Wenyuan ge edition.

Zheng Qingzhi 鄭清之 (1176–1251). *Anwantang ji* 安晚堂集. In *Siku quanshu,* Wenyuan ge edition.

Zheng Yuejing 鄭曰敬 (ca. 1901). *Xihu baiyong* 西湖百詠. In Wang Guoping, ed., *Xihu wenxian jicheng,* vol. 27.

Zhonghua Shuju Bianjibu 中華書局編輯部. *Song Yuan fangzhi congkan* 宋元方志叢刊. Beijing: Zhonghua Shuju: Xinhua Shudian Beijing Faxingsuo, 1990.

Zhou Bida 周必大 (1126–1204). *Erlaotang zazhi* 二老堂雜誌. In Wang Guoping, ed., *Xihu wenxian jicheng,* vol. 6.

Zhou Hui 周輝 (b. 1126). *Qingbo zazhi* 清波雜志. In *Siku quanshu,* Wenyuan ge edition.

Zhou Mi 周密 (1232–1298). *Guixin zashi* 癸辛雜識. Beijing: Zhonghua Shuju, 1988.

———. *Pinzhou yudi pu* 蘋洲漁笛譜. In *Siku quanshu*, Wenyuan ge edition.

———. *Qidong yeyu* 齊東野語. In Wang Guoping, ed., *Xihu wenxian jicheng,* vol. 13.

———. *Wulin jiushi* 武林舊事. In Meng Yuanlao, et al., *Dongjing meng hua lu (wai si zhong).*

Zhou Qingyuan 周清源 (ca. 16th–17th century). *Xihu erji* 西湖二集. Shanghai: Shanghai Guji Chubanshe, 1990.

Zhou Zizhi 周紫芝 (1082–1155). *Taicang timi ji* 太倉稊米集. In *Siku quanshu,* Wenyuan ge edition.

Zhu Guozhen 朱國禎 (1557–1632). *Yongchuang xiaopin* 涌幢小品. In *Siku quanshu,* Wenyuan ge edition.

Zhu Mu 祝穆 (d. 1255). *Fangyu shenglan* 方輿勝覽. In *Siku quanshu,* Wenyuan ge edition.

Zhu Peng 朱彭 (1731–1803). *NanSong guji kao* 南宋古跡考. In *Siku quanshu,* Wenyuan ge edition.

Zhu Tinghuan 朱廷煥 (ca. 1634). *Zengbu Wulin jiushi* 增補武林舊事. In *Siku quanshu,* Wenyuan ge edition.

Zhuang Chuo 莊綽 (ca. 12th century). *Jilei bian* 雞肋編. In *Siku quanshu,* Wenyuan ge edition.

Secondary Sources

Altenburger, Roland. "Layered Landscape: Textual and Cartographical Representations of Hangzhou's West Lake, 16th–18th Centuries." In *Entangled Landscapes: Early Modern China and Europe*, edited by Yue Zhuang and Andrea Riemenschnitter, 115–43. Singapore: NUS Press, 2017.

Aoyama, Sadao 青山定雄. *Tō Sō jidai no kōtsū to chishi chizu no kenkyū* 唐宋時代の交通と地誌地圖の研究. Tokyo: Yoshikawa Kobunkan, 1963.

Baker, R. H. Alan. *Geography and History: Bridging the Divide*. Cambridge, UK: Cambridge University Press, 2003.

Barnhart, Richard. "Shining Rivers: Eight Views of the Hsiao and Hsiang in Sung Painting." In *International Colloquium on Chinese Art History: Proceedings*, edited by International Colloquium on Chinese Art History and National Palace Museum, 45–95. Taipei: National Palace Museum, 1992.

Benn, James A. *Tea in China: A Religious and Cultural History*. Honolulu: University of Hawai'i Press, 2015.

Bol, Peter. "Reconceptualizing the Order of Things in Northern and Southern Song." In *The Cambridge History of China, vol. 5, pt. 2: Sung China, 960–1279*, edited by John W. Chaffee, Denis Crispin Twitchett, and John King Fairbank, 665–726. Cambridge, UK: Cambridge University Press, 2015.

———. "The Rise of Local History: History, Geography, and Culture in Southern Song and Yuan Wuzhou." *Harvard Journal of Asiatic Studies* 61, no. 1 (June 2001): 37–76. https://doi.org/10.2307/3558587.

———. *This Culture of Ours: Intellectual Transitions in T'ang and Sung China*. Stanford, CA: Stanford University Press, 1992.

Brook, Timothy. *The Confusions of Pleasure: Commerce and Culture in Ming China*. Berkeley: University of California Press, 1998.

Bush, Susan, and Hsiao-yen Shih. *Early Chinese Texts on Painting*. Cambridge, MA: Published for the Harvard-Yenching Institute by Harvard University Press, 1985.

Cahill, James. "The Imperial Painting Academy." In *Possessing the Past: Treasures from the National Palace Museum, Taipei*, edited by Wen Fong, James C. Y Watt, and Guoli Gugong Bowuyuan, 159–99. New York: Metropolitan Museum of Art, 1996.

———. *The Lyric Journey: Poetic Painting in China and Japan*. Cambridge, MA: Harvard University Press, 1961.

———. *The Restless Landscape: Chinese Painting of the Late Ming Period*. Berkeley: University Art Museum, 1971.

Campany, Robert Ford. *Strange Writing: Anomaly Accounts in Early Medieval China*. Albany: State University of New York Press, 1996.

Campbell, Duncan. "The Ten Scenes of West Lake." *China Heritage Quarterly* 28 (December 2011). Last accessed August 5, 2018. http://www.chinaheritagequarterly.org/features.php?searchterm=028_scenes.inc&issue=028.

Cao Jiaqi 曹家齊. *Songdai de jiaotong yu zhengzhi* 宋代的交通與政治. Beijing: Zhonghua Shuju, 2017.

Chang, Kang-i Sun, and Stephen Owen, eds. *The Cambridge History of Chinese Literature*. 2 vols. Cambridge, UK: Cambridge University Press, 2010.

Chang, Michael G. *A Court on Horseback: Imperial Touring and the Construction of Qing Rule, 1680–1785*. Cambridge, MA: Harvard University Asia Center, 2007.

Chen Guocan 陳國燦. "NanSong shimin jieceng tanxi 南宋市民階層探析." In *NanSong shi ji NanSong ducheng Lin'an yanjiu*, vol. 1, edited by He Zhongli, 160–80. Beijing: Renmin Chubanshe, 2009.

Chen Hui 陳暉. "*Xihu fansheng quanjing tu* wei NanSong yuanhua kao 《西湖繁盛全景圖》為南宋院畫考." In *Xihu wenlan: Xihu wenhua yantaohui lunwen jicui* 西湖文瀾: 西湖文化研討會論文集粹, edited by Zhongguo Shehui Kexueyuan Kaogu Yanjiusuo 中國社會科學院考古研究所, 257–60. Hangzhou: Hangzhou Chubanshe, 2015.

Chen Xiaofa 陳小法, "Xuezhou Dengyang yu Hangzhou Xihu 雪舟等楊與杭州西湖," *Xihu xue luncong* 西湖學論叢 7 (2015): 7–18.

Chen Ye 陳野. *NanSong huihua shi* 南宋繪畫史. Shanghai: Shanghai Guji Chubanshe, 2008.

Cheng, Hsiao-wen. "Traveling Stories and Untold Desires: Female Sexuality in Song China, 10th–13th Centuries." PhD diss., University of Washington, 2012.

Cheng Meng 成蔭. "NanSong Lin'an Xihu jingqu jieri youle chutan 南宋臨安西湖景區節日遊樂初探." *Sichuan shifan daxue xuebao* 四川師範大學學報 34, no. 6 (November 2007): 124–28.

Cheng Meng 成蔭 and Wang Xi 王曦. "Guanfang gonggong fuwu yu NanSong Xihu lüyou 官方公共服務與南宋西湖旅遊." *Yibin xueyuan xuebao* 宜賓學院學報 8 (August 2005): 19–21.

Cheng Minsheng 程民生. "Songren shenghuo shuiping ji bizhi kaocha 宋人生活水平及幣值考察." *Shixue yuekan* 史學月刊, no. 3 (2008): 100–111.

City University of Hong Kong Chinese Civilisation Centre. *China: Five Thousand Years of History and Civilization*. Hong Kong: City University of Hong Kong Press, 2007.

Clunas, Craig. *Elegant Debts: The Social Art of Wen Zhengming, 1470–1559*. Honolulu: University of Hawai'i Press, 2004.

———. *Pictures and Visuality in Early Modern China*. Princeton, NJ: Princeton University Press, 1997.

———. *Superfluous Things: Material Culture and Social Status in Early Modern China*. Honolulu: University of Hawai'i Press, 2004.

Cohen, Erik. "A Phenomenology of Tourist Experiences." *Sociology* 13, no. 2 (1979): 179–201. https://doi.org/10.1177/003803857901300203.

Cohen, Monique, Nathalie Monnet, and Bibliothèque Nationale de France. *Impressions de Chine*. Paris: Bibliothèque Nationale, 1992.

Collins-Kreiner, Noga, and Yael Zins. "Tourists and Souvenirs: Changes through Time, Space and Meaning." *Journal of Heritage Tourism* 6, no. 1 (2011): 17–27. https://doi.org/10.1080/1743873X.2010.515312.

Cresques, Abraham, and Georges Grosjean. *Mapamundi, the Catalan Atlas of the Year 1375*. Dietikon-Zurich: Urs Graf, 1978.

Cresswell, Tim. *Place: An Introduction*. Chichester, West Sussex: Wiley, Blackwell, 2015.

Cronon, William. *Nature's Metropolis: Chicago and the Great West*. New York: W. W. Norton, 1992.

Dai Huafen 戴華芬. "Xihu de meili yu aichou: Shilun NanSong shiqi Xihu lüyou huodong de geshi fengmao 西湖的美麗與哀愁—試論南宋時期西湖旅遊活動的各式風貌." MA thesis, Tsinghua University, 2002.

Davis, Richard. *Wind against the Mountain: The Crisis of Politics and Culture in Thirteenth-century China*. Cambridge, MA: Council on East Asian Studies, Harvard University, 1996.

de Pee, Christian. "Circulation and Flow: Immanent Metaphors in the Financial Debates of Northern Song China (960–1127 CE)." *History of Science* 56, no. 2 (2018): 168–95. https://doi.org/10.1177/0073275317724706.

———. "Nature's Capital: The City as Garden in *The Splendid Scenery of the Capital* (*Ducheng jisheng*, 1235)." In Lam, et al., eds., *Senses of the City*, 179–204.

———. "Notebooks (*biji*) and Shifting Boundaries of Knowledge in Eleventh-Century China." *The Medieval Globe* 3, no. 1 (2017): 129–68. https://doi.org/10.17302/TMG/3-1.6.

———. "Purchase on Power: Imperial Space and Commercial Space in Song-Dynasty Kaifeng, 960–1127." *Journal of the Economic and Social History of the Orient* 53, no. 1–2 (2009): 149–84. https://doi.org/10.1163/002249910X12573963244322.

———. "Urban Acupuncture: Care and Ideology in the Writing of the City in Eleventh-Century China." In *Ancient and Modern Practices of Citizenship in Asia and the West: Care of the Self*, edited by Gregory Byrne Bracken, 171–92. Amsterdam: University of Amsterdam Press, 2019.

De Weerdt, Hilde Godelieve Dominique. "The Cultural Logics of Map Reading: Text, Time, and Space in Printed Maps of the Song Empire." In *Knowledge and Text Production in an Age of Print: China, 900–1400*, edited by Lucille Chia, Hilde Godelieve Dominique De Weerdt, and E. J. Brill, 239–70. Leiden-Boston: Brill, 2011.

———. *Information, Territory, and Networks: The Crisis and Maintenance of Empire in Song China*. Cambridge, MA: Harvard University Asia Center, 2015.

Dott, Brian Russell. *Identity Reflections: Pilgrimages to Mount Tai in Late Imperial China*. Cambridge, MA: Harvard University Asia Center, 2004.

Duan, Xiaolin 段晓琳. "A Comparative Study of Two Series of Printed West Lake Ten Views." In *Meishuxue boshisheng guoji xueshu luntan lunwenji* 美術學博士生國際學術論壇論文集, edited by Li Song 李松 and Ding Ning 丁寧, 224–49. Xi'an: Shaanxi Normal University Press, 2012.

———. "Scenic Beauty outside the City: Tourism around Hangzhou's West Lake in the Southern Song (1127–1276)." PhD diss., University of Washington, 2014.

———. "Ten Views of West Lake." In *Visual and Material Cultures in Middle Period China*, edited by Patricia B. Ebrey and Shih-shan Susan Huang, 151–92. Leiden: Brill, 2017.

Duan, Yuming 段玉明. "Kaifeng Daoist Temples in the Southern Song Dynasty Hangzhou: Research in Actual Examples of Religious Cultural Changes." *Frontier History China* 2, no. 2 (2007): 145–65. https://doi.org/10.1007/s11462-007-0010-z.

Ebrey, Patricia Buckley. *Accumulating Culture: The Collections of Emperor Huizong*. Seattle: University of Washington Press, 2008.

———. *Emperor Huizong*. Cambridge, MA: Harvard University Press, 2014.

———. "Taking Out the Grand Carriage: Imperial Spectacle and the Visual Culture of Northern Song Kaifeng," *Asia Major* (Third Series) 12, no. 1 (1999): 33–66.

———. "Women, Money, and Class: Sima Guang and Song Neo-Confucian Views on Women." *Women and the Family in Chinese History*, edited by Patricia B. Ebrey, 10–38. New York: Routledge, 2002.

Ebrey, Patricia Buckley, and Peter N. Gregory, eds. *Religion and Society in T'ang and Sung China*. Honolulu: University of Hawai'i Press, 1993.

Ebrey, Patricia Buckley, and Shih-shan Susan Huang, eds. *Visual and Material Cultures in Middle Period China*. Leiden: Brill, 2017.

Egan, Ronald. "Crime, Violence, and Ghosts in the Lin'an Stories in *Yijian zhi*." In Lam, et al., eds., *Senses of the City*, 149–78.

———. "Nature and Higher Ideals in Texts on Calligraphy, Music, and Painting." in *Chinese Aesthetics: The Ordering of Literature, the Arts, and the Universe in the Six Dynasties*, edited by Zong-qi Cai, 277–309. Honolulu: University of Hawai'i Press, 2004.

———. *The Problem of Beauty: Aesthetic Thought and Pursuits in Northern Song Dynasty China*. Cambridge, MA: Harvard University Asia Center, 2006.

Elman, Benjamin A. *From Philosophy to Philology: Intellectual and Social Aspects of Change in Late Imperial China*. Los Angeles: UCLA Press, 2001.

Fang Hao 方豪. "Songdai fojiao dui lüyou zhi gongxian 宋代佛教對旅遊之貢獻." *Dongfang zazhi* 東方雜誌 5, no. 3 (1971): 33–44.

Fong, Wen 方聞. *Beyond Representation: Chinese Painting and Calligraphy, 8th–14th Century*. New Haven: Yale University Press, 1992.

Fujiwa Rumi 原瑠美. "Saiko hirakiei shōshi Minami Sō Linan kenkyū ni yose te 西湖開濬小史南宋臨安研究によせて." *Chuo Journal of Asian History* 34 (2010): 125–57.

Genovese, Eugene D., Leonard Hochberg, and Edward Whiting Fox. *Geographic Perspectives in History*. Oxford: B. Blackwell, 1989.

Gernet, Jacques. *Daily Life in China, On the Eve of the Mongol Invasion, 1250–1276*. Stanford, CA: Stanford University Press, 1962.

Gerritsen, Anne. "Visions of Local Culture: Tales of the Strange and Temple Inscriptions from Song-Yuan Jizhou." *Journal of Chinese Religions* 28, no. 1 (2000): 69–92. https://doi.org/10.1179/073776900805306685.

Hansen, Valerie. *Changing Gods in Medieval China, 1127–1276*. Princeton, NJ: Princeton University Press, 1990.

Hargett, M. James. *Jade Mountains and Cinnabar Pools: The History of Travel Literature in Imperial China*. Seattle: University of Washington Press, 2018.

———. *On the Road in Twelfth-Century China: The Travel Diaries of Fan Chengda (1126–1193)*. Stuttgart: Steiner Verlag Wiesbaden, 1989.

———. "Sketches." In *The Columbia History of Chinese Literature*, edited by Victor H. Mair. New York: Columbia University Press, 2001.

———. "Song Dynasty Local Gazetteers and Their Place in the History of Difangzhi Writing." *Harvard Journal of Asiatic Studies* 56, no. 2 (December 1996): 405–42. https://doi.org/10.2307/2719404.

Harrist, E. Robert. "Site Names and Their Meaning in the Garden of Solitary Enjoyment." *Journal of Garden History* 13 (1993): 199–212. https://doi.org/10.1080/01445170.1993.10412488.

Hartwell, Robert. "A Revolution in the Chinese Iron and Coal Industries in the Northern Sung, 960–1126 A.D.." *Journal of Asian Studies* 21, no. 2 (February 1962): 153–62.

Hawkes, Jacquetta. *A Land*. London: Collins, 2012.

He, Qiliang 何其亮, "The Project of Dredging the West Lake in the 1950s and Its Ecological Consequences." Paper presented at the Annual Conference of the Association for Asian Studies, Washington, DC, March 2018.

He Zhongli 何忠禮. *NanSong shi ji NanSong ducheng Lin'an yanjiu* 南宋史及南宋都城研究. Beijing: Renmin Chubanshe, 2009.

Hofmann, Martin. "The Biographer's View of Craftsmanship." In *Of Knowledge: Technology in Chinese History*, edited by Dagmar Schäfer, 283–97. Leiden: Brill, 2011.

Honda Osamu 本田治. "Sō Dai Kōshū oyobi kōhai chi no suiri to suiri soshiki 宋代杭州及び後背地の水利と水利組織." In Umehara, ed., *Chūgoku kinsei no toshi to bunka*, 125–51.

Hu Shiying 胡士瑩. *Huaben xiaoshuo gailun* 話本小說概論. Beijing: Zhonghua Shuju, 1980.

Huang, Chi-Chiang. "Elite and Clergy in Northern Sung Hangchou: A Convergence of Interest." In *Buddhism in the Sung*, edited by Peter N. Gregory and Daniel Aaron Getz, 295–339. Honolulu: University of Hawai'i Press, 1999.

Huang, Shi-shan Susan. "Tianzhu Lingqian: Divination Prints from a Buddhist Temple in Song Hangzhou." *Artibus Asiae* 67, no. 2 (2007): 243–96.

Hucker, Charles O. *A Dictionary of Official Titles in Imperial China*. Beijing: Beijing Daxue Chubanshe, 2008.

Hur, Nam-lin. *Prayer and Play in Late Tokugawa Japan: Asakusa Sensōji and Edo Society*. Cambridge, MA: Harvard University Asia Center, 2000.

Hymes, Robert. "Marriage, Descent Groups, and the Localist Strategy in Sung and Yuan Fu-chou." in *Kinship Organization in Late Imperial China 1000–1940*, edited by Patricia Buckley Ebrey and James L. Watson, 95–136. Berkeley: University of California Press, 1996.

I Lo-fen 衣若芬. "'Landscape Like a Picture' and 'Landscape in the Picture': On the Song and Yuan Poems on the 'Xiaoxiang' Landscape Paintings 「江山如畫」與「畫裡江山」: 宋元題「瀟湘」山水畫詩之比較." *Zhongguo wenzhe yanjiu jikan* 中國文哲研究集刊 23 (2003): 33–70.

———. "A New Exploration on Qing Palace's Collection of Ming Dynasty Artist Wang Fu's painting—'The Eight Views of Beijing' 玉堂天上: 清宮舊藏明代「北京八景圖」新探." *Gugong xuekan* 故宮學刊 16 (2016): 283–96.

Idemitsu Sachiko 出光佐千子. *Ike Taiga no "Seikozu" nitsuite: "Shinkei" no gogi nikansuru ichi kōsatsu* 池大雅の「西湖図」について: 「真景」の語義に関する一考察. Shushi Gakui Ronbun: Keio Gijuku Daigaku, 2000.

Ihara Hiroshi 伊原弘. *Chūgoku Kaifū no seikatsu to saiji: Egakareta Sōdai no toshi seikatsu* 中国開封の生活と歳時 : 描かれた宋代の都市生活. Tokyo: Yamakawa Shuppansha, 1991.

———. *Sōdai Chūgoku o tabisuru* 宋代中國を旅する. Tokyo: NTT Huppan, 1995.

Inglis, Alister David. *Hong Mai's Record of the Listener and Its Song Dynasty Context*. Albany: State University of New York Press, 2006.

Jiang Qingqing 姜青青. *"Xianchun Lin'an zhi" Songban "jingcheng situ" fuyuan yanjiu* 《咸淳臨安志》宋版《京城四圖》復原研究. Shanghai: Shanghai Guji Chubenshe, 2015.

Jin Wenjing 金文京. "Xihu zai Zhong Ri Han: Lüetan fengjing zhuanyi zai DongYa wenxue zhong de yiyi 西湖在中日韓——略談風景轉移在東亞文學中的意義." In *DongYa wenhua yixiang zhi xingsu* 東亞文化意象之形塑, edited by Shih Shou-Chien 石守謙 and Liao Zhaoheng 廖肇亨, 141–66. Taipei: Yunchen Wenhua Shiye Gufen Youxian Gongsi, 2001.

Kracke, A. Edwin, Jr. "Sung K'ai-feng: Pragmatic Metropolis and Formalistic Capital," in *Crisis and Prosperity in Sung China*, edited by John W. Haeger, 49–77. Tucson: University of Arizona Press, 1975.

Kubin, Wolfgang. *Zhongguo wenren de ziranguan* 中國文人的自然觀. Translated by Ma Shude 馬樹德. Shanghai: Shanghai Renmin Chubanshe, 1990.

Lam, Joseph, Shuen-fu Lin, Christian de Pee, and Martin Powers, eds. *Senses of the City: Perceptions of Hangzhou in the Southern Song (1127–1179)*. Hong Kong: Chinese University of Hong Kong Press, 2017.

Lee, Hui-shu. "The Domain of Empress Yang (1162–1233): Art, Gender and Politics at the Southern Song Court." PhD diss., Yale University, 1994.

———. *Empresses, Art, and Agency in Song Dynasty China*. Seattle: University of Washington Press, 2010.

———. *Exquisite Moments: West Lake and Southern Song Art*. New York: China Institute Gallery. Distributed by Art Media Resources, 2001.

———. "Picturing West Lake: Reflections of a Cultural Space." Paper presented at the "When Shall West Lake Be Without Song or Dance?" Conference, University of Michigan, October 2011.

———. "*Wulin jiushi*: *Xihu qingqu tu* yu Lin'an shengjing 武林舊事:《西湖清趣圖》與臨安勝景." Paper presented at the "Liang Song shuhua chuanxi yu yanjiu guoji xueshu luntan 兩宋書畫傳習與研究國際學術論壇" Conference, China Academy of Art, Hangzhou, September 2017.

Lee, John. "Recent Studies in English on the Tang-Song transition: Issues and Trends." *Guoji Zhongguo xue yanjiu* 國際中國學研究 2 (December 1999): 365–83.

Lefebvre, Henri. *The Production of Space*. Oxford: Blackwell, 1991.

Li Hsiao-ti 李孝悌, ed. *Zhongguo de chengshi shenghuo: Shisi dao ershi shiji* 中國的城市生活: 十四到二十世紀. Taipei: Lianjing Chuban Shiye Gongsi, 2005.

Li Huarui 李華瑞. *Songdai jiu de shengchan he zhengque* 宋代酒的生產和征榷. Baoding: Hebei Daxue Chubanshe, 1995.

Li Lincan 李霖燦. "Ye Xiaoyan de *Xihu tu* ji qita 葉肖巖的西湖圖及其他." *Gugong wenwu yuekan* 故宮文物月刊 28 (July 1985): 126–31.

Li Yumin 李玉珉. "Xihu shijing tezhan 西湖十景特展." *Gugong wenwu yuekan* 156 (March 1996): 98–117.

Li Zehou 李澤厚. *Mei de lichen, Huaxia meixue, Meixue sijiang* 美的歷程 華夏美學 美學四講. Hefei: Anhui Wenyi Chubanshe, 1994.

Lian, Xinda. "How Does an Objective Correlative Objectify? West Lake as the Site for Patriotic Sentiment in Southern Song Lyrics." In Lam, et al., eds., *Senses of the City*, 205–34.

Lin, Fan. "The Local in the Imperial Vision: Landscape, Topography, and Geography in Southern Song Map Guides and Gazetteers." *Cross-Currents: East Asian History and Culture Review*, no. 23 (2017): 10–39. Last accessed August 17, 2019. http://cross-currents.berkeley.edu/e-journal/issue-23.

Lin, Li-Chiang 林麗江. "A Study of the *Xinjuan hainei qiguan*, a Ming Dynasty Book of Famous Sites." In *Bridges to Heaven: Essays on East Asian Art in Honor of Professor Wen C. Fong*, edited by Jerome Silbergeld, Dora C. Y. Ching, Judith G. Smith, and Alfred Murck, 779–812. Princeton, NJ: Princeton University Press, 2011.

Lin, Shuen-fu. "Wen Jiweng of the Late Southern Song: The Man, His Life, and His Poem." *West Lake Tsinghua Journal of Chinese Studies* 39, no. 1 (March 2009): 63–124.

Lin Zhengqiu 林正秋 and Jin Min 金敏. *NanSong gudu Hangzhou* 南宋故都杭州. Zhengzhou: Zhongzhou shuhuashe: Henansheng Xinhua Shudian Faxing, 1984.

———. "Xihu gudai shujun zhili shi tanshu 西湖古代疏浚治理史探述," *Xihu xue luncong* 3 (2010): 56–67.

Ling Yuzhi 凌郁之. *Hong Mai nianpu* 洪邁年譜. Shanghai: Shanghai Guji Chubanshe, 2006.

Liu, Gang 劉剛. "The 'Loss' of Purity: Changes and Persistence in the Cultural Memory of the Cold Spring Pavilion." *Frontiers of Literary Studies in China* 8, no. 2 (2014): 205–24.

———. "The Poetics of Miscellaneousness: The Literary Design of Liu Yiqing's *Qiantang Yishi* and the Historiography of the Southern Song." PhD diss., University of Michigan, 2010.

Liu, Lihong. "Collecting the Here and Now: Birthday Albums and the Aesthetics of Association in Mid-Ming China." *Journal of Chinese Literature and Culture* 2, no. 1 (2015): 43–91. https://doi.org/10.1215/23290048-2887553.

Liu Chunying 劉春迎. "Cong BeiSong Dongjing waicheng de kaogu faxian tan BeiSong shiqi de yingzaochi 從北宋東京外城的考古發現談北宋時期的營造尺." *Wenwu* 文物, no. 2 (2008): 54–60.

Liu Fang 劉方. *Shengshi fanhua: Songdai Jiangnan chengshi wenhua de fanrong yu bianqian* 盛世繁華: 宋代江南城市文化的繁榮與變遷. Hangzhou: Zhejiang Daxue Chubanshe, 2011.

Liu Qiugen 劉秋根 and Ren Huanhuan 任歡歡. "Songdai nüxing shishang xiaofei 宋代女性時尚消費." *Hebei xuekan* 河北學刊 31, no. 3 (May 2011): 71–77.

Liu Zhiyuan 劉志遠. *Nanhai yihao de kaogu shijue* 南海一號的考古試掘. Beijing: Kexue Chubanshe, 2011.

Loehr, Max. *The Great Painters of China*. New York: Harper & Row, 1980.

Lomine, Loykie. "Tourism in Augustan Society 44BC–AD69." In *Histories of Tourism: Representation, Identity, and Conflict*, edited by John K. Walton, 69–87. Clevedon, UK: Channel View Publications, 2005.

Lu Xun 魯迅. *Selected Works of Lu Hsun*. Translated by Xianyi Yang and Gladys Yang. Peking: Foreign Languages Press, 1956.

Luo, Yinan 羅祎楠. "A Study of the Changes in the Tang–Song Transition Model." *Journal of Song-Yuan Studies*, no. 35 (2005): 99–127.

Ma, Lawrence. *Commercial Development and Urban Change in Sung China (960–1279)*. Ann Arbor: University of Michigan, 1971.

McDowall, Stephen. *Qian Qianyi's Reflections on Yellow Mountain: Traces of a Late-Ming Hatchet and Chisel*. Hong Kong–London: Hong Kong University Press. Distributed by Eurospan, 2009.

Meyer-Fong, Tobie. *Building Culture in Early Qing Yangzhou.* Stanford, CA: Stanford University Press, 2003.

Milburn, Olivia. *Urbanization in Early and Medieval China: Gazetteers for the City of Suzhou.* Seattle: University of Washington Press, 2015.

Mitchell, W. J. T. *Iconology: Image, Text, Ideology.* Chicago: University of Chicago Press, 1986.

———. *Landscape and Power.* Chicago: University of Chicago Press, 1994.

Miyazaki Noriko 宮崎法子. "Saiko wo meguru kaiga 西湖をめぐる絵画." In Umehara, ed., *Chūgoku kinsei no toshi to bunka*, 199–246.

Moerman, D. Max. *Localizing Paradise: Kumano Pilgrimage and the Religious Landscape of Premodern Japan.* Cambridge, MA: Harvard University Asia Center. Distributed by Harvard University Press, 2005.

Mote, W. Frederick. "A Millennium of Chinese Urban History: Form, Time, and Space Concepts in Soochow." *Rice University Studies* 59, no. 4 (Fall 1973): 35–65.

Mou Zhenyu 牟振宇. "NanSong Lin'an cheng simiao fenbu yanjiu 南宋臨安城寺廟分布研究." *Hangzhou shifan daxue xuebao* 杭州師範大學學報 1 (2008): 95–101.

Moule, A. C. *Quinsai: With Other Notes on Marco Polo.* Cambridge, UK: Cambridge University Press, 1957.

Murck, Alfreda. "Eight Views of the Hsiao and Hsiang Rivers by Wang Hong." In *Images of the Mind*, edited by Wen C. Fong 方聞, 214–35. Princeton: The Art Museum, Princeton University, 1984.

———. *Poetry and Painting in Song China: The Subtle Art of Dissent.* Cambridge, MA: Harvard University Asia Center for the Harvard-Yenching Institute, 2000.

Naquin, Susan. *Peking: Temples and City Life, 1400–1900.* Berkeley: University of California Press, 2000.

Naquin, Susan, and Yu Chün-fang. *Pilgrims and Sacred Sites in China.* Berkeley: University of California Press, 1992.

Nenzi, Laura. *Excursions in Identity: Travel and the Intersection of Place, Gender, and Status in Edo Japan.* Honolulu: University of Hawai'i Press, 2008.

Nolan, Mary Lee, and Sidney Nolan. "Religious Sites as Tourism Attractions in Europe." *Annals of Tourism Research* 19, no. 1 (1992): 68–78. https://doi.org/10.1016/0160-7383(92)90107-Z.

Nyíri, Pál. *Scenic Spots: Chinese Tourism, the State, and Cultural Authority.* Seattle: University of Washington Press, 2006.

Osawa Masaaki 大沢正昭. "Tōdai henkakuki no rekishiteki igi 唐代変革期の歴史的意義." *Rekishi Hyōron* 357 (1980).

Ouyang Guang 歐陽光. *SongYuan shishe yanjiu conggao* 宋元詩社研究叢稿. Guangzhou: Guangzhou Gaodeng Jiaoyu Chubanshe, 1996.

Owen, Stephen. *Remembrances: The Experience of the Past in Classical Chinese Literature.* Cambridge, MA: Harvard University Press, 1986.

Polo, Marco, Henri Cordier, and Henry Yule. *The Book of Ser Marco Polo, the Venetian: Concerning the Kingdoms and Marvels of the East.* London: J. Murray, 1903.

Polo, Marco, and Komroff Manuel. *The Travels of Marco Polo, the Venetian.* New York: H. Liveright, 1903.

Powers, Martin. "Picturing Time in Song Painting and Poetry." In Lam, et al., eds., *Senses of the City*, 55–72.

Quan Hansheng 全漢昇. "BeiSong Bianliang de shuchuru maoyi 北宋汴梁的輸出入貿易." *Zhongguo jingji shi luncong* 中國經濟史論叢, 87–200. Hong Kong: Xianggang Zhongwen Daxue Xinya Shuyuan Xinya Yanjiusuo, 1972.

Raj, Razaq, and Nigel D. Morpeth. *Religious Tourism and Pilgrimage Festivals Management: An International Perspective*. Wallingford, UK: CABI Publisher, 2007.

Relph, Edward C. *Place and Placelessness*. Los Angeles: Sage Publications, 2016.

———. "Spirit of Place and Sense of Place in Virtual Realities." *Techné: Research in Philosophy and Technology* 10, no. 3 (2007): 17–25. https://doi.org/10.5840/techne20071039.

Ridgway, Benjamin B. "Imagined Travel: Displacement, Landscape, and Literati Identity in the Song Lyrics of Su Shi (1037–1101)." PhD diss., University of Michigan, 2005.

———. "Touring the City in Southern Song China: The Popular Poetics of 'Hundred-Poem' Collections on Jiankang and Hangzhou in the 13th century." Paper presented at the Second Conference on Middle Period Chinese Humanities, Leiden, September 2017.

Robson, James. *Power of Place: The Religious Landscape of the Southern Sacred Peak (Nanyue) in Medieval China*. Cambridge, MA: Harvard University Asia Center, 2009.

Rowe, G. Peter. *Making a Middle Landscape*. Cambridge, MA: MIT Press, 1991.

Shaw, Gareth, and Allan M. Williams. *Tourism and Tourism Spaces*. London: Sage Publications, 2004.

Shiba Yoshinobu 斯波義信. *Commerce and Society in Sung China*. Translated by Mark Elvin. Ann Arbor: University of Michigan, Center for Chinese Studies, 1970.

———. "Sō to Kōshū no shōgyō kaku 宋都杭州の商業核." In Umehara, ed., *Chūgoku kinsei no toshi to bunka*, 125–51.

———. *Songdai Jiangnan jingjishi yanjiu* 宋代江南經濟史研究. Translated by Fang Jian 方健 and He Zhongli 何忠禮. Nanjing: Jiangsu Renmin Chubanshe, 2011.

Shih Shou-Chien 石守謙. *Shanming guying: Zhongguo shanshuihua he guanzhong de lishi* 山鳴谷應 : 中國山水畫和觀眾的歷史. Taipei: Shitou Chuban Gufen Youxian Gongsi, 2017.

———. *Yidong de Taohuayuan: DongYa shijie zhong de shanshuihua* 移動的桃花源: 東亞世界中的山水畫. Beijing: Shenghuo Dushu Xinzhi Sanlian Shudian, 2015.

Simmel, Georg. "Fashion." *The American Journal of Sociology* 62, no. 6 (May 1957): 541–58. https://doi.org/10.1086/222102.

Song Renzheng 宋仁正. "Songdai de Xihu yu Hangzhou 宋代的西湖與杭州." MA thesis, National Chengchi University, 2004.

State Administration of Cultural Heritage of People's Republic of China. "West Lake Cultural Landscape of Hangzhou." *UNESCO*, 2011. Last accessed August 5, 2018. https://whc.unesco.org/uploads/nominations/1334.pdf.

Sun Liang 孫良. "NanSong shiqi Hangzhou fojiao wenhua chutan 南宋時期杭州佛教文化初探." *Xihu xue luncong* 2 (2008): 74–79.

Sun Xun 孫旭. "Songdai Hangzhou simiao yanjiu 宋代杭州寺院研究." MA thesis, Shanghai Normal University, 2010.

Tang Guizhang 唐圭璋 and Zhou Ruchang 周汝昌. *TangSong ci jianshang cidian* 唐宋詞鑒賞辭典. vol. NanSong, Liao, Jin, Yuan. Shanghai: Shanghai Cishu Chubanshe, 1988.

Thorp, Robert L., and Ellis Richard Vinograd. *Chinese Art and Culture*. New York: Harry A. Abrams, 2001.

Tuan, Yi-Fu 段義孚. *Space and Place: The Perspective of Experience*. Minneapolis: University of Minnesota Press, 1977.

———. *Topophilia: A Study of Environmental Perception, Attitudes, and Values*. Englewood Cliffs, NJ: Prentice-Hall, 1974.

———. "A View of Geography." *The Geographical Review* 81, no. 1 (January 1991): 99–107. https://doi.org/10.2307/215179.

Umehara Kaoru 梅原郁, ed. *Chūgoku kinsei no toshi to bunka* 中國近世の都市と文化. Kyoto-shi: Kyoto Daigaku Jinbun Kagaku Kenkyujo, 1984.

Urry, John, and Larsen Jonas. *The Tourist Gaze 3.0*. London: Sage Publications, 2011.

Virag, Curie. "The Ethics of Visualization: Structure and Feeling in Song Landscape Aesthetics." Paper presented at the Conference on Middle Period China, 800–1400, Boston, June 2014.

von Glahn, Richard. *The Sinister Way: The Divine and the Demonic in Chinese Religious Culture*. Berkeley: University of California Press, 2004.

Wang, Liping. "Emperor Kangxi's Southern Tours and the Qing Restoration of West Lake." *China Heritage Quarterly* 28 (December 2011). Last accessed August 5, 2018. http://www.chinaheritagequarterly.org/features.php?searchterm=028_kangxi.inc&issue=028.

———. "Paradise for Sale: Urban Space and Tourism in the Social Transformation of Hangzhou, 1589–1937." PhD diss., University of California, San Diego, 1997.

———. "Tourism and Spatial Change in Hangzhou, 1911–1927." In *Remaking the Chinese City: Modernity and National Identity, 1900 to 1950,* edited by Joseph Esherick, 107–20. Honolulu: University of Hawai'i Press, 2000.

Wang, Y. Eugene 汪悅進. "Tope and Topos: The Leifeng Pagoda and the Discourse of the Demonic." In *Writing and Materiality in China: Essays in Honor of Patrick Hanan,* edited by Patrick Hanan, Zeitlin T. Judith, Lydia He Liu, and Ellen Widmer, 488–552. Cambridge, MA: Harvard University Asia Center, 2003.

Wang Zhongyao 王仲尧. "NanSong Lin'an ji MingQing Hangzhou daojiao gongguan kao 南宋臨安及明清杭州道教宮觀考." *Hangzhou shifan daxue xuebao* 杭州師範大學學報 6 (November 2005): 42–46.

West, Stephen. "The Interpretation of a Dream: The Sources, Evaluation, and Influence of the *Dongjing meng hua lu*." *T'oung Pao* 71, no. 1–3 (1985): 63–108.

———. "The Pains of Pleasure: The Lanterns of Kaifeng." In Lam, et al., eds., *Senses of the City*, 109–48.

———. "Playing with Food: Performance, Food, and Aesthetics of Artificiality in the Sung and Yuan." *Harvard Journal of Asiatic Studies* 57, no. 1 (1997): 67–106.

Wooldridge, Chuck. *City of Virtues: Nanjing in an Age of Utopian Visions*. Seattle: University of Washington Press, 2015.

Wright, Arthur. "The Cosmology of the Chinese City," in *The City in Late Imperial China*, edited by G. William Skinner, 33–74. Stanford: Stanford University Press, 1977.

Wu, Pei-yi. "An Ambivalent Pilgrim to T'ai Shan in the Seventeenth Century." In *Pilgrims and Sacred Sites in China,* edited by Susan Naquin and Yu Chün-fang, 65–88. Berkeley: University of California Press, 1992.

Wu Gangyi 吳剛毅. "Lu Hong jiqi huaji wei'e yuanliu kaojian 盧鴻及其畫跡偽訛源流考鑑." MA thesis, Taiwan Shifan Daxue Meishuxi, 1998.

Wu Renshu 巫仁恕. *Pinwei shehua: WanMing de xiaofei shehui yu shidafu* 品味奢華: 晚明的消費社會與士大夫. Taipei: Zhongyang Yanjiuyuan, Lianjing Chuban Shiye Youxian Gongsi, 2007.

———. *Youyou fangxiang: MingQing Jiangnan chengshi de xiuxian xiaofei yu kongjian bianqian* 優游坊廂：明清江南城市的休閑消費與空間變遷. Taipei: Zhongyang Yanjiuyuan Jindaishi Yanjiusuo, 2013.

Wu Songdi 吳松弟. "NanSong yimin yu Lin'an wenhua 南宋移民與臨安文化." *Lishi yanjiu* 歷史研究, no. 5 (2006): 35–50.

Wu Ya-ting 吳雅婷. "Dushan: BeiSongren de yuedu xingwei yu shan de renshi 讀山: 北宋人的閱讀行為與山的認識." Paper presented at the Second Conference on Middle Period Chinese Humanities, Leiden, September 2017.

———. "Movement Matters: Sociocultural Connotations of Travel Activity During the Song Era 移動的風貌: 宋代旅行活動的社會文化內涵." PhD diss., National Taiwan University, 2007.

Xiao Peng 蕭鵬. "Xihu yinshe kao 西湖吟社考." *Cixue* 詞學 7 (1989): 88–91.

Xie, Jing. "Disembodied Historicity: Southern Song Imperial Street in Hangzhou." *Journal of the Society of Architectural Historians* 75, no. 2 (June 2016): 182–200.

Xu Jijun 徐吉軍. *NanSong ducheng Lin'an* 南宋都城臨安. Hangzhou Shi: Hangzhou Chubanshe, 2008.

Yang Junbo 楊俊博. "BeiSong Dongjing siyuan lüyou xiyinwu ji lüyou huodong yanjiu 北宋東京寺院旅遊吸引物及旅遊活動研究." MA thesis, Henai University, 2006.

Yang Ming 楊鳴 and Fang Yi 方憶. "Riben zaoyuan kongjian zhong de Xihu jingguan yixiang 日本造園空間中的西湖景觀意象." *Xihu xue luncong* 5 (2013): 67–75.

Yu, Chün-fang. "Pu-to Shan: Pilgrimage and the Creation of the Chinese Potalaka." In *Pilgrims and Sacred Sites in China*, edited by Susan Naquin and Yu Chün-fang, 190–245. Berkeley: University of California Press, 1992.

Zhang, Ellen Cong. "Communication, Collaboration, and Community, Inn-wall Writing during the Song (960–1279)." *Journal of Sung Yuan Studies* 35 (2005): 1–27.

———. "The Culture of Travel in Song China (960–1276)." PhD diss., University of Washington, 2003.

———. Introduction to *Record of the Listener: Selected Stories from Hong Mai's Yijian Zhi*, by Hong Mai, xi–xxxvi. Translated by Cong Ellen Zhang. Indianapolis: Hackett Publishing, 2018.

———. "To Be 'Erudite in Miscellaneous Knowledge:' A Study of Song (960–1279) *Biji* Writing." *Asia Major* 25, part 2 (2012): 43–77.

———. *Transformative Journeys: Travel and Culture in Song China*. Honolulu: University of Hawai'i Press, 2011.

Zhang Hongsheng 張宏生. "Consciousness of Adversity and the Spirit of Innovation: Jiang Kui's 'Poems on Past Travels' and the Urban Culture of Hangzhou in the Southern Song." Translated by Liu Gang. In Lam, et al., eds., *Senses of the City*, 73–108.

Zhang Huiru 張慧茹. "NanSong Hangzhou shuihuanjing yu chengshi fazhan hudong guanxi yanjiu 南宋杭州水環境與城市發展互動關係研究." MA thesis, Shaanxi Normal University, 2007.

Zhang Shiqing 張十慶. *Wushan shisha tu yu NanSong Jiangnan chansi* 五山十刹圖與南宋江南禪寺. Nanjing: Dongnan Daxue Chubanshe, 2000.

Zhao Shiyu 趙世瑜. *Kuanghuan yu richang: MingQing yilai de miaohui yu minjian shehui* 狂歡與日常: 明清以來的廟會與民間社會. Beijing: Shenghuo Dushu Xinzhi Sanlian Shudian, 2002.

Zhao Xinggen 趙杏根. "Songdai fangsheng yu fangshengwen yanjiu 宋代放生與放生文研究." *Shangrao shifan xueyuan yuanbao* 上饒師範學院院報 32, no. 2 (April 2012): 3–10.

Zheng Zhenduo 鄭振鐸. *Zhongguo gudai banhua congkan* 中國古代版畫叢刊. Shanghai: Shanghai Guji Chubanshe, 1988.

Zhu, Jianfei. *Chinese Spatial Strategies: Imperial Beijing, 1420–1911*. London: Routledge Curzon, 2004.

Zhu Kezhen 竺可楨. "Zhongguo lishi shang de hanzai 中國歷史上的旱災." In *Zhu Kezhen quanji* 竺可楨全集, vol. 1, edited by Fan Hongye 樊洪業, 494–98. Shanghai: Shanghai Keji Jiaoyu Chubanshe, 2004.

Zhuang Shen 莊申. *Tang Lu Hong caotang shizhi tujuan kao* 唐盧鴻草堂十志圖卷考. Taipei: Zhongyang Yanjiuyuan Lishi Yuyan Yanjiusuo, 1960.

Zhuansun Zhangjie 顓孫張傑. "Lin'an fosi yu lüyou wenhua yanjiu 臨安的佛寺與旅遊文化研究." MA thesis, Shanghai Normal University, 2005.

GLOSSARY-INDEX

Note: Works are listed under the author or artist; anonymous works and anthologies are listed as main entries.